Jesse Feiler

Sams **Teach Yourself**

Objective-C

in  24 Hours

Second Edition

SAMS 800 East 96th Street, Indianapolis, Indiana, 46240 USA

Sams Teach Yourself Objective-C in 24 Hours, Second Edition

ISBN-13: 978-0-672-33449-8
ISBN-10: 0-672-33449-6

Library of Congress Control Number: 2013954664

Printed in the United States of America

First Printing March 2014

Trademarks

All terms mentioned in this book that are known to be trademarks or service marks have been appropriately capitalized. Sams Publishing cannot attest to the accuracy of this information. Use of a term in this book should not be regarded as affecting the validity of any trademark or service mark.

Warning and Disclaimer

Every effort has been made to make this book as complete and as accurate as possible, but no warranty or fitness is implied. The information provided is on an "as is" basis. The author and the publisher shall have neither liability nor responsibility to any person or entity with respect to any loss or damages arising from the information contained in this book.

Special Sales

For information about buying this title in bulk quantities, or for special sales opportunities (which may include electronic versions; custom cover designs; and content particular to your business, training goals, marketing focus, or branding interests), please contact our corporate sales department at corpsales@pearsoned.com or (800) 382-3419.

For government sales inquiries, please contact governmentsales@pearsoned.com.

For questions about sales outside the U.S., please contact international@pearsoned.com.

Editor-in-Chief
Greg Wiegand

Executive Editor
Loretta Yates

Development Editor
Sondra Scott

Marketing Manager
Stephane Nakib

Managing Editor
Kristy Hart

Senior Project Editor
Lori Lyons

Copy Editor
Karen Annett

Indexer
Erika Millen

Proofreader
Kathy Ruiz

Technical Editor
Robert McGovern

Publishing Coordinator
Cindy Teeters

Cover Designer
Mark Shirar

Compositor
Nonie Ratcliff

Manufacturing Buyer
Dan Uhrig

Contents at a Glance

Table of Contents

About the Author

Jesse Feiler is a developer and author. He has been an Apple developer since before it became fashionable, and has worked with mobile devices starting with Apple's Newton and continuing with the iOS products (iPhone, iPod touch, and iPad).

His books include *Sams Teach Yourself Core Data in 24 Hours*, *Data-Driven iOS Apps for iPad and iPhone with FileMaker Pro*, *FileMaker Pro in Depth* (Sams/Pearson), *Database-Driven Web Sites* (Harcourt), *Learning iCloud Data Management* (Addison Wesley/Pearson), and *iOS App Development for Dummies* (Wiley).

He has written about Objective-C and the Apple frameworks beginning with *Rhapsody Developer's Guide* (AP Professional) and *Mac OS X Developer's Guide* (Morgan Kaufmann).

He is the author of *MinutesMachine*, the meeting management software for iPad, as well as Saranac River Trail app for iPhone and iPad. There are more details at champlainarts.com.

A native of Washington DC, he has lived in New York City and currently lives in Plattsburgh, NY. He can be reached at northcountryconsulting.com.

Acknowledgments

As always, Carole Jelen at Waterside Productions has provided help and guidance in bringing this book to fruition. At Pearson, Loretta Yates has helped move this book from an idea to an actual book. Along the way, the book and author have benefited from technical suggestions from Robert McGovern. The production staff kept the book on track and helped clarify text.

We Want to Hear from You!

As the reader of this book, you are our most important critic and commentator. We value your opinion and want to know what we're doing right, what we could do better, what areas you'd like to see us publish in, and any other words of wisdom you're willing to pass our way.

We welcome your comments. You can email or write to let us know what you did or didn't like about this book—as well as what we can do to make our books better.

Please note that we cannot help you with technical problems related to the topic of this book.

When you write, please be sure to include this book's title and author as well as your name and email address. We will carefully review your comments and share them with the author and editors who worked on the book.

Email: consumer@samspublishing.com

Mail: Sams Publishing
         ATTN: Reader Feedback
         800 East 96th Street
         Indianapolis, IN 46240 USA

Reader Services

Visit our website and register this book at informit.com/register for convenient access to any updates, downloads, and errata that might be available for this book.

Introduction

If you want to develop native apps for OS X or for iOS, the language in which you write them is Objective-C. (You can write web-based apps using Safari extensions and HTML5.)

Because Apple's development environment builds on the frameworks of Cocoa and Cocoa Touch, what you have to write is the code that is specific to your own app. All the basic functionality is provided by Cocoa and the frameworks; you do not have to write any code to manage menus, for example (in most cases), and you don't have to worry about implementing complex view structures on iOS such as navigation bars and split views. The code that you write is very specific code that fits into the existing frameworks. It might be code that overrides or extends an existing method, or it might be new methods that are unique to your own app.

Who Should Read This Book

Even though the code that you write might not be extensive, you do have to understand the syntax and structure of Objective-C in order to write it and to understand the code that Apple provides for you.

You should have some basic experience with programming in order to read this book, but it is designed to bring you up to speed on the major prerequisites to understanding Objective-C, including the concepts of object-oriented programming. The book assumes that you have at least a basic understanding of the C programming language on which Objective-C is based. Don't worry if you are far from a C expert; the concepts used in Objective-C are the basics.

What This Book Covers

Objective-C has been the language of choice for the Cocoa environments and, before them, the NeXTSTEP and Rhapsody environments. Theoretically, it can be used in other contexts, but in practice, it is the language of these environments. Sometimes, drawing the line between Objective-C syntax and elements of the Cocoa environments and frameworks can be very difficult. This book focuses on the language itself. It provides a number of examples from code in the Cocoa frameworks as well as code in the examples from developer.apple.com and the templates built in to Xcode, but the primary focus is on the language. The book includes information on how to use the Xcode development tool because, for all intents and purposes, you have to use it to write Objective-C code.

Downloading the Sample Files

You can download examples from the author's website at northcountryconsulting.com or from the publisher's site at informit.com/title/9780672334498.

How This Book Is Organized

There are five parts to this book. You can focus on whichever one addresses an immediate problem, or you can get a good overview by reading straight through. As with all of the Sams Teach Yourself books, as much as possible each hour is made to stand on its own so that you can jump around to learn in your own way. Cross-references throughout the book help you find related material.

Part I: Getting Started with Objective-C

This part gives you the high-level view of Objective-C.

▶ Hour 1, "Overview of the Developer Program—Here you see how to register to become an Apple developer and gain access to the resources on developer.apple.com. You can choose from various options, but you must register before you can do any meaningful development work.

▶ Hour 2, "Object-Oriented Programming with Objective-C"—This hour shows you how Objective-C builds on top of C. It also covers how Objective-C implements object-oriented concepts and manages inheritance.

▶ Hour 3, "Using Object-Oriented Features in Objective-C"—Objective-C is a dynamic language that relies on messaging. Those concepts are explained here so that you can begin to implement your own apps.

▶ Hour 4, "Using Xcode 5"— This is the integrated development environment (IDE) you use to develop apps. You'll see how to work with new features that make your coding faster and catches errors even before you build your app. Xcode integrates the Git source code repository so that you can easily track your code on your own Mac, a networked Mac, or a public repository such as GitHub.

▶ Hour 5, "Using Compiler Directives"—Compiler directives help you manage files and use the preprocessor to prepare code for the compiler itself.

Part II: Working with the Objective-C Basics

This part of the book delves into the concepts of messaging, classes, selectors, building blocks, and memory.

▶ **Hour 6, "Exploring Messaging and a Testbed App"**—Messaging is the heart of Objective-C. You send messages rather than call methods or functions, and the difference between Objective-C and other languages is significant.

▶ **Hour 7, "Declaring a Class in an Interface File"**—This hour explores the basics of declaring a class. You see how to import other files and use forward declarations for classes and protocols.

▶ **Hour 8, "Declaring Instance Variables in an Interface File"**—You can assign instance variables to classes. You also see how to deal with static typing and the scope of instance variables.

▶ **Hour 9, "Declaring Properties in an Interface File"**—Objective-C lets you declare properties of a class in your interface file rather than declaring variables. The property declaration provides more features than a simple C variable declaration. Furthermore, the compiler can synthesize the accessors for the property based on the property declaration.

▶ **Hour 10, "Declaring Methods in an Interface File"**—Method declarations in Objective-C provide the same functionality that they do in other languages, but the details in this message-based environment are different.

▶ **Hour 11, "Declaring Actions in an Interface File"**—Actions are typically triggered by user actions in the interface. You declare them in your interface files and manage their interactions with Interface Builder.

▶ **Hour 12, "Routing Messages with Selectors"**—The target-action pattern is the basis for message routing; it is explained in this hour. You also see how to use selectors and the SEL data type.

▶ **Hour 13, "Building on the Foundation"**—Throughout Objective-C, you find certain patterns repeated over and over. These include its data types and the concept of mutable and immutable versions of them.

▶ **Hour 14, "Defining a Class in an Implementation File"**—After all those declarations, you get down to actually defining the code behind the declarations in this hour.

▶ **Hour 15, "Organizing Data with Collections"**—Arrays are one of the core features of programming languages. Objective-C adds additional collection objects, including dictionaries and sets. This hour covers how to use them.

▶ **Hour 16, "Managing Memory and Runtime Objects"**—Whether you are running on a mainframe or supercomputer or a relatively small mobile device, memory is a critical resource. There are many tools to help you manage memory, but in most cases, you still need to do something and understand what your choices are. This hour introduces you to Automatic Reference Counting (ARC), the modern way to manage Objective-C memory; it also shows you how garbage collection has been used in the past.

Part III: Expanding and Extending Classes

One of the differences between Objective-C and other object-oriented languages is that you can expand and extend classes in a variety of ways and not just by subclassing them.

▶ **Hour 17, "Extending a Class with Protocols and Delegates"**—Next to the ability to override classes, protocols and delegates are the most commonly used way for adding functionality to a variety of classes.

▶ **Hour 18, "Extending a Class with Categories and Extensions"**—Categories and extensions let you add methods and even variables to existing classes—even those for which you might not have the source code.

▶ **Hour 19, "Using Associative References and Fast Enumeration"**—These relatively recent additions to Objective-C enable you to become a power programmer. You can add and remove associations at runtime, which gives you more flexibility with your instance variables. Fast enumeration also speeds your runtime performance and might mean that you have less code to write yourself.

▶ **Hour 20, "Working with Blocks"**—Blocks provide the ability to create and use sections of code that are portable and anonymous. You can use them as arguments of methods or functions, typically as completion handlers for completion routines, handlers, and errors, as well as for specific types of functionality, such as sorting and view manipulation. The concept is borrowed from languages such as C, Ruby, Python, and Lisp; it has been part of Objective-C since Mac OS X 10.6 (Snow Leopard) and iOS 4.0.

Part IV: Beyond the Basics

Exception and error handling, queues and threading, the debugger, and Xcode debug gauges allow you to analyze and improve your projects and their performance.

▶ **Hour 21, "Handling Exceptions and Errors"**—As in many languages, you can set up try/catch/finally structures to catch exceptions as close as possible to the place where they happen. In this hour, you see how to use them and how to integrate them with the debugger.

▶ **Hour 22, "Grand Central Dispatch: Using Queues and Threading"**—Even on small mobile devices, you have the ability to manage multiprocessing. This hour shows you the techniques that are available for multiprocessing.

▶ **Hour 23, "Working with the Debugger"**—During development with Xcode, you can use the debugger and console to improve your code. This hour shows you the basics and explores break points, preferences, and some advanced debugging techniques.

▶ **Hour 24, "Using Xcode Debug Gauges for Analysis"**—Although debugging can help you get rid of bugs, you need to monitor your app's performance. Memory leaks aren't bugs unless they crash your app, but with these tools you can spot them before the damage is done. Debug gauges are a simple graphical interface on top of the more sophisticated Instruments app; both are discussed here.

Part V: Appendixes

The appendixes provide additional reference material that can help you with the concepts in the book. There is even more material on developer.apple.com and on the author's website at northcountryconsulting.com.

▶ **Appendix A, "C Syntax Summary"**—Objective-C is a thin layer built on top of C. This appendix reviews the basic C syntax that matters for Objective-C. Much of it is reimplemented for you in the frameworks of Cocoa, so this appendix walks you through what is left.

▶ **Appendix B, "Apps, Packages, and Bundles"**—Your app on Mac OS X or iOS is actually a collection of files, including code, resources such as data stores and images, and property lists. This is a high-level overview so that you can understand what it is you are building with Xcode and Objective-C.

▶ **Appendix C, "Archiving and Packaging Apps for Development and Testing"**—This overview gives you the basic information you need to know to share your apps with testers and through the App Store. It is not just a matter of copying files.

HOUR 1
Overview of the Developer Program

What You'll Learn in This Hour

▶ Exploring Objective-C

▶ Gaining access to Apple's developer program and its tools

▶ Exploring Xcode and its workspace window

Introducing Objective-C

Objective-C was developed in the early 1980s by Brad Cox and Tom Love. It was licensed by Steve Jobs's company, NeXT, in 1988, where it was used to develop the first two key frameworks of the NeXTSTEP operating system—Application and Foundation Kits. When Apple purchased NeXT in 1996, the projects moved to Cupertino, California. At Apple, NeXTSTEP became Rhapsody and then morphed into OS X; since then, another transformation led it to become the iPhone OS and then iOS (it was becoming too difficult to explain to people why the iPad used the iPhone OS). You can find Application Kit (AppKit) in the operating systems today along with a direct descendant of the Foundation Kit—Core Foundation.

One of the primary purposes of Objective-C was to prove that it was not difficult to add object-oriented programming capabilities to the C programming language. Objective-C was envisioned as a lightweight superset of C, and that is what was implemented.

This cursory summary of 30 years of Objective-C brings you up to date on some of the key points in the evolution of Objective-C. Looking at Objective-C today, some of the high points (and, at the time, often much-debated and contentious issues) are not relevant to many people. Rather than looking back, you (and this book) can focus on the present and the future.

NOTE

It is important to consider why people learn Objective-C today. The primary reason to learn Objective-C today is because you want to write apps for OS X or iOS.

Writing apps for OS X or iOS is the reason to learn Objective-C, but Objective-C is not all you need. You also need the Xcode development tool. If you want to test on iOS devices or submit apps to the Mac App Store or the App Store, you need to register as a developer with Apple. With those items, you are ready to get started developing for OS X or iOS.

Enrolling as an Apple Developer

Most of the time, you register as a developer at developer.apple.com. The terms and conditions vary from country to country, and they have changed and will probably continue to change as Apple's business changes. You need to choose your program and then select the type of enrollment you want. Certain program resources, such as basic documentation, do not require registration or enrollment, and they are available to anyone with a web browser. You can easily see what is available by going to developer.apple.com and not logging in.

TIP

If you see "Hi, Guest" on many pages, you are not logged in. If you are greeted by name, then a cookie has been used to log you in and you see resources that might not be available to unregistered guests.

For a personal account, the entire process is automated so you can be enrolled in a matter of minutes as long as you have a credit card handy to pay the basic program fee of $99 per year for a Mac OS or iOS membership.

NOTE

How Old Do You Have to Be to Enroll?

You must be at least the age of majority in the country where you live. The age of majority in many countries is 18. In part, this is because you need to accept a legal agreement with regard to the conditions of the enrollment. If you are younger than the age of majority, keep reading: There are ways to legally enroll and get to work.

Choosing Your Program

There are three developer programs. Each program has a Dev Center with sample code and demos. In addition, there is a developer library for each program with videos, references, guides, examples, and other documentation. Access to each of these programs depends on the level of enrollment you have. You do not need a paid registration to access the basic reference information for any of these programs. However, as you see in the following section, paid enrollments in the Mac OS and iOS programs give you more access.

▶ **Mac**—The basic membership is $99 per year.

▶ **iOS**—The basic membership is $99 per year.

▶ **Safari**—This program is free.

The basic membership adds access to beta software, developer discussion boards, and an invitation to purchase tickets for developer events such as Apple's Worldwide Developer Conference (WWDC). In the last several years, basic members have also been able to access videos of most of the WWDC sessions without an additional charge through iTunes.

The Mac OS and iOS programs include the ability to submit apps to the relevant App Store. With the iOS program, it also includes the ability to use the software simulator for iPhone or iPad apps. In addition, two technical support incidents are provided in the annual membership; you can buy more for $50 each. This support is provided by Apple engineers from the Developer Technical Support (DTS) team. They can help you over a technical hurdle as well as give you assistance in finding your way through the vast array of resources on developer.apple.com.

TIP

DTS Support

It is important to note that DTS does not provide support for prereleased (beta) software. However, the developer discussion boards are particularly helpful with problems of that kind; Apple engineers provide technical support in that forum to all registered developers who are interested in a particular topic. DTS support is separate from bug reporting: It is support for your use of Apple's software.

TIP

Watch Your DTS Calendar

If you do not use them, your technical support incidents expire at the end of your membership year. You can check your status on http://developer.apple.com in the Member Section. If you find yourself with an unused technical support incident, you might want to ask one of those questions you have always thought of asking someday, even if it is not relevant to a project you are working on at the moment.

Selecting Your Membership Category

The Mac OS and iOS programs let you register in various categories. The categories change from time to time; you can find an overview of the current categories and programs at developer. apple.com/programs/. These are the categories as of the writing of this book:

▶ **Personal**—This is the category most people use. It registers you as a person. As noted, you must be over the age of majority in the country where you live. You are able to build apps and submit them to the appropriate App Store. You also get the resources that let you test your app on iOS devices rather than just on the software simulator that runs on your Mac. To install your test app on an iOS device with a personal membership, that device's identification must be entered into your Xcode environment.

▶ **Business**—A business membership enables you to add other registered developers to your team so that they can install test apps through their own accounts. This solves the problem of working with someone who is far away when you both are working on the same iOS app. Note that the teams you set up are for each app you work on; you give access to other developers only to the app you want them to use. The cost is $99 per year. You can convert a personal membership to a business membership if you are eligible. This requires additional documentation and review by Apple as described on developer.apple.com.

NOTE

Eligibility for Business Memberships

Check with developer.apple.com to see if you are eligible for a business membership. In the United States at this time, businesses that are organized as sole proprietorships (doing business as or DBA businesses) are not eligible for business memberships. Partnerships and corporations (including Subchapter-S corporations) are eligible.

▶ **University Team (iOS only)**—This program allows an instructor at a university to set up a team for up to 200 students. It is available to degree-granting institutions of higher learning. The program is free.

TIP

This is the route to follow if you are under the age of majority (in most countries, younger than 18).

▶ **Enterprise Program (iOS only)**—This program enables you to develop and distribute apps within your organization without going through the App Store. The cost is $299 per year.

Registering for Your Apple ID

You need an Apple ID to identify yourself. If you have an iTunes account, you have an Apple ID. You have an Apple ID if you had a Mobile Me account or now have an iCloud account. There is no charge for an Apple ID. You can have multiple Apple IDs. In fact, you may be required to do so: If you publish on iBooks, you need an Apple ID—and you cannot use it for the App Store so you will need to create a separate one.

Setting Up the Development Environment

The heart of your development environment for Objective-C is Xcode, the Integrated Development Environment (IDE) running on your Mac. Even if you have not registered for a developer program, you can freely download it from the Mac App Store. (If you want unreleased beta versions of Xcode, you must be a registered developer, but much of the documentation is available in the public sections of developer.apple.com.)

Your development environment includes Xcode and its Objective-C language. It also includes frameworks such as Cocoa (on OS X) and Cocoa Touch (on iOS). This book focuses specifically on Objective-C, so although examples often use the various frameworks, they are not described in any detail except for their use in Objective-C code.

Talking Xcode

You build projects with Xcode. A project is normally a fully contained set of files that can be moved from one location or computer to another. You can see this as you explore developer. apple.com with its sample code projects. You can download each one and place it anywhere you want on your computer, build it, and run it. You can change settings to make a project access specific files in your environment, but that comes at the expense of portability.

If you need to manage your source code, Xcode has a subset of Git and Subversion commands integrated into its interface. You cannot do every detailed task that Git or Subversion provides with the Xcode commands, but you can certainly do the important source version control tasks. In fact, many people do not even know what is not implemented in the Xcode interface to Git because they simply do not use commands beyond the basics.

NOTE

About Git

As noted on the Git website at http://git-scm.com/, Git is a fast version control system. It is free and open source, supporting distributed development, branching and merging, and other modern source code version control tools.

Xcode comes with a variety of project templates for iOS and Mac OS. These are built in and are separate from the examples you can download from developer.apple.com. Whereas the examples downloadable from developer.apple.com are fully implemented projects you can use as models, the built-in templates are starting points. Many of them work without any further effort on your part, but what they do is provide a starting place for you to build on. For example, the Cocoa Application template for OS X puts up an empty window and a menu bar with basic commands.

Project Info

Every project has basic information about the project that includes the following:

▶ **Deployment target**—This is the earliest version of the SDK for which the project is targeted.

▶ **Configurations**—Most projects have at least a debug and release configuration from the start. You can add or delete others.

▶ **Localizations**—You can use localization to translate your project into various languages. Localization is built into the Cocoa and Cocoa Touch frameworks.

Targets

Each project starts with a single target; you can add new ones. A target is usually an app. Each target can have its own identifier and version number along with its own icons, bundles, and so forth. Some of the Mac OS templates provide a target for users along with another target that is built for Spotlight to use. In many cases, there is no need to distinguish between a project and its target if there is only one target.

For iOS projects, you can specify the device (or universal to build for both iPad and iPhone). On OS X as well as iOS, you specify the user interface for the target.

An increasingly common use of targets is to create an Xcode project with one target for iOS and another for OS X. Both targets can share some common code so that you can easily maintain a project with apps for both platforms.

Introducing the Xcode Workspace

Xcode uses a complex workspace window that packs a great deal of information into a compact and flexible interface. On Mavericks OS X 10.9, the full-screen option from the View menu or the full-screen button at the top right of a traditional window is a good choice with Xcode 5—at least at the beginning.

Because the Xcode workspace window can be configured in many different ways, the first step to understanding the tool that you will be working with is to look at the workspace window components. This section begins with an introduction to those components and then continues with a Try It Yourself activity for you to experiment with.

NOTE

Working with Figures

Note that the sequence of figures in this section is designed to introduce you to the workspace window. If you launch Xcode, you are greeted by a splash screen (probably—it's an option) and by a project window that will likely look similar to one of the later figures in this sequence. But to get started, look at Figure 1.1, which shows you an editing window that might be familiar to you from other editing environments.

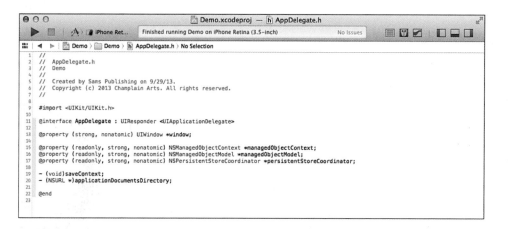

FIGURE 1.1
Edit your source code.

Almost everything in this window is configurable—the fonts, the colors, and the presence of absence of line numbers. At the top left, the right-pointing arrow builds and runs your code; the square stops it. Status updates such as "Finished running Demo on iPhone Retina (3.5-inch)" appear in the center of the window. At the top right are two trios of buttons. The rightmost set controls the optional panes of the window that you can show and hide. (Don't worry: The rest of the interface is explained later on in this hour.) The button on the left of this trio controls the navigator. Use it to show and hide the navigator at the left of the window, as shown in Figure 1.2.

You can hide the navigator with another click of the mouse. Click on the rightmost of those buttons to show the utilities area, as shown in Figure 1.3.

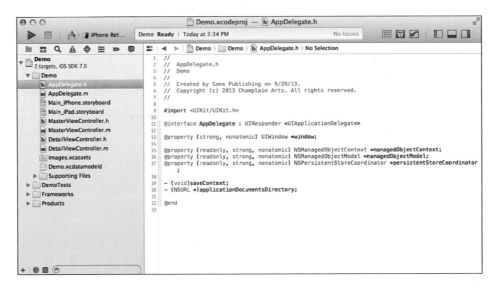

FIGURE 1.2
Show the navigator area.

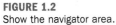

FIGURE 1.3
Show the utilities area.

The utilities area has two configurable panes. Drag the top of the library pane up from the bottom to show both utilities and the library, as shown in Figure 1.4.

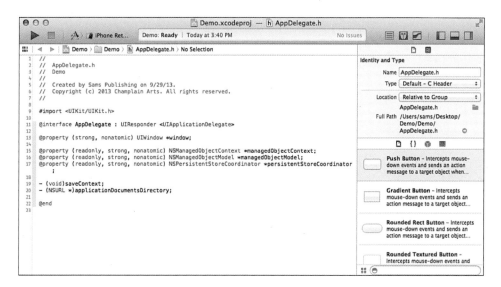

FIGURE 1.4
Show the library.

You can resize the window, as shown in Figure 1.5.

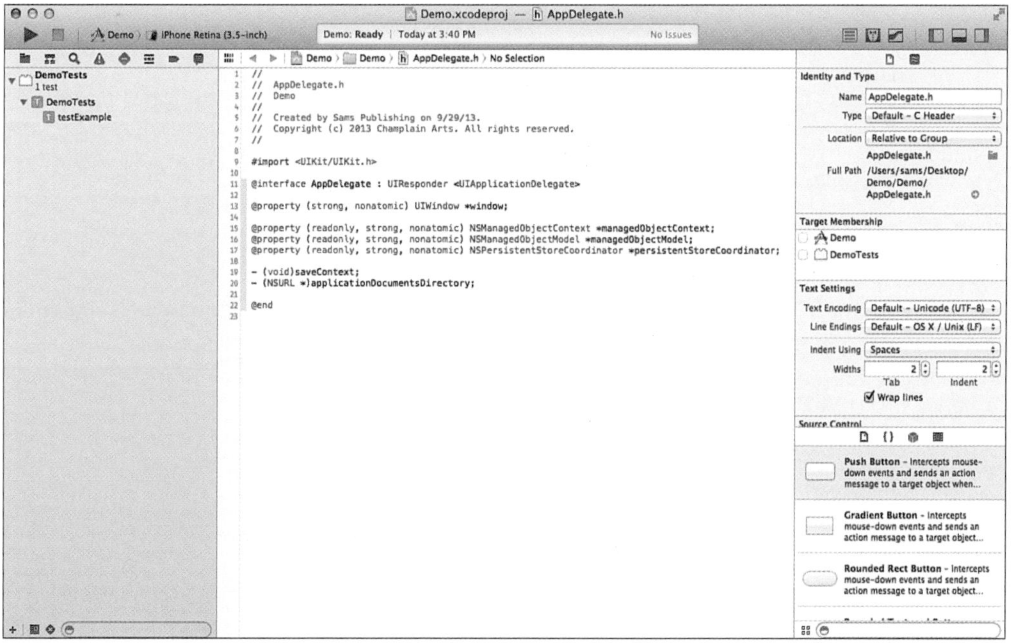

FIGURE 1.5
Resize the window.

If your code listing is short, there will be blank space at the bottom. Click the central button of the trio to bring up the debug pane, as shown in Figure 1.6. You'll notice that the navigator has changed. That's because Figure 1.6 shows the workspace window as it typically is when you are running your app (using the right-pointing triangle in the top left of the window).

You now have an overview that should let you create your first project.

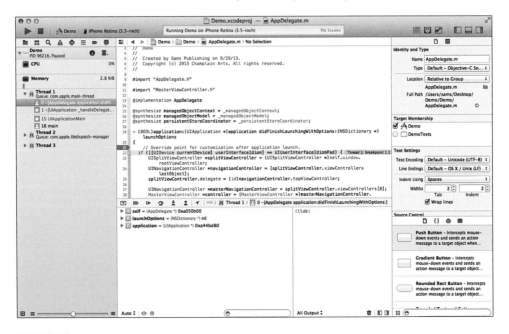

FIGURE 1.6
Show the debug pane.

Getting Up and Running with Your First Project

The best way to find out more about using Xcode is to use one of the built-in templates. Build and run it, and you have a basic app on which you can build your own functionality. From the standpoint of this book, what you have is a large amount of Objective-C code that you can study and work with as you read on.

▼ TRY IT YOURSELF

Create Your First Project

Here is a high-level introduction to the Xcode workspace where you work. Unlike most other tasks in this book, the steps in this task can be done in any order as you explore. Also, note that much of the behavior can be modified with preferences, so your results might look a bit different.

1. Create a new project from one of the built-in templates. You might see a splash screen with the option to do that as soon as you launch Xcode. That splash screen also lets you turn it off in the future, which is why you might not see it. In any case, you can use File, New, New Project to open the sheet shown in Figure 1.7.

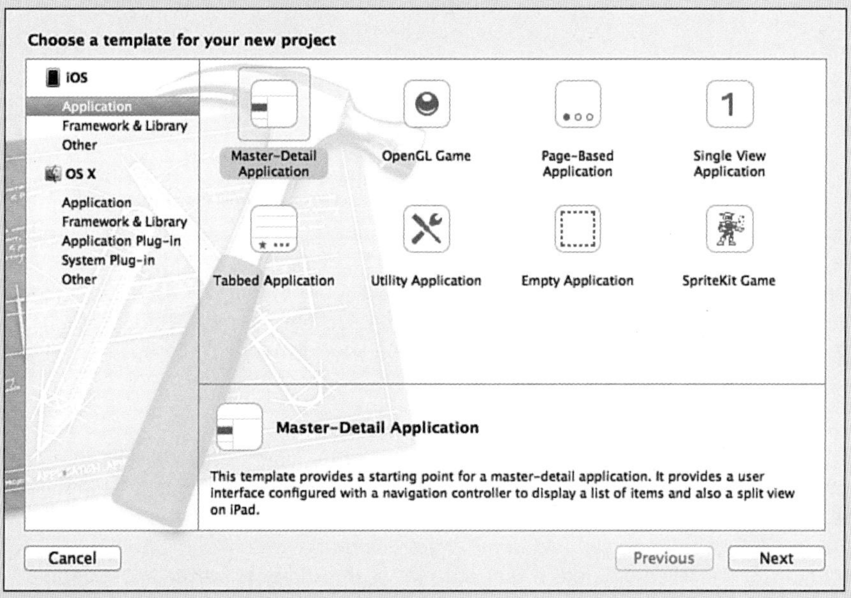

Choose a template for your new project

iOS
  Application
  Framework & Library
  Other
OS X
  Application
  Framework & Library
  Application Plug-in
  System Plug-in
  Other

Master-Detail Application   OpenGL Game   Page-Based Application   Single View Application

Tabbed Application   Utility Application   Empty Application   SpriteKit Game

Master-Detail Application

This template provides a starting point for a master-detail application. It provides a user interface configured with a navigation controller to display a list of items and also a split view on iPad.

Cancel   Previous   Next

FIGURE 1.7
Create a new project.

In these steps, the template used is the iOS Master-Detail Application template from the iOS section. You are asked to name the project and choose the folder where it will be created. Don't bother with any of the other sections.

2. The workspace window opens.

3. Explore your project. Show and hide the parts of the workspace window.

4. Use the right-pointing triangle at the top of the window to run your project. Just to the right of the right-pointing triangle and the square, you'll find buttons that let you choose how to run it: Choose one of the simulators (it doesn't matter which one).

Summary

This hour has provided an overview of Objective-C and how it fits into your development environment along with the Cocoa and Cocoa Touch frameworks and Xcode. Objective-C is a superset of C so it builds on everything in C adding just what is necessary to create a full-featured object-oriented environment.

You have also seen the basics of Xcode—the tool you'll use to build your code, your interface, and even set your app's icons and launch images.

Q&A

Q. How do you start writing apps for iOS and OS X if you are too young to be a registered developer?

A. You have two routes available to you. If you attend a school that is eligible for the University Developer Program, you might be able to join through them. Otherwise, you can browse developer.apple.com and read the documentation. Go to the Mac App Store and buy Xcode so you can start writing code. (Even though Xcode is free, the store transactions always use the word *buy*.) You are neither able to place your apps in either the Mac App Store or the original App Store for iOS apps nor test on iOS devices, but you can hone your skills and develop apps that can be used to showcase your skills.

Q. What are the best settings for Xcode preferences?

A. Use whatever is most comfortable for you. As you are getting used to Xcode, one strategy is to create a new user account in System Preferences. Remember that Xcode is installed so that all users on a computer can use it. This enables you to use your test account to explore the preferences. When you find some preferences that you like, move them to your main account. You can even delete the test account at that time. However, most people who use Xcode a lot constantly adjust the workspace depending on what project they are doing and what part of the project they are working on.

Workshop

Quiz

1. How do you get a copy of Xcode?

2. How do you control the workspace window?

Quiz Answers

1. Register at developer.apple.com. There are various registration categories that are designed for different types of developers. The paid levels of developer registration include technical support assistance (two incidents for the basic programs). The developer programs often let you download prerelease versions of Xcode, the operating systems, and other software. You can buy the shipping version of Xcode for free from the Mac App Store.

2. Control the workspace window with buttons in the toolbar, menu commands, and preferences.

Activities

Even though you may be chomping at the bit to start writing your own Objective-C code, take the time to explore several Xcode templates (at least two). Get used to the workspace window, and make certain to build them with the settings before you have modified them. In the case of the basic OS X Cocoa application (the basis for most of your OS X work), the basic template puts up an empty window. It is supposed to do that, so do not think you have done something wrong. Your job is to fill that window.

HOUR 2
Object-Oriented Programming with Objective-C

What You'll Learn in This Hour

▶ Understanding Objective-C and its objectives

▶ Using object-oriented principles and good programming style

▶ How inheritance works in the Objective-C world

Object-Oriented Programming in the Objective-C World

Object-oriented programming is probably the most commonly used programming paradigm today, but there is no clear definition of what it is. The most common informal description (not definition) is that it is a style of programming in which the basic building blocks are objects— combinations of methods and variables that represent concepts or physical objects in a program. The ability to build a program in which the program components map directly to objects and concepts in the physical world can make it easier for people to develop software because on one level they are dealing with the objects and concepts about which they are trying to build software.

Beyond this basic concept of objects, a variety of other concepts can come into play. These concepts include data abstraction, encapsulation, messaging, modularity, polymorphism, and inheritance. (That list is from the Wikipedia article on object-oriented programming.) Objective-C incorporates all of those, and in this hour you find out more about data abstraction, encapsulation, and modularity. The other concepts are introduced in subsequent hours.

Implementing Object-Oriented Programming

Although this book focuses on Objective-C and does not compare it with other languages, it is important to point out that in the 1960s when object-oriented programming became popular, there was disagreement over how to go about developing actual programs. There were two schools of thought:

▶ **Object-oriented languages**—Over the years, a number of languages have been built specifically to work with object-oriented programming. These included Simula, Ruby, Eiffel, and Smalltalk.

▶ **Object-oriented additions**—Partly because of the difficulty of retraining programmers on a totally new language, many hybrid languages have been developed. These include C++ and C# as well Objective-C. Object-oriented features have been added to languages such as PHP and even FORTRAN and COBOL.

Building Object-Oriented Projects

When you have an object-oriented language, you can start to build object-oriented projects, but that is just the starting point. There are several ways to proceed, but because Objective-C is used almost exclusively for building OS X and iOS projects, the focus in this section is on them.

One of the major objectives of object-oriented programming is making it easier to reuse existing code. When you encapsulate code into formal objects with well-structured interfaces, you should be able to reuse that code, and your investment in it can pay off in a variety of later uses.

Code reuse is a critical component of Apple's development environments. Object-oriented programming and its implementation in Objective-C provide the basis of reuse. The structure of reuse on iOS and OS X relies on frameworks. Frameworks are sets of related classes (and a few nonclass entities) that implement functional areas of interest to developers. Frameworks are essentially organizational tools for the classes they contain. Your involvement with frameworks consists of importing the ones necessary to your project; you actually interact with, use, and subclass the classes within a framework. (It is also possible to create your own frameworks, but that is beyond the scope of this book. You can find documentation of the process on developer. apple.com.)

The set of frameworks that you deal with forms either Cocoa or Cocoa Touch. Each has two aspects: one for runtime and one for development.

TIP

In this book, if no distinction is made regarding the environment, then you can assume the reference is to both environments.

When you create Cocoa projects, you commonly start from a template in Xcode. (You also may start from an example on developer.apple.com.) In both cases, the import directives for the appropriate frameworks are already provided, but you can also add any necessary import directives.

Looking at the Frameworks

You will most commonly deal with two sets of frameworks. As noted previously, these are primarily organizational structures; you find references to them in the documentation you see in Xcode's Organizer and elsewhere. On OS X, the various frameworks themselves are organized into five layers:

▶ User Experience

▶ Application Frameworks

▶ Graphics and Media (Application Services)

▶ Core Services

▶ Underpinning the whole structure is the Darwin kernel

On iOS, there are five layers:

▶ Application

▶ Cocoa Touch

▶ Media

▶ Core Services

▶ Core OS

As is common in layered architectures, each layer can refer to layers below it but cannot refer to layers above it. Thus, frameworks in Core Services can rely on classes in Core OS (iOS) and Darwin (OS X), but not on anything in the higher layers, such as media and interface-handling classes.

Within this structure, there are two frameworks on which your projects almost always rely. On OS X, they are

▶ AppKit in Application Frameworks

▶ Core Foundation in Core Services

On iOS, they are

▶ UIKit in Cocoa Touch

▶ Foundation in Core Services

Although the frameworks are collections of classes for the most part, they also contain some other entities. In particular, Core Foundation and Foundation contain C elements such as structs and typedefs. This ability to use native C in an Objective-C project is important to this structure.

Creating C with Objects

Objective-C started from C, "the language of the UNIX operating system," as Brian W. Kernighan and Dennis M. Ritchie put it in the introduction to their classic book, *The C Programming Language*. C itself is a relatively terse language (the preface to the first edition refers to its "economy of expression"). C played a critical role in the development of object-oriented languages around 1980: Both C++ and Objective-C started as C programs to convert their native syntax to compilable C code. C++ was heavily influenced by Simula, whereas Objective-C's main influence was Smalltalk. The relative merits of the two object-oriented offspring of C have been hotly debated over the years.

Today, Objective-C is perhaps most widely known as the language of OS X and iOS. Comparisons to other languages are largely irrelevant. What does matter is the basic C syntax that is outlined for you in Appendix A, "C Syntax Summary," if you need a refresher.

Start Thinking in Objective-C

Just as with a natural language, if you start thinking in a language you know well and then mentally translate it into the new language, it takes you much longer to learn the new language. Much of what you know about computer languages in general still applies in Objective-C, and the basics of object-oriented programming apply as well. For many people, the biggest difference between Objective-C and languages such as C itself or C++ is that Objective-C looks different. The next section introduces you to the heart of this difference: methods and messaging.

TIP
Don't translate the concepts and syntax of the following sections. Use what natural language instructors call total immersion: Jump right in and start writing Objective-C.

Understanding Data Abstraction

Data abstraction is one of the key principles behind Objective-C. Abstraction is not simply a computer term; it is widely used in other areas. It is the process of considering a number of ideas or objects together and leaving out the differences among them so that what remains is the abstraction that is common to all of them. It can be an exercise in logic or philosophy or a children's game such as, "What do these things have in common?" If the things are a monkey, a goldfish, and a person, the answer might be that they are all animals. That is one abstraction of those objects.

A key part of abstraction is hiding details that are irrelevant to the abstraction so that the abstracted information is more recognizable. That aspect of data abstraction is critical in Objective-C. In the language, its use, and its best practices, the hiding of object details makes the abstractions usable. Hiding is very important in Objective-C.

When you have abstract objects with their differences hidden, you can write code to manipulate the objects. With the differentiations hidden, your code can safely ignore the differences. It is important to learn and remember this principle of hiding differentiations from the abstract objects. Many people mistakenly start out with Objective-C (and other languages, but the focus here is on Objective-C) by dealing with the differentiations that should be hidden.

Thus, if you create a bank account class, to the outside world it should look and function the same way whether it is a savings account or a checking account. The class probably can report its current balance and perhaps pending transactions. Subclasses might be able to report attributes specific to savings or checking accounts, but the abstract bank account class probably cannot do that because reporting on checks that have not yet cleared is not something that a savings account can do (unless it is a hybrid account where you can write checks against the savings account).

Considering Classes and Instances

As is the case in many programming languages, you can define entities in your code. You can write functions and methods in many languages, and you can declare classes in many object-oriented languages. However, having written a function or method means very little unless you actually call it. By the same token, declaring a class has no meaning unless you actually create an *instance* of the class.

Exploring Encapsulation

Encapsulation is related to data abstraction, and it can be demonstrated by writing some pseudocode for a bank account class, as shown in Listing 2.1.

Although this is pseudocode, it begins to introduce a few Objective-C syntax elements that are described in detail in Part II, "Working with the Objective-C Basics."

LISTING 2.1   Pseudocode for a Bank Account Class

```
#import "BankAccount.h"

@implementation BankAccount

#define checking 1
#define saving 2
#define investment 3

- (float)balance: (int) accountType
{
  switch (accountType) {
    case checking:
       //set returnValue ...
       break;

    case saving:
       //set returnValue ...
       break;

    case investment:
       //set returnValue ...
       break;

    default:
       //set returnValue ... (maybe to nil)
       break;
  }
  return returnValue;

}

@end
```

This is a method of a bank account class that returns the balance for that account. You pass in the account type, and depending on the account type, different routines fire to return the necessary value.

The structure shown here demonstrates the principle of encapsulation by breaking it. The bank account class does abstract the particularities of each type of account. You call this method and pass in whatever type of account you are interested in, so you might think that you have abstracted the class data.

But the notion of encapsulation added to data abstraction suggests that the abstract object should be self-sufficient. If you have an instance of a bank account class, you should be able to ask it for its balance, and, without you passing in any additional information, the self-contained (encapsulated) class can do whatever is necessary.

This approach means that within the bank account class, you need to store the account type.

Listing 2.2 shows pseudocode for a bank account class header.

LISTING 2.2   Bank Account Header

```
@interface BankAccount : NSObject
{
  @private int accountType; //variable declaration
}

- (float *)balance; //method declaration

@end
```

Because the account type is stored within the object, the method to return the bank account's balance already has that information. The code shown previously in Listing 2.1 can be converted to use that internal value, as shown in Listing 2.3.

LISTING 2.3   Bank Account Balance from an Internal Account Type Variable

```
#import "BankAccount.h"

@implementation BankAccount

#define checking 1
#define saving 2
#define investment 3

- (float *)balance
{
  switch (accountType) {
    case checking:
      //set returnValue ...
      break;

    case saving:
      //set returnValue ...
      break;

    case investment:
      //set returnValue ...
      break;
```

```
   default:
     //set returnValue ...
     break;
 }
 return returnValue;


}

@end
```

In Listing 2.2, the header of this class, you see that the account type variable is declared as private, which means that it is accessible only from within the class. The only part of the class that is visible to the outside world is the method that returns the balance. It does that based on its own internal data (the account type, and, presumably, transaction data). This bank account class is both abstracted and encapsulated. From the outside, all it can do is return its balance based on its internal values. Anyone accessing this class doesn't need to know how it does what it does.

Note that in Listing 2.3 everything about the internal workings of the class is hidden. The values of the different types of bank accounts are not exposed. This type of structure might be useful to protect your code from external changes. When you create a bank account instance, you might set its account type by passing in a parameter that might be a string such as "Super Saver Account." The translation of that string, which is controlled by the marketing area of the bank, to an internal type of account can happen when the specific bank account instance is created; from then on, the terminology of the marketing area is independent of the internal functions of the bank accounts. Likewise, you can change the functionality of an account type without changing anything that is exposed to the outside world. (This happens in banking when regulations change across a banking system, forcing new types of calculations.)

GO TO ▶ Hour 8, "Declaring Instance Variables in an Interface File," p. 111, for more about setting the scope of instance variables, such as making them private, public, or protected.

Using Accessors to Manage Encapsulation

An important tool for managing encapsulation is the use of *accessors*, which are small methods that let you access the instance variables of an object without referring to them directly. Accessors sometimes simply retrieve or set the value of a variable, but they also may perform transformations and modifications. For example, in a number of framework accessor methods in the Core Data framework, an accessor creates an essential element of the Core Data stack if it does not yet exist. Having created it, the object can then return it quickly the next time it is asked for.

Managing Inheritance in the Objective-C World

As you see throughout this book, Objective-C approaches subclassing and inheritance in more varied ways than many other object-oriented languages do. The basics of inheritance are simple. You declare a *base object*, which may have its own methods and instance variables. Following good Objective-C programming practice, the instance variables are accessed through accessors and are not visible to other classes.

GO TO ▶ Hour 9, "Declaring Properties in an Interface File," p. 127, to see how to use declared properties to automatically generate accessors.

You can declare class methods in the class interface (a .h file) or in the implementation file (a .m file). Methods declared in the interface file are visible to other classes, but you can hide methods from the outside world by declaring them inside the implementation. Hiding methods in the implementation file helps to increase the encapsulation of the class.

GO TO ▶ "Using Class Extensions" in Hour 18, "Extending a Class with Categories and Extensions," p. 245, to see how to hide your class's methods.

You then proceed to override your base object. Each class that overrides the base object inherits the methods and variables of the base object. It can *override* them so that if your base object has a method called init, you can control how subclasses deal with that method. You have three basic choices:

- ▶ **Invoke**—If your base class declares init, when you call init on a subclass, the base class's init method is invoked.

- ▶ **Override**—If you have declared an init method in a subclass, calling init on the subclass invokes the subclass's init method.

- ▶ **Override and invoke**—As part of a subclass's override of a base class method, you can always call [super init] (or whatever the name of the base class method is).

This means that you can combine the functionality of the base class with additional or replacement functionality in its subclasses. If you subclass a subclass, you can use calls to super to invoke the various implementations of the method up through the base class. From the object-oriented standpoint, what you see is that the base object and its descendants all implement in one way or another this particular method—something that the abstract object should implement (such as reporting the balance in a bank account).

All of this is standard for object-oriented programming. Objective-C expands on the concept of inheritance in a variety of ways. Inheritance and subclassing provide an orderly way of integrating code from other objects into your own object. Primarily this is from superclasses of your own object.

However, Objective-C offers several ways to integrate code from other structures into your own object. In addition to inheritance, these are

▶ **Protocols**—These are sets of methods that can be adopted by classes. The class that adopts the protocol then implements the methods of the protocol; if a class adopts a protocol, know that you can invoke any of the protocol's methods. (A protocol's methods can be marked as optional, and in that case you have to make certain that you are only invoking those methods that are required or are implemented.) Each class that adopts a protocol implements it in its own way, often with its own variables. The protocol structure in some ways implements some features of multiple inheritance. The methods of the protocol may appear in several classes that are otherwise unrelated. The idea that only the inheritance chain lets you share methods is augmented in this way.

▶ **Categories**—Whereas protocols can be adopted by any class, categories consist of methods that are added to a specific class at runtime. You can use categories to add methods to an existing class for which you do not have the source code.

▶ **Extensions**—Sometimes called anonymous categories, extensions are declared and implemented in the implementation of a class (typically the .m file). Extensions can add methods and properties to a class. They also can redefine properties (such as changing readonly to readwrite). They are now commonly used to declare methods and properties that are totally private to the class itself.

Summary

In this hour, you read about the design principle behind Objective-C as well as how it implements object-oriented programming objectives. In particular, you have seen how data abstraction and encapsulation are implemented in Objective-C so that you can write elegant, efficient, and maintainable object-oriented code. You have also seen how Objective-C implements a variety of architectures that allow for data reuse and sharing. With Objective-C, it is not just a matter of inheritance because you also have categories, extensions, and protocols to use.

Q&A

Q. Why do categories, extensions, and protocols matter in Objective-C?

A. They allow you to reuse code in other ways than by creating subclasses. This can mean that your class hierarchies in Objective-C might be flatter than they are in languages in which the only way to share code is to subclass it.

Q. Why does encapsulation matter?

A. Along with data abstraction, it means that your objects are self-contained. The only attributes and functions that are exposed to the outside world are those that are common to all instances of the class. This can make ongoing maintenance easier.

Workshop

Quiz

1. If you override a method of a superclass, is it automatically invoked as well?

2. Why are accessors important?

Quiz Answers

1. No. If you want to invoke the method of a superclass, you must call it with code such as [`super myMethod`]. Typically, that is either the first or last line of your override.

2. They allow you to set and get values for instance variables without directly touching the variables themselves. They also let you do some additional work such as adjusting or creating other variables and properties.

Activities

Explore the Cocoa frameworks on developer.apple.com or with Organizer in Xcode. If you read the overview of each one, you find a list of its classes, and you see which ones will be most important to you. Pay particular attention to UIKit in Cocoa Touch and AppKit in OS X.

Using Object-Oriented Features in Objective-C

Communicating to Methods with Messages

Perhaps the biggest difference between Objective-C and languages such as C++ is its messaging syntax as well as the way people talk about it. Objective-C has classes just as other object-oriented languages do, and those classes can have methods within them. You communicate with those methods with messages. A message is enclosed within square brackets, and it consists of the name of the object to which it is being sent followed by the message itself.

The implementation files that you create carry the .m suffix because originally they were referred to as message files that contained the code for the messages defined in the header (.h) files. (This is possibly an apocryphal tale, but the importance of messaging in Objective-C is undisputed.)

NOTE

There is an ulterior purpose to this section. It does help you to understand how to communicate with Objective-C methods and messages, but the examples begin with the messages that you use to allocate and initialize objects.

Looking at a Simple Message

Here is a simple message that is sent to an object called myObject, which is assumed to be of type NSObject—the object that is the root class of most class hierarchies in Objective-C.

```
[myObject init];
```

This message calls the init method on `myObject`.

Methods can return a value. If a method returns a value, you can set it to a variable as in the following:

```
myVariable = [myObject init];
```

Declaring a Method

When you declare a simple method, you use an Objective-C variation on C function syntax. NSObject, the root class of almost all of the Objective-C objects you use, does declare an init method.

The following is the declaration that supports the messages shown in the previous section:

```
- (id)init
```

As you might surmise, the init method shown here returns a result of type id. (You find out more about id shortly.)

The minus sign at the start of the method is an important part of the declaration: It is the method type. It indicates that this is a method that is defined for instances of a class. Any instance of the class in which this declaration is used can invoke this method.

To put it another way, you (or an instance of a class) can send the init message to any instance of this class. Because this is the NSObject superclass of every other object, that means you can send the init message to any instance of any class.

There is more on allocating and initializing objects later in this hour.

Using Class Methods

The minus sign at the start of the method shown in the previous section indicates that it is an instance method. There is another type of method in Objective-C: a class method. It is indicated by a plus sign.

A message to an instance method can be sent to any instance of that class subject to constraints for that specific class. Whereas you call an instance method on an instance of a class, you call a class method on the class itself. No instance is involved.

Class methods are used most frequently as *factory methods*. Perhaps the most common class method is alloc. For NSObject, its declaration is

```
+ (id)alloc;
```

Whereas you send init to an instance, as in this case:

```
[myObject init];
```

alloc allocates an uninitialized instance of a class as in

```
[MyClass alloc];
```

This returns an instance of MyClass. As you can see in the declaration, this result is of type id. It is time to explore that type.

Working with id—Strongly and Weakly Typed Variables

Objective-C supports strongly and weakly typed variables. When you reference a variable using a strong type, you specify the type of the variable. The actual variable must be of that type or a subclass of that type; if it is a subclass, it is, by definition, the type of all of its superclasses.

In Cocoa, you can declare a variable as:

```
NSArray *myArray
```

This means you could be referring to an object of type NSMutableArray, which is a subclass. You can write the same code to work with elements of the array no matter what its actual type is. If necessary, you might have to coerce a specific instance to the subclass that you want (if you know that is what it is).

id is the ultimate weakly typed variable; it could be any class. That is why it is used as the return type from alloc. alloc is a class method on NSObject so if you call it on an NSArray, you get an instance of NSArray returned through id.

NOTE

instanceType

A new keyword, instanceType, is available when working with related result types. By convention, methods beginning with names such as init and alloc always return objects that are an instance of the class type that receives the message. Thus, [MyClass init] returns an instance of MyClass. Init is declared as returning an id, but with this convention it is the related type. You can now use instanceType instead of id to specify that the returned value is the same type as the receiver's type (that is, MyClass in this example). Because instanceType turns out to be more specific than id at compile time, it is preferable to use in these cases because it can allow for more error checking. As you can see from the examples in this hour, many types of the code you write already use specific variables of the correct type; however, instanceType in declarations of your own methods can make that more likely.

Nesting Messages

Messages can be nested within one another. You could write the following:

```
myObject = [MyClass alloc];
myObject = [myObject init];
```

This would use the class method of MyClass to allocate a new instance of MyClass, which you immediately assign to myObject.

You can nest them together as follows:

```
myObject = [[MyClass alloc] init];
```

The rules for nesting square brackets are the same as for nesting parentheses——the innermost set is evaluated first.

TIP

Xcode gives you a big assist by enabling you to set a preference to match brackets as you type.

Looking at Method Signatures and Parameters

alloc and init are very good basic examples because they have no parameters. Most methods in any language do have parameters. For example, you can write an area function that takes two parameters (height and width) and returns the product as its return value.

Other languages generally specify a name and a type for each parameter, and so does Objective-C. However, it adds another dimension: It labels each parameter.

This labeling means that the code is more readable, but you do have to understand what is going on when there is more than one parameter. When there is no parameter, the message is simply the receiver and the name of the method:

```
[myObject init];
```

If there is a parameter, it follows the method name. In the message, a colon precedes the parameter itself. For example, in `NSSet`, you can initialize a set with an `NSArray` using code like this:

```
mySet =[NSSet alloc];
[mySet initWithArray: myArray];
```

The declaration needs to specify not only the parameter name, which is used in the code of the method, but also its type:

```
(instanceType)initWithArray:(NSArray *)array;
```

The second and subsequent parameters are also labeled. The difference is that the first parameter is labeled in effect by the name of the method. If you add more parameters, their names and types are needed; they are preceded by a keyword (which, in the case of the first parameter is the method name). Here is another `NSSet` method. It initializes an `NSSet` to the elements of another `NSSet` (the first parameter). The second parameter specifies whether the elements of the first set are to be copied or not.

Here is a typical invocation:

```
[mySet: initWithSet: aSet copyItems:YES];
```

Here is the declaration:

```
(instanceType)initWithSet:(NSSet *)set copyItems:(BOOL)flag
```

In documentation (and in this book), the signature sometimes is compressed to be the result, method name, and parameters so that the previous declaration is shown as

```
(instanceType)initWithSet:copyItems:
```

Allocating and Initializing Objects

The messages shown in this hour have demonstrated how you can allocate and initialize objects. Because these processes are used so extensively in Objective-C, it is worthwhile to take a few moments to look more carefully at these messages.

As noted previously, you most often create instances of classes by calling `alloc`. This is a class method of `NSObject`, which means it is available to any class in the frameworks or in your own code. You simply send a message to the class, and you get back a new instance.

```
MyClass *newInstance = [MyClass alloc];
```

Immediately thereafter, you initialize the newly created instance, most often with a call to `init` or a related method.

```
newInstance = [newInstance init];
```

As noted previously, you can combine these two messages into one line of code.

```
MyClass *newInstance = [[MyClass alloc] init];
```

It makes sense that `alloc` returns an object that you can place in an instance variable. You might be surprised that `init` also returns an object. The reason for this is that after you have created the new object, the call to `init` might not only set instance variables and other settings, but it also might decide to replace the allocated object with another one. That is the one that you should use thereafter.

By convention, initializer names start with `init`. They might have additional parameters, such as these various initializers for `UIBarButtonItem` in Cocoa Touch:

- `initWithBarButtonSystemItem:target:action:`
- `initWithCustomView:`
- `initWithImage:style:target:action:`
- `initWithTitle:style:target:action:`
- `initWithImage:landscapeImagePhone:style:target:action:`

Initializers may set various properties of the object being created; they also may take various routes to complete the initialization. If you create a series of initializers, there are two rules to follow:

▶ The first step in an initializer is to call [super `init`]. This ensures that the basic object is there and complete.

▶ Initializers can call other initializers that each performs some initialization. The most complete initializer (that is, the one that sets all of the properties rather than just some of them) is the designated initializer. The others are secondary initializers.

It is a good practice to put all of the initializers together in your code, possibly using a `#pragma mark` – section. This separates the initializers and, in the list of methods in the jump bar for a file, the pragma section names will appear.

Summary

In this hour, you have seen the messaging structure that is at the heart of Objective-C. It is not just another way of talking about the calling of methods that other languages use; it is a different way of constructing software. You see in later hours how the messaging architecture helps to implement dynamic aspects of Objective-C programs.

The common `alloc` and `init` methods have been used in this hour as examples. You have also seen how you can work with them and construct a hierarchy of designated and secondary initializers to construct your runtime objects.

Q&A

Q. Why does `init` return an `id`?

A. By returning an `id`, which is often a reference to the object on which it was called, it allows `init` to substitute a new object for the original one. Increasingly, the declarations are being changed to use the new `instanceType` return value, which allows for more error checking. Each new release of iOS adds more of these revisions.

Q. What is the difference between a class method and an instance method?

A. You must have an instance of a class to use an instance method; you can simply call a class method with the class name (that is, you do not need an instance). Class methods are often used as factory methods to create new instances of the class.

Workshop

Quiz

1. How do you differentiate class and instance methods in your code?

2. When do you call [super `init`] in an initializer?

Quiz Answers

1. Class methods begin with +; instance methods begin with −.

2. This is the first thing you do. You might go up through a hierarchy, but you have to have all of the superclasses created and initialized before you continue with your own.

Activities

Browse the Cocoa frameworks to see how messages are structured. Get used to the sequence of labeled parameters in the messages. It might take a while to be comfortable reading them, but remember that this is the environment in which you are going to be working.

HOUR 4
Using Xcode 5

What You'll Learn in This Hour

▶ Creating an Xcode project
▶ Using source code repositories
▶ Committing changes to Git
▶ Using Git branches

Getting to Work with Xcode

Now that you have seen the basics of Objective-C and its use with object-oriented programming, you can start to write code. As noted previously, today the overwhelming majority of Objective-C programs are written for use on OS X and iOS; most of them are written using Xcode, Apple's development tool.

NOTE

Getting Xcode

The simplest way to get Xcode is from the Mac App Store. The price is right (free). Before the existence of the Mac App Store, Xcode was distributed as a free download or on the installation disc(s) for the operating system. In those scenarios, the Xcode files were installed in a root-level folder called Developer, thus making them available to all user accounts on the Mac in question. Now, Xcode is just another app installed in the root-level Applications folder so all user accounts on the Mac have access to it. The root-level Developer folder is gone, and your Xcode files now live in your own account. This only matters to you if you used Xcode in the past or if you are referring to documentation that is now out of date. Customarily, developer preview editions of Xcode are available on developer.apple.com to registered developers. Those versions are sometimes distributed in other ways, which are described on developer.apple.com if necessary.

Xcode is a complete development environment that includes editors for text-based code, user interfaces, and Core Data data models. It comes with debugging tools, as well as a variety of extra tools you need for building and managing your projects.

As of this writing, the current version of Xcode is 5. Xcode 4 was a major change from Xcode 3, including a new single-window interface and the integration of the user interface design tool, Interface Builder (previously a separate program), into Xcode and the addition of storyboarding for iOS apps. Xcode 5 is another major change that continues the simplification started in Xcode 4. In Xcode 5, debugging tools are more closely integrated with Xcode itself along with more extensive support for Git repositories (this is discussed throughout this hour). In addition, the interface of Xcode 5 shows how some of the major design principles of iOS 7 can be applied to Mac apps. (Xcode has always served as somewhat of a testbed for new interface technologies.)

The download of Xcode typically contains the SDKs for the current and various previous versions of the operating systems for iOS and OS X. For that reason, during the development process of a new OS, revisions to the SDKs are typically reflected in revisions to Xcode. Furthermore, in 2012 and 2013, a further pattern emerged that may or may not continue. In both of these years, the new version of iOS was released a few weeks before the new version of OS X. A version of Xcode was released for the new version of iOS and the current version of OS X. A few weeks later, a minor ("dot") release of Xcode reflected the new OS X version.

Most of the time, you use Xcode to build projects from built-in Xcode templates that include several frameworks for OS X or iOS. You write code that customizes and adds on to those frameworks for your own project's needs.

NOTE

This book does not go into the frameworks you use because the goal of the book is to help you learn Objective-C itself. Still, it is important to know how your code is going to be arranged in an Xcode world.

With Xcode, you create *projects*. Each project can have several targets. In the simplest case, you have a single target for your project, but you can also have several targets (such as a full version and a lite version or an OS X version and an iOS version). You can switch among the targets to build them separately in Xcode.

▼ TRY IT YOURSELF

Create a New Xcode Project

These steps provide a quick review of how to get started with an Xcode project. You've seen them before in Hour 1, "Overview of the Developer Program." These steps provide a bit more details about the options you have as you create a new project.

In Hour 5, "Using Compiler Directives," you'll go through them again in even more detail. Partly this is to introduce you to the process, but it's also because the purpose of building the project changes from hour to hour. In Hour 1, the purpose was to get you started as quickly as possible with Xcode. In this hour, the purpose is to build a project so that you can use the Xcode source control options to manage changes. And in Hour 6, "Exploring Messaging and a Testbed App," the purpose will be to create a testbed app that you can use to experiment with Objective-C syntax.

Here's how to create a new Xcode project:

1. Launch Xcode.

   The first time you launch it, you see the splash screen shown in Figure 4.1. The check box at the bottom left enables you to choose whether or not to see it in the future. If you do not see it, you can always reopen it from Window, Welcome to Xcode or ⌘-Shift-1.

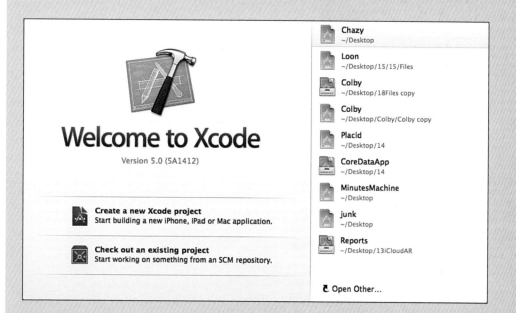

FIGURE 4.1
Create a new project from the Xcode splash screen.

2. Click Create a New Xcode Project to open the window shown in Figure 4.2. Select the operating system and template you want to use.

3. Select the templates for each of the operating systems. For this experiment, choose the Master-Detail Application template for iOS.

   Figure 4.3 shows the templates for OS X.

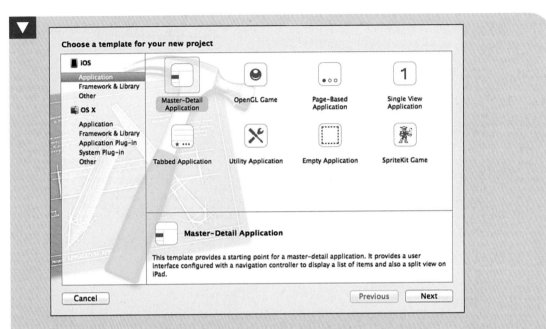

FIGURE 4.2
Review the iOS templates.

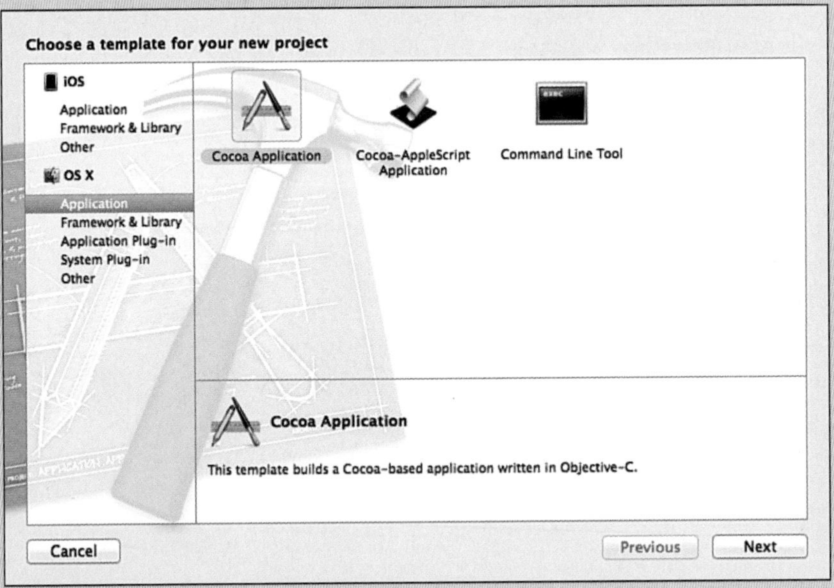

Choose a template for your new project

iOS
Application
Framework & Library
Other

OS X
Application
Framework & Library
Application Plug-in
System Plug-in
Other

Cocoa Application   Cocoa-AppleScript   Command Line Tool
                     Application

Cocoa Application

This template builds a Cocoa-based application written in Objective-C.

Cancel   Previous   Next

FIGURE 4.3
You can switch to OS X templates.

4. On the next screen (see Figure 4.4), name the project and provide additional information.

TIP

The choices and settings differ for iOS and OS X projects as well as for different templates within them, but you always name the project.

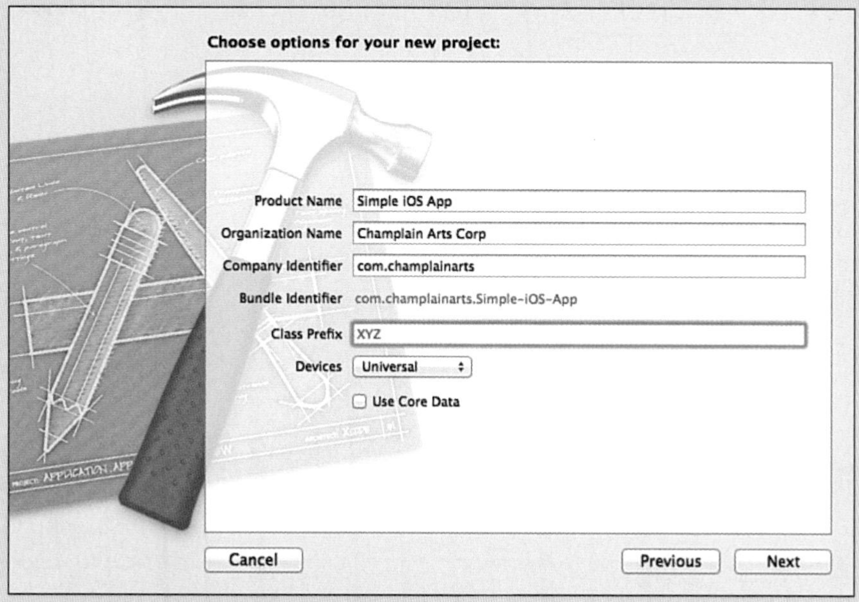

Choose options for your new project:

Product Name	Simple iOS App
Organization Name	Champlain Arts Corp
Company Identifier	com.champlainarts
Bundle Identifier	com.champlainarts.Simple-iOS-App
Class Prefix	XYZ
Devices	Universal
	☐ Use Core Data

Cancel   Previous   Next

FIGURE 4.4
Set the name and options for your project.

5. Provide a location for the project and create a source code repository, as shown in Figure 4.5. From the pop-up menu, choose My Mac for the location.

Make sure to check the Create Git Repository on My Mac check box source code repository. There is more on Git in particular and source code repositories in general in the next section.

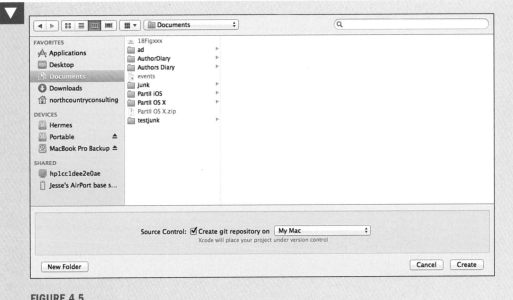

FIGURE 4.5
Review the location and create a Git source code repository.

Keeping Track of Your Source Code

In Step 5 of the Try It Yourself activity, "Create a New Xcode Project," you set the check box
to create the Git source code repository. In this section, you explore what Git in particular and
source code repositories in general are and how they can make your life easier as you develop
a project. You may wonder why you need to worry about them at this point in your Objective-C
programming adventures. The reason is simple: By the time your projects and files are so many
that you need a source code management system, it is often too late to implement one easily.
Thus, source code management joins security, multiuser architectures, and runtime version control of data structures as issues you should confront before you need them.

NOTE

What Doesn't Need Version Control?

A one-time test or experiment that you plan to definitely discard does not need source control management. You write it, test whatever it is you want to test, and then you throw it away. You may actually save some or all of the code so that you can refer to the relevant section or snippet that solved
a problem you might need to address in larger systems. For many people, considering the trade-off
between not having source control for a project that needs it and having source control for a project
that doesn't really need it is not a challenge: When in doubt, use it.

Xcode supports both Subversion and Git with a common interface for both. However, it creates repositories only for Git, which is why it is used in this hour. Both Subversion and Git can be controlled from the command line in the Terminal app. Because Subversion is a client/server version control system rather than a distributed one, Git and its distributed architecture make it easier to integrate into Xcode in a totally automated manner.

Exploring Source Code Control

When software development moved beyond consisting of a single file for each program or app, it started to become more difficult to manage the various project files. On top of that, when more than one developer—maybe in more than one location—was working on a project, it became necessary to automate the management of the various files. Source code repositories were born. In multiple-developer, multiple-location situations, there are not only multiple files in a project, but also multiple versions of each file. The complexity of storing these files and, most important, knowing which versions of which files make up a single version of the project as a whole quickly becomes hard to manage.

TIP

Finding Out More About Version Control

Wikipedia is a terrific resource, particularly for technology issues. Start by looking up Git and then follow whatever links interest you. This section provides only a high-level overview of the Git interface in Xcode.

A key aspect of source code management is the ability to check out files from the repository and modify them in your own directory. When you are done, you can check the code back in. In both the check-in and checkout processes, you are allowed to add a comment about what you have done, and perhaps what you plan on doing next. (Using these comments is definitely a best practice.) In addition to your optional comment, the source code management software automatically captures the date and time of the check-in/checkout as well as the user's name. Thus, you have a management record of the files.

Using Forks and Branches

Whether you are working with other developers or are working on your own, there are times when you do not simply want to check out files and then check them back in. Sometimes you want to fork or branch the code.

In the case of branching, you create an independent branch or series of check-ins and check-outs that remain within the overall project. Depending on the project and the development, you might eventually merge a branch back into the main branch, or a branch might become the main branch. However it is handled, the intention of branching is to create multiple development paths within a single project. In the case of forking, you might take an existing project, copy it (with permission, of course), and then continue development on the separate fork.

TIP

Using Branches in a Classroom

One example of branching is when a single project is placed in a source code repository for a class. Each student can then check out a branch independently of the other students. The teacher and students can view the various branches to see how different people have addressed the same problems in the project. Think about how you would accomplish the same results if each student worked in a separate set of files in separate directories. For even a small class with fewer than a dozen people, you could quickly wind up with people manipulating more than a hundred files in various projects.

The problem of source code management was addressed in two primary ways. Starting in the mainframe era, the notion of management of any kind of data was generally solved by storing the data in a centralized location (think databases) and in a client/server scenario.

With the advent of fast networks, it became feasible to decentralize the storage of the shared data, and that is what Git does. There is no centralized repository; rather, there can be many repositories, each of which is complete.

In practical terms, for most people working on their own Xcode projects, there is only one repository: their own. There is no need to sync it with other copies of the repository because there are none. This means that although Git can manage multiple repositories on a peer-to-peer basis, the only commands that you need to worry about are the commands to check in or check out a file, create a branch, or merge a branch.

The final thing you need to worry about is the check box shown previously in Figure 4.5. Check it to create your Git repository on your own computer—and you are ready to go.

TIP

The History of Git

Git is free software initially developed by Linus Torvalds for handling the source control needs of the Linux Kernel project. It is distributed under the GNU Public License (GPL), version 2.

Working in a Source Code Repository World

There are two points to remember as you move into the world of source code repositories:

▶ **Everything is a version or a revision.** If you want to split hairs, you can even suggest that the first version of a file posted to a repository is itself a revision—a revision from nothing to that first version.

▶ **Trust the version control.** For many people, the hardest thing to learn is to stop managing files and versions themselves. Before embarking on an attempt to solve a problem, many developers are used to copying the project files to a new directory so that, if there are problems, they can revert to a known version. This is no longer necessary. You can create a branch if you want, but you can also check out files to modify them and discard the modifications. All of the file and naming manipulation can be handled by the version control system.

TIP
As you might have noticed, in this book the terms *source code control* and *version control* are used interchangeably. There are subtle differences, but for all intents and purposes, they are the same thing.

Because you will be relying on the version control software to keep track of the versions of your code along with your comments as you check files in and out, you do not need to name files to reflect their test status. This can be a difficult habit to break, but unless you do, you will not reap the benefits of source code management software. Furthermore, you will make your development environment more complicated.

Establish a naming convention for your files and stick to it. With Xcode, the naming convention can be very simple: Accept the Xcode default names. You can set up a class prefix as shown previously in Figure 4.4 to add a default prefix to new files. Make certain that the prefix has to do with the files (for example, who owns licensed code in them) and does not reflect the state of the file, such as test or development. Those considerations can be managed very well with source code control. Prefixes enable you to prevent namespace collisions between existing code and your new code. They also can help you keep track of where code you have included from other developers and open sources comes from.

Thus, when you create and name your project, consider that you are naming what will be the project in all of its configurations—test, production, enhancements, and so forth. Use the production name in most cases.

TIP
There is one exception to this. You might want to have a single alternate version of the project with its own name. This can facilitate testing on a sandboxed app environment where the name matters.

Using Git with Xcode

If you have created a new project as described in the Try It Yourself activity, "Create a New Xcode Project," you have an iOS app that can run as is. It does not do much, but it builds and runs, and, most important, it provides a shell with which you can test your Objective-C code.

Without making any changes, build the project. Click the Run arrow at the left of the toolbar in the Xcode window and select where to run it. If you have created an iOS project, your choices will be an actual device or the simulator, which has a variety of hardware configurations built in to it, as shown in Figure 4.6.

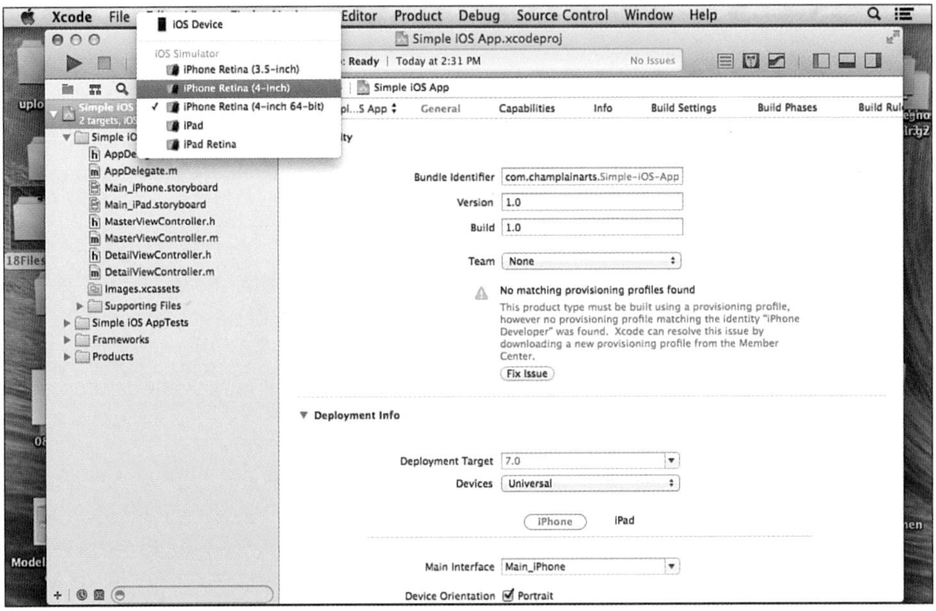

FIGURE 4.6
Build and run the project.

You may see a message about a missing provisioning profile. If you are just testing Objective-C code, you can ignore that message. If you are using the frameworks that implement iCloud and access to shared services, you must resolve the issue; for the projects in this book, however, you should be okay.

When it runs, you'll see the app as shown in Figure 4.7. You can use the simulator's menu commands to rotate the simulated device.

NOTE

Local and Remote Repositories for Git

If you create a git repository as shown previously in Figure 4.5, you'll want to see it and be able to use it within Xcode. However, you won't see it in the Finder. It is a hidden file (starting with a period) inside your project's directory. That way, if you move the directory elsewhere, you'll still have your repository. However, if you move the individual files, you'll lose the repository unless you go back and show invisible files and move it.

Git (including the Git interface in Xcode) enables you to manage remote repositories as well as a local one. The most common way of doing this is to clone a remote repository. You can then work on your local copy and, when you are ready, synchronize it back to the remote version. This is described at the end of this hour in "Using a Remote Repository."

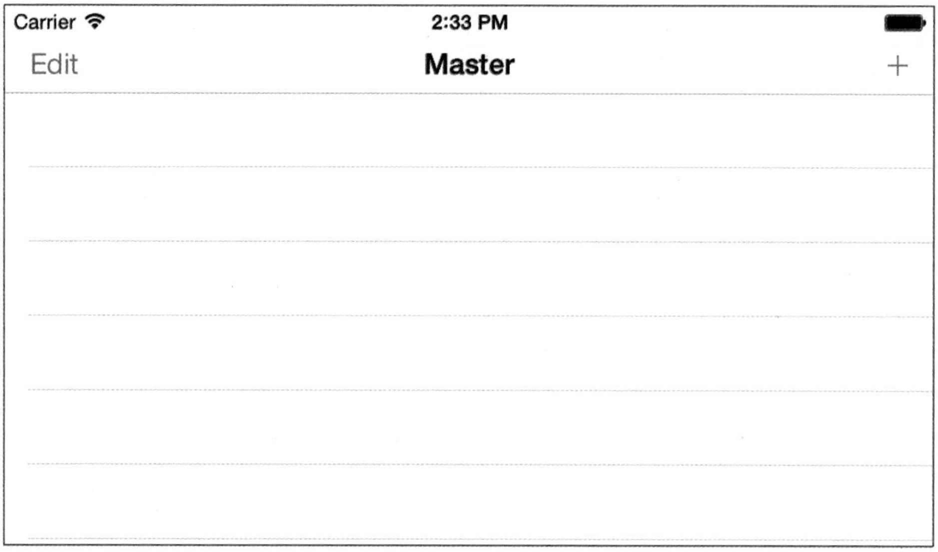

Carrier 🔋	2:33 PM	🔋
Edit	**Master**	+

FIGURE 4.7
View the app on the simulator.

After you start to use Git, you will see what it can do (and how you can do it).

TRY IT YOURSELF ▼

Use Git to Track Changes

Now that you have an app up and running, the best way to learn about Git is to use it. Before continuing, make certain that you do have an app created, as in the Try It Yourself activity, "Create a New Xcode Project." Then, follow these steps:

▼

1. Select the working copy of your app and choose Configure from the submenu, as shown in Figure 4.8.

    You may see repositories other than the one you have just created.

TIP

If you do not see the project you have just created, create a new project and make certain to indicate that you want a Git repository.

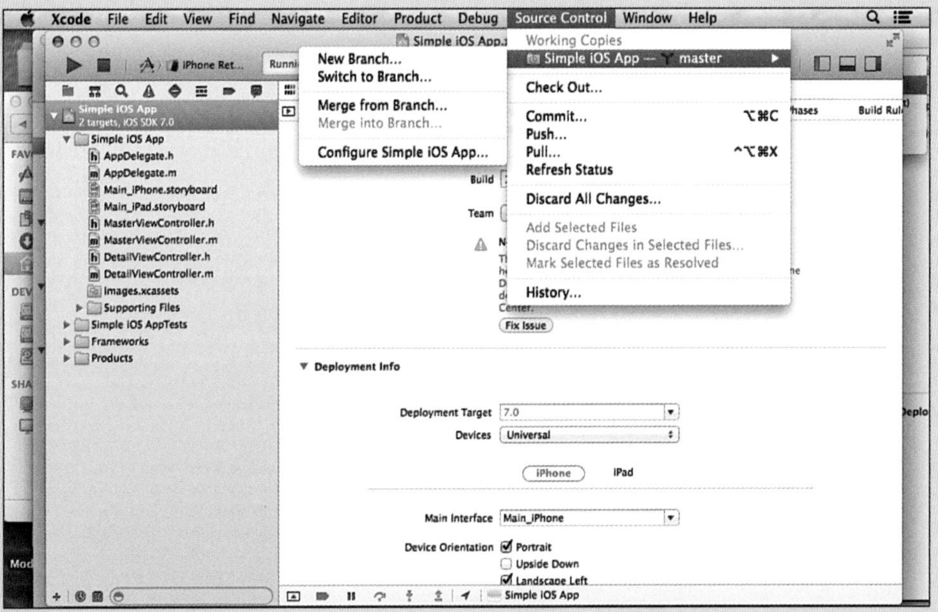

FIGURE 4.8
Configure your repository.

2. Check that the local repository has been created, using the command Source Control, History as shown in Figure 4.9.

3. Make a change to a file in the project.

    In Figure 4.10, you see a traditional C language-style comment added at the top of AppDelegate.h. Note the badge (the letter M) indicating a modification to the file in the project navigator. (It might take a moment or two for it to show up.)

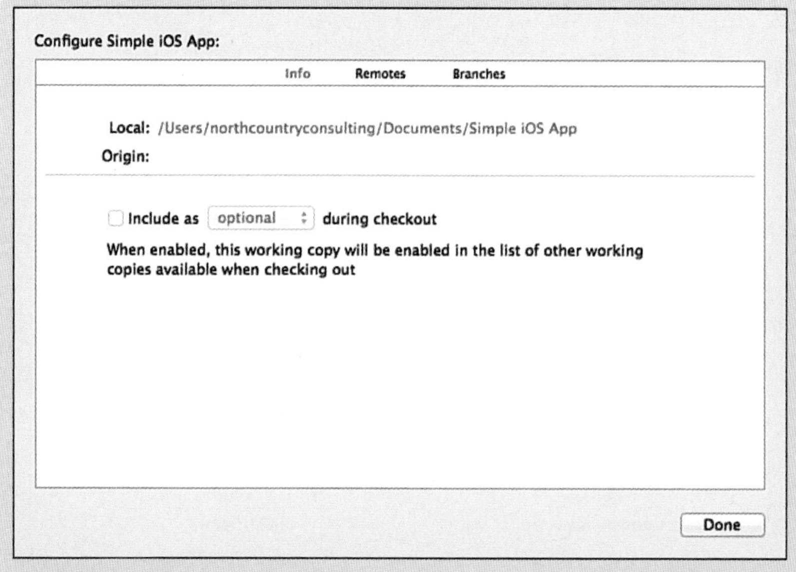

Configure Simple iOS App:
Info
Remotes
Branches
Local: /Users/northcountryconsulting/Documents/Simple iOS App
Origin:
Include as optional during checkout
When enabled, this working copy will be enabled in the list of other working copies available when checking out
Done

FIGURE 4.9
Verify the local repository.

Simple iOS App.xcodeproj — AppDelegate.h
iPhone Ret...
Running Simple iOS App on iPhone Retina (4-inch)
No Issues
Simple iOS App
2 targets, iOS SDK 7.0
Simple iOS App
AppDelegate.h
M
AppDelegate.m
Main_iPhone.storyboard
Main_iPad.storyboard
MasterViewController.h
MasterViewController.m
DetailViewController.h
DetailViewController.m
Images.xcassets
Supporting Files
Simple iOS AppTests
Frameworks
Products
Simple iOS App > Simple iOS App > AppDelegate.h > No Selection
//
// AppDelegate.h
// Simple iOS App
//
// Created by North Country Consulting on 10/6/13.
// Copyright (c) 2013 Champlain Arts Corp. All rights reserved.
//
#import <UIKit/UIKit.h>
// this is a comment to test Git
@interface AppDelegate : UIResponder <UIApplicationDelegate>
@property (strong, nonatomic) UIWindow *window;
@end
Simple iOS App

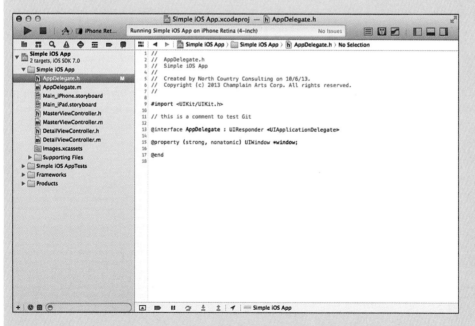

FIGURE 4.10
Make a change to a file.

4. Commit the change by choosing Source Control, Commit.

5. Review the changes.

Figure 4.11 shows you the changes (right) and the previous version (left). Check that they are OK. If they are, type a commit message at the bottom of the window and click Commit in the lower right. You use the check boxes in the project navigator to add or remove changed files from the commit. You also can use the check mark in the gutter between the changes and original version to accept or reject an individual change.

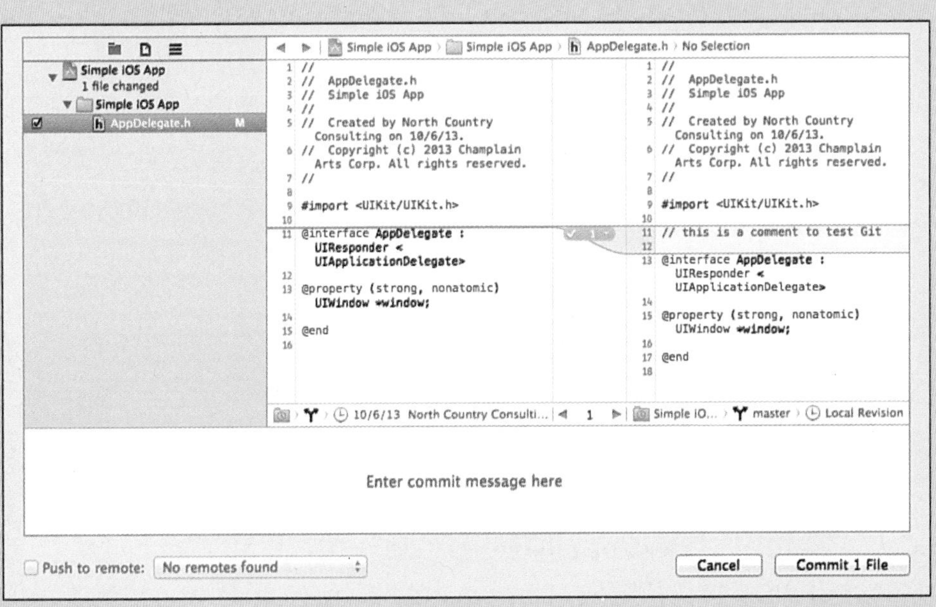

FIGURE 4.11
Review the changes.

6. If you do not provide a description of your changes, you will not be able to commit them (see Figure 4.12).

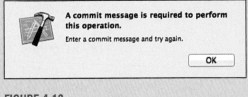

FIGURE 4.12
You must have a commit message.

7. Provide the commit message and commit the changes. The M in the project navigator will disappear (there may be a brief delay).

8. Review the history with Source Control, History, as shown in Figure 4.13.

You can review individual changes to each file in a commit.

Project history:	Q▾ Search commit messages
Today	

North Country Consulting
4:00 PM
e91165907bc9
Show 1 modified file
This is a test commit message.

North Country Consulting
2:18 PM
7a29585129a8
Show 19 modified files
Initial Commit

[Done]

FIGURE 4.13
Review the history of changes.

There's one additional point to bring up. You can configure each of your working copies using Configure <Your Project Name> in the submenu shown in Figure 4.8. As you can see in Figure 4.14, one of the configuration settings lets you choose which side the original code and the modified code is shown on.

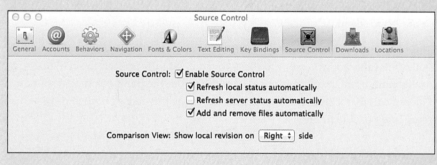

Source Control

General   Accounts   Behaviors   Navigation   Fonts & Colors   Text Editing   Key Bindings   Source Control   Downloads   Locations

Source Control: ☑ Enable Source Control
☑ Refresh local status automatically
☐ Refresh server status automatically
☑ Add and remove files automatically

Comparison View: Show local revision on [Right ⬍] side

FIGURE 4.14
Configure the display.

You have seen the basics of using Git: creating a repository, making a change, and committing it. Moving beyond the basics is not so much a matter of getting more complicated but, rather, of mastering a few special cases.

▼ **TRY IT YOURSELF**

Discard Changes

Note that canceling a commit (refer to Figure 4.11) leaves the modifications still in the file and uncommitted. You might want to do this if you're not finished testing the change. Sometimes, though, you want to discard the changes and start over from the last commit, as you see in the following steps:

1. Select the file or files you want to back out in the project navigator. It should be marked as changed with M (modified) or A (added).

2. Choose Source Control, Discard All Changes.

3. You will need to confirm the discard.

4. Changes for the selected files are backed out from the files, and the files are marked as unmodified. At this point, the changes are gone from the repository and from the file itself. If you worry about being able to go back in case of an emergency, if you are using Time Machine (and you should be), you can always do a special backup, or you can create a separate branch in your repository.

When you review your changes before committing them, it is sometimes easy to decide whether to commit or discard them. There are also cases where you know as you are embarking on a series of changes that they might not work. In such a case, it is often not just a matter of a few lines of code, but a matter of significant changes to several files—sometimes over a period of time as you explore a new architecture or interface. In those cases, branches are a good solution. You create a branch and work within it. You can commit changes as you go along. When you are at a stopping point, you might decide that the new branch is the way to move forward, and you can merge it back into the main branch.

On the other hand, you might decide that the branch has been a good experiment and learning process, but it really is not the way you want to move forward with the project. In such a case, you can revert to the main branch and continue committing from the point before you split off the new branch or you can merge in the changes. You can delete the unused branch or keep it around for reference and possible future use.

Use Branches

Before creating a new branch, you might want to commit all uncommitted changes. You do not have to do so, but it is often easier to make certain that the project is in a stable and known condition. If you have a choice, work from a version that works even if it does not contain every feature. Then, you can create a branch and, if you break the code, at least you can return to something stable. Here are the steps to follow to create a new branch:

1. Use the submenu shown previously in Figure 4.8 to create a new branch.

2. Name the new branch (see Figure 4.15). (Spaces are not allowed in branch names.)

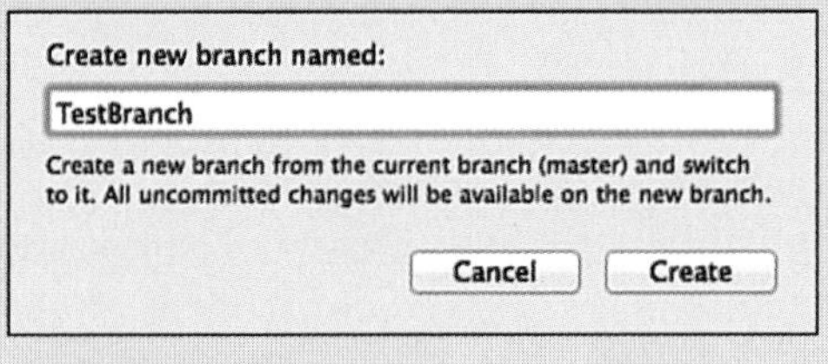

Create new branch named:

```
TestBranch
```

Create a new branch from the current branch (master) and switch to it. All uncommitted changes will be available on the new branch.

Cancel   Create

FIGURE 4.15
Name the new branch.

3. You are automatically switched to the new branch. You can verify this by choosing Switch to Branch from the workspace submenu. As you see in Figure 4.16, all branches are listed in the center of the sheet; the current branch is identified in the text at the bottom. You can switch back and forth. Figure 4.16 shows the perspective when you switch back to the master branch after having created a branch for testing.

4. Modify a line of code to your project and commit it with a comment. If you added a comment line to AppDelegate.h to test committing changes, you can delete it now and commit that change.

5. Use Source Control, History to view changes, including this one.

6. Using the Source Control submenu, switch back to the main branch. The sheet shown in Figure 4.16 shows the master branch as a branch to which you can switch from the current branch (TestBranch).

7. Use Source Control, History to view the history of the current branch. Because you have switched back to the master branch, the last commit from Step 6 on TestBranch is not shown.

8. From the Source Control submenu, you can use Merge from Branch or Merge into Branch to combine two branches. Note that from the master branch, Merge into Branch is not possible.

FIGURE 4.16
Switch to a branch.

Using a Remote Repository

The source control commands you have seen in this hour work in general with both Subversion and Git. As noted, the biggest difference between the two approaches is that Subversion is a client/server architecture and Git is a distributed architecture. However, because Git is designed for a distributed environment and because it is integrated into Xcode's interface when you create a new project, it is easier for many people to use.

NOTE

Using Subversion on a Single Computer

Even though Subversion is a client/server architecture, for a small project you can install it on your own computer so that you are both the client and the server. This is the same sort of thing that you do when you build a website and host it on your own computer for testing.

The first step in using a remote repository is to either create one or gain access to one. Fortunately, this is remarkably easy to do. If you search the Web for "Git Hosting," you find a variety of vendors that provide the service. Their prices vary, so it is worth your time to look at their rates. Perhaps the biggest provider is Github.com. In common with some other services, they offer a free account for open source projects. For private repositories, their prices currently start at $7 a month.

Version control is essential on large-scale projects, and often open source projects are very large scale. If you want to participate in an open source project, the first step often is connecting to the source code repository and downloading the existing code.

Some organizations run their own semiprivate repositories. For example, a school might set up Git on one of its servers and allow students and faculty to connect to it.

If you want to create a remote repository, normally you open an account with a vendor or with your organization. You then create the repository using whatever tools are provided to you. After it is created, you or others can connect to it and get to work.

The standard practice with Git is to clone a repository on which you want to work. Each distributed copy of the project is managed on its own, and the changes are then merged back. With Subversion, you check out the code. With Subversion, committing changes to your local copy automatically merges them back to the main version. (You might want to review the commit interface, as shown previously in Figure 4.11.)

With Git, the commits to your local copy of the repository are distinct from the updating and merging of the remote repository, although the interface that lets you review, merge, and discard changes is similar. After you have committed your local changes, you can use Source Control, Push to move them back to the shared repository.

TRY IT YOURSELF ▼

Check Out or Clone a Repository

After you have located a shared repository, the next step is to check out a copy (from a Subversion repository) or to clone a Git repository. Here are the steps to clone a Git repository:

1. In the Accounts tab of Xcode Preferences, use the + at the bottom left to create a new repository. The shortcut menu shown in Figure 4.17 appears.

2. Specify the location of the repository you want to clone. You can either use the HTTPS or the ssh address shown in github or your own remote repository.

3. When requested, provide the username, password, and a brief description of the remote repository.

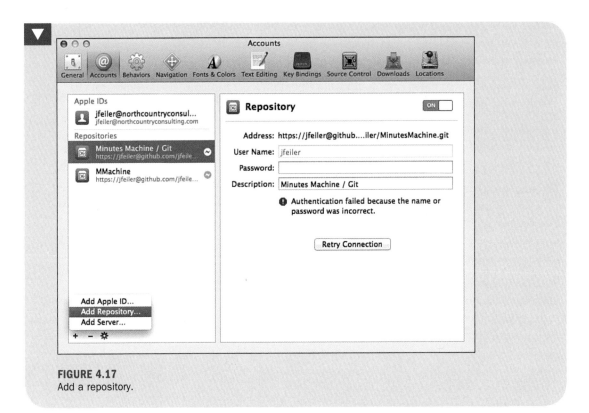

FIGURE 4.17
Add a repository.

You now work with your copy of the repository as you would with any other repository on your local computer. Use Source Code, Push with Git to merge your changes to the remote repository. With Subversion, this is provided as part of the regular Commit command.

You can also use Source Control, Check Out and choose the Repositories tab to check out a project as a new Xcode project on your Mac. You can find more information on Git at http://git-scm.com/.

There's one final point to mention. You saw in Figure 4.5 that you can automatically create a Git repository on your Mac when you create a project. If you are running Git on a server, you can choose that server to create the new repository. Eventually, that pop-up menu will contain the names of all local servers that are running Git.

Summary

This hour explored the Xcode interface to source control management. Both Subversion and Git are supported, although Git, which is designed as a distributed source control tool, is more strongly supported because it fits neatly into Xcode.

Q&A

Q. Why does source control matter?

A. When you identify versions of your software, you can keep track of the project's evolution. More important, all of the code is in one place, and you do not accumulate a variety of copies of your project inside folders with names like Friday Test, Restructured Database, and the like. Perhaps most useful is that you can back out changes without searching through various disk archives and backups.

Q. When do you use a branch?

A. A branch is a series of updates that start from the master (or another branch) and continue with revisions. You can merge a branch back into the master or other branch, or simply abandon it and continue with the main branch.

Workshop

Quiz

1. What is the difference between Commit in Subversion and Git?

2. Why is there a difference between Commit for Subversion and Git?

Quiz Answers

1. With Subversion, Commit updates the shared repository. With Git, you have to push changes to the shared repository after the commit.

2. Because Git is a distributed architecture, you have a complete copy of the repository on your local computer and can merge changes without disturbing the shared repository (which, in fact, is shared mostly in the fact that it is one of many repositories).

Activities

Create an OS X app in Xcode using the OS X Cocoa Application template. You can call is Simple Mac App. Without any further work, you can run it and see that you have an app with a window and functioning menu bar. You'll use it in the next hour.

Browse Github.com to see the features it offers (and that many other hosting services offer). Open source projects are often available for download, so experiment by connecting to an open source repository with Github or another product and browse the files.

HOUR 5
Using Compiler Directives

What You'll Learn in This Hour

▶ Exploring code from a template
▶ Working with prefix headers
▶ Controlling compilation with compiler directives
▶ Reviewing the file structures of your code

Exploring Your Projects

If you have followed the steps in Hour 4, "Using Xcode 5," you now have your first Xcode project built in Objective-C. It doesn't do much, but it's a start. If opens a split-view controller that lets you enter data. The built-in functionalities are quite impressive when you think about it. Between the frameworks and the templates, you've got code to handle rotation of the iOS mobile devices (not to mention the fact that a single codebase can be used for both iPhone and iPad).

If you built Simple Mac App as described in Exercises in Hour 4 (you should build it to continue on), you'll have an app that implements a menu bar and basic commands as well as a window—all without writing any code beyond the templates.

The structure of the projects is the same as most of the projects you will build with Xcode, so this hour walks you through the few lines of code that have been generated for you. When you understand the structure, you can start to add your own code.

The iOS and OS X apps have many similarities, but they are described in separate sections in this hour. As you become more adept at Objective-C and the frameworks, it can be very useful to compare how similar things are done differently in iOS and in OS X. However, most people who are just starting out (like you) find it easier to focus on the specific operating system they want to work with, so the iOS and OS X sections are presented separately.

Looking at the iOS Project

When you have created your project from a template, look at it in the project navigator. Figure 5.1 shows the Simple iOS App. You might have to open a few of the groups (remember that the file folder icon represents an Xcode group and not a folder on a disk), but this is basically what you see. Over time, some of the files might have been renamed or replaced, and that might happen in the future (in fact, it is a good bet that it will happen), but the overall structure remains as you see it in Figure 5.1.

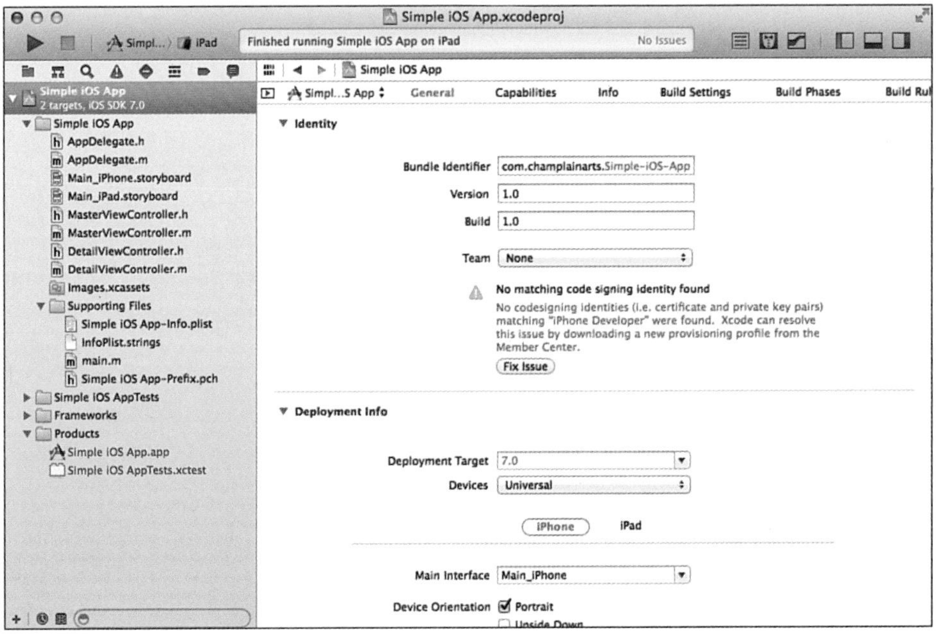

FIGURE 5.1
Explore your new iOS project.

The basics of the project, including its bundle identifier and build and version numbers, are shown at the top. They are all editable. If you followed the steps in Hour 4, you will see that no signing identity has been found. The project can be built and run on the simulator without being signed, so this warning is not dealt with in this book. You can find more information on code signing at developer.apple.com if you are a registered developer.

Looking at the OS X Project

In the case of Simple Mac App, your project will look like Figure 5.2.

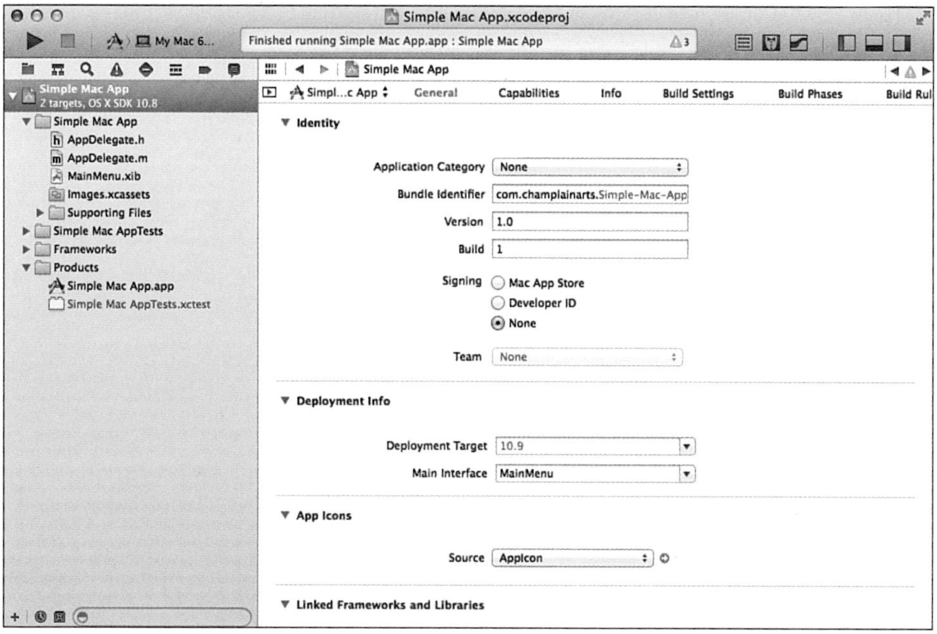

FIGURE 5.2
Explore your new Mac project.

You'll see that there is no code signing identity for the Mac version. As is the case with iOS and the simulator, you can proceed with the rest of the book and come back to code signing when you want to distribute your app. Your app must be signed to use the Mac App Store and certain capabilities that require the security of code signing such as iCloud. Find more information on code signing at developer.apple.com.

Looking at Both Projects

The Products group might show your app in red. Red filenames indicate that the files are missing. After you build your project, the app file turns to black to indicate that it now exists on disk.

CAUTION

Watch Out for Missing Files

It's a warning sign if other files are shown in red. If you have created a new project from a template and any of the files other than the products are missing, something is wrong. Quit Xcode and delete the project. Then re-create it.

Your project contains a variety of files. The extensions indicate what types of files they are. This book focuses on the Objective-C language itself, so you can skip over the framework files (although they must be there for you to build and run your code). You can also ignore the .xib files on OS X, which specify the user interface to your app, including the menu commands on OS X. .strings and .rtf files contain text that might appear in the app. Similarly, you can skip over the storyboard files on iOS, which also provide the interface.

plist files are property lists. These are XML files containing a dictionary with key-value pairs. plist files are used extensively to store settings for apps. You update these files indirectly as you set your project's settings, as was shown in Figure 5.1.

Precompiled headers (.pch) can contain prefix headers that are automatically included in each file's compilation. As with the plist files, you update them through the project interface. And, as with the plist files, you rarely need to change the default settings.

The .pch files demonstrate *compiler directives*, which are the primary topic of this hour, but before moving on to the files themselves, note the two other file types in the project navigator: .h and .m.

.h has commonly been used for header files in C (and other languages), and that is also the role of the .h files in Objective-C. Objective-C is built on messaging, and originally the files that implemented the actual message instructions (that is, the files with the code for the header files) were given the extension .m.

Almost all of the files that you write are these Objective-C .h and .m files.

Working with Compiler Directives

The files for your project are short, and they make it easy for you to look at the structure and contents. All of the files use *compiler directives*, so that is a good place to start your analysis.

Compiler directives are instructions to the compiler that are processed before the actual compilation of the file. For this reason, they are sometimes referred to as preprocessor directives or preprocessor commands.

Working with Basic Directives

The building block for many of the directives described in this section is the macro definition directive: #define. In its simplest form, a macro defines a replacement for a string. For example,

```
#define pi 3.14159265
```

enables you to write code such as

```
x = pi * 2;
```

Before compilation begins, that line of code is converted to

```
x = 3.14159265 * 2;
```

Another form of macro definition enables you to define a function-like macro in which one or more values are included in the macro. You can supply values in your code as you invoke the macro.

TIP

Although macro definitions are convenient ways for hard-coding unchanging values such as pi, they are also used as flags to indicate the presence or absence of certain features.

When used in this way, all you care about is whether or not a certain identifier has been defined as a macro. Thus the line

```
#ifdef pi
```

merely tells you whether or not pi has been defined as a macro. It tells you nothing about its value. When used as a flag in this way, a section of code is typically processed or not based on whether or not some identifier is defined. You can use both `#ifdef` or `#ifndef` depending on whether you want to test the positive or negative outcome.

You introduce the conditional with a test such as the one shown earlier. You then follow it with lines of code (the *controller text*) and #endif statement as in the following:

```
#ifdef pi
//do something with pi
#endif
```

All of this is standard C practice, and, in fact, it is common in one form or another in almost every programming language today.

Looking at Prefix Headers

You now know enough to look at the prefix headers. They are automatically prefixed to all source files. They're a good place to insert customized logging macros that you may create as well as global version controls. They often check to see if something is defined; if it is, certain files are imported. The prefix headers are part of the templates, and the versioning and importing in them can be used in most cases without modification.

The convention of a double-underscore at the beginning and end of an identifier is used to indicate that this is an internal value.

A common C directive is `#include`. It is used to include an external file in the compilation just as if it were part of the file being processed. A problem with `#include` is that it is very easy to get circular references that result in code (particularly declarations) being included more than once and thereby generating compiler errors.

TIP
___

With Xcode, you can use `#import` instead of `#include` to avoid these issues. If a file has already been imported, a second `#import` directive has no effect.

Listing 5.1 shows the `.pch` file for an iOS app.

LISTING 5.1 Prefix Header for Simple iOS App

```
//
// Prefix header for all source files of the 'Simple iOS App'
// target in the 'Simple iOS App' project
//

#import <Availability.h>

#ifndef __IPHONE_5_0
#warning "This project uses features only available in iOS SDK
5.0 and later."
#endif

#ifdef __OBJC__
   #import <UIKit/UIKit.h>
   #import <Foundation/Foundation.h>
#endif
```

This prefix header begins by unconditionally importing a file that happens to have the version defined in it. Note that the test is for a definition of __IPHONE_5_0, which is the definition for IOS SDK 5.0 and later. This is actually a fairly common type of collision between an internal term (__IPHONE_5_0) and a marketing term (iOS 5.0).

If __IPHONE_5_0 is not defined, a warning is presented that something is missing.

Then, to see if Objective-C is available the test is if __OBJC__ is defined. If it is, the Cocoa Touch files are imported.

Listing 5.2 shows the automatically generated .pch file for the simple Mac app used in Hour 4.

LISTING 5.2   Prefix Header for Simple Mac App

```
//
// Prefix header for all source files of the 'Simple Mac App'
// target in the 'Simple Mac App' project
//

#ifdef __OBJC__
  #import <Cocoa/Cocoa.h>
#endif
```

This code checks to see if __OBJC__ is defined. In this case, __OBJC__ is defined when you are working in an Objective-C environment. If it is defined, then the Cocoa framework is imported, and that brings up the next directive: #import.

Thus, in Listing 5.2, if you have an Objective-C compiler, the Cocoa.h file from the Cocoa framework is imported. The < and > indicate a file that is taken from a framework—in this case, Cocoa.

Looking at Plain C Code in main.m

As noted previously, you can compile ordinary C code through the Objective-C compiler. That happens in both the OS X and the iOS versions of the template. In both cases, a function called main in a file called main.m starts the app running.

Listing 5.3 shows the code for iOS. The names of the functions are different for iOS and OS X, but the functionality is basically the same.

LISTING 5.3   main.m (iOS)

```
//
//  main.m
//  Simple iOS App
//
//  Created by Jesse Feiler on 11/10/13.
//  Copyright (c) 2013 Champlain Arts Corp. All rights reserved.
//

#import <UIKit/UIKit.h>

#import "AppDelegate.h"
```

```
int main(int argc, char *argv[])
{
  @autoreleasepool {
    return UIApplicationMain(argc, argv, nil,
      NSStringFromClass([AppDelegate class]));
  }
}
```

Listing 5.4 shows this bootstrap code in OS X.

LISTING 5.4   main.m (OS X)

```
//
//  main.m
//  Simple Mac App
//
//  Created by Jesse Feiler on 11/10/13.
//  Copyright (c) 2013 Champlain Arts Corp. All rights reserved.
//

#import <Cocoa/Cocoa.h>

int main(int argc, const char *argv[])
{
  return NSApplicationMain(argc, (const char **)argv);
}
```

NOTE

File Header Information

The information at the top of the files in Listings 5.3 and 5.4 is omitted from the other listings in this book, but it is always produced in the files themselves. It is text drawn from the name of the file, the name of the project, the clock, and other user information. Because it is all a comment, you can modify it if you want.

Investigating Header (.h) Files

You have already seen the basics of the files in your project. In this section, you look at the header (.h) files and discover a new compiler directive syntax.

The first Objective-C class in your project for both iOS and OS X is AppDelegate. In keeping with convention, the class has two files—AppDelegate.h and AppDelegate.m.

Listing 5.5 shows the `AppDelegate` header file for iOS.

The template imports the UIKit framework, which is the basic framework for Cocoa Touch. After that, you have three Objective-C compiler directives. Objective-C compiler directives begin with @ rather than the # for C compiler directives. (Although `#import` is an extension to the C compiler directives implemented with Xcode, it is treated as the other C compiler extensions and so begins with #.)

GO TO ▶ `@interface` and `@end` are described later in this hour in "Using Objective-C Compiler Directives." `@property` is described in Hour 9, "Declaring Properties in an Interface File," p. 127.

LISTING 5.5 `AppDelegate.h` (iOS)

```
#import <UIKit/UIKit.h>

@interface AppDelegate : UIResponder <UIApplicationDelegate>

@property (strong, nonatomic) UIWindow *window;

@end
```

Listing 5.6 shows the `AppDelegate` header file for OS X. It begins by importing Cocoa.h from the Cocoa framework. You do not have to worry about duplicate declarations because `#import` takes care of that for you.

LISTING 5.6 `AppDelegate.h` (OS X)

```
#import <Cocoa/Cocoa.h>

@interface AppDelegate : NSObject <NSApplicationDelegate>

@property (assign) IBOutlet NSWindow *window;

@end
```

Looking Inside Message (.m) Files

The companion .m files to the .h files are described in this section. There is not much new to note except that `@implementation` is discussed later in this hour in the "Using Objective-C Compiler Directives" section.

In Listing 5.7, you see the AppDelegate.m file for iOS. It's a lengthy listing, but notice that most of it consists of commented-out code for methods you typically implement. All of those methods contain nothing except the comments with the exception of `application:didFinish` `LaunchingWithOptions:`. If you compare that line of code with the comparable code in Listing 5.8, you see that it is structured differently.

GO TO ▶ Hour 17, "Extending a Class with Protocols and Delegates," explores the reasons for that difference.

The code inside that method in Listing 5.7 implements some window handling on iOS that is managed differently on OS X.

LISTING 5.7 `AppDelegate.m (iOS)`

```
#import "AppDelegate.h"

@implementation AppDelegate


- (BOOL)application:(UIApplication *)application
  didFinishLaunchingWithOptions:(NSDictionary *)launchOptions
{
    self.window = [[UIWindow alloc] initWithFrame:
      [[UIScreen mainScreen] bounds]];
    // Override point for customization after application launch.
    self.window.backgroundColor = [UIColor whiteColor];
    [self.window makeKeyAndVisible];
    return YES;
}


- (void)applicationWillResignActive:(UIApplication *)application
{
  /*
  Sent when the application is about to move from active to inactive state. This
  can occur for certain types of temporary interruptions (such as an incoming
  phone call or SMS message) or when the user quits the application and it begins
  the transition to the background state.
  Use this method to pause ongoing tasks, disable timers, and throttle down OpenGL
  ES frame rates. Games should use this method to pause the game.
  */
}


- (void)applicationDidEnterBackground:(UIApplication *)application
{
  /*
  Use this method to release shared resources, save user data, invalidate timers,
  and store enough application state information to restore your application to
  its current state in case it is terminated later.
  If your application supports background execution, this method is called instead
  of applicationWillTerminate: when the user quits.
  */
```

```
}

- (void)applicationWillEnterForeground:(UIApplication *)application
{
  /*
  Called as part of the transition from the background to the inactive state; here
  you can undo many of the changes made on entering the background.
  */
}

- (void)applicationDidBecomeActive:(UIApplication *)application
{
  /*
  Restart any tasks that were paused (or not yet started) while the application
  was inactive. If the application was previously in the background, optionally
  refresh the user interface.
  */
}

- (void)applicationWillTerminate:(UIApplication *)application
{
  /*
  Called when the application is about to terminate.
  Save data if appropriate.
  See also applicationDidEnterBackground:.
  */
}

@end
```

In Listing 5.8, you see the .m AppDelegate file for OS X.

LISTING 5.8   AppDelegate.m (OS X)

```
#import "AppDelegate.h"

@implementation AppDelegate

- (void)applicationDidFinishLaunching:
    (NSNotification *)aNotification
{
  // Insert code here to initialize your application
}

@end
```

Using Objective-C Compiler Directives

Objective-C compiler directives begin with @. You often use them to describe portions of a file. In the .h files, for example, @interface marks the beginning of the header interface code. That section is terminated by @end.

In the .m files, @implementation marks the beginning of the implementation, and it is terminated by @end.

Other common Objective-C compiler directives are used to introduce forward declarations such as @class MyClass or @protocol MyProtocol, which are defined in other parts of your code. (Forward declarations are promises that something will be declared later on; but in the meantime, you can use it in the code you are writing.)

Strings in Objective-C are delimited with

```
@"this is a string"
```

where the @ alerts the compiler that a string follows.

Summary

In this hour, you have seen the compiler directives that let you communicate with the preprocessor. You have also seen the basic structure of interface (.h) and message (.m) files.

Q&A

Q. What do prefix headers do?

A. They usually contain defines that determine what gets compiled. Frequently they control conditional compilation based on what versions of SDKs are installed.

Q. How do you include C code in an Objective-C project?

A. C code is placed in a file with the extension .m just like any other Objective-C source code you write to implement a method. You can also use it inside other files. C compiles without issues (providing there are no syntax errors) in the compilers used in Xcode.

Workshop

Quiz

1. What is the difference between `#include` and `#import`?

2. How do you specify a string literal in Objective-C?

3. What is the significance of files shown in red in the project navigator?

Quiz Answers

1. `#include` includes the specified file without regard for whether or not it has already been included. This can lead to duplicate declarations if a file is included twice. `#import` only imports the file once, and it ignores subsequent `#import` directives for the same file.

2. Use the Objective-C compiler directive symbol `@` as in `x = @"mystring";`.

3. Files in red are missing. They might have been moved on disk, or they might be not-yet-built project files.

Activities

Explore one of the other templates for either iOS or OS X. Build and run it to see what happens. Test to see what commands are built in.

HOUR 6
Exploring Messaging and a Testbed App

What You'll Learn in This Hour

▶ Setting up a testbed app

▶ Creating a branch to test with

▶ Sending a message to an interface element

Setting Up the Testbed Apps

Now that you have a high-level understanding of Objective-C and the development environment, this part of the book helps you write and run code so that you can explore exactly how things work. Because this is no longer a world in which you can write a few lines of Hello World code to test things out, you need an app that you can experiment with. Fortunately, it is easy to create one, and that is the first thing to do in this hour.

It's a good thing that it's so easy to do because you'll create two testbed apps—one for iOS and one for OS X. Objective-C is the same on both operating systems. Cocoa on OS X and Cocoa Touch on iOS are very similar, but they are different. So in order to have a testbed app ready for testing, you need to either create both of them or pick the one that you're most interested in. For many people, it is easier to implement just one of these apps and then come back to the other one when they want to explore it.

Before starting, however, remember that you are creating an app that contains thousands of lines of code. Your fingers will not get sore, though, because that code is packaged into the various frameworks that you use in your app. Both of the testbed apps are very simple: They put up a window.

This is a very simple task, but it is the prototype for a large number of tasks that you need to perform. If you want to experiment with setting the color of an object, add it to your window and write the coloring code. Then put that app aside and experiment with changing the font in a text field. Once you have the testbed app in place, you'll have a platform for exploring the Objective-C syntax in the rest of this book.

One easy way to reuse your testbed app is to use a Git source code repository, which, as you saw in Hour 4, "Using Xcode 5," you can create and manage through Xcode. You can create the basic project that just puts up the empty window on OS X or iOS. Then, each time you want to experiment with something, just create a new branch to test that code out. In this case, for example, the first branch is the branch that adds a text field and colors the text blue. Later on, you can add other branches with other adventures. The technical term for such a base for experimentation is testbed, and that is what this project is called.

▼ TRY IT YOURSELF

Build the Basic Test App on iOS

The first step is to build the basic app and set up its repository. Follow these steps:

1. Create a new Xcode project based on the iOS Single View Application template.

2. Use the settings shown in Figure 6.1. (Substitute your own name. If you don't have your own domain name, you can make one up as long as you are using the app only for yourself.)

   The name of the project is Testbed iOS. Choose Universal for Devices. Even if you only implement either the iPad or iPhone version, you'll have the code ready to implement the other later on if you want.

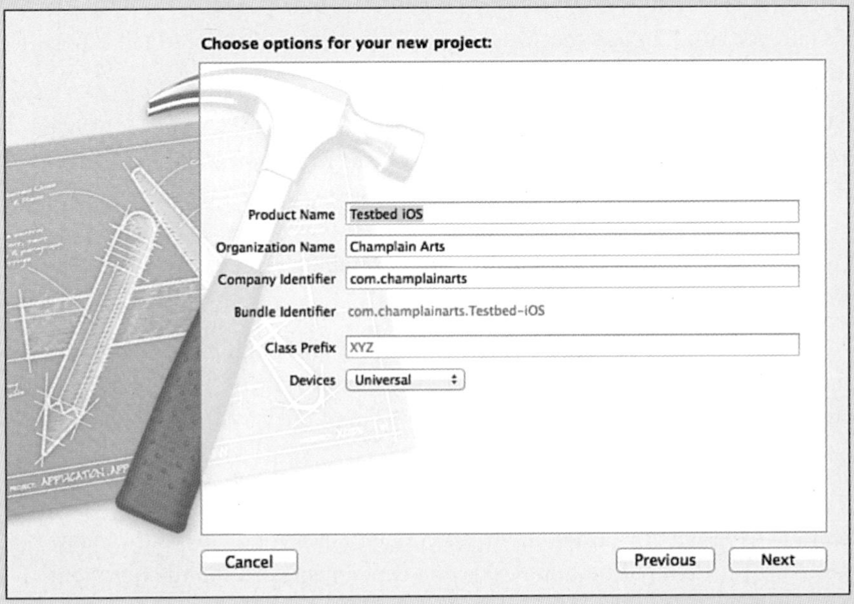

FIGURE 6.1
Create the Testbed project for iOS.

3. Save the project wherever you want.

4. Test the project. Choose a simulator from the Scheme menu to the right of the Run button at the left of the toolbar, as shown in Figure 6.2. There may be a warning about a missing code sign identity: Ignore it. Then, click to build and run the project. It will take several moments for the simulator to launch. You won't see much—just a blank window. If you scroll to the top, you'll see the status bar with the current date. It's not much, but your first app is running!

FIGURE 6.2
Run the app.

TRY IT YOURSELF ▼

Build the Basic Test App on OS X

For the OS X version, the steps are comparable:

1. Create a new Xcode project based on the OS X Cocoa Application template.

2. Use the settings shown in Figure 6.3. The name of the project is Testbed OS X and you don't need any other options. However, you do need to enter your own identity.

▼ TIP

If you don't have your own domain name, you can make one up as long as you are using the app only for yourself.

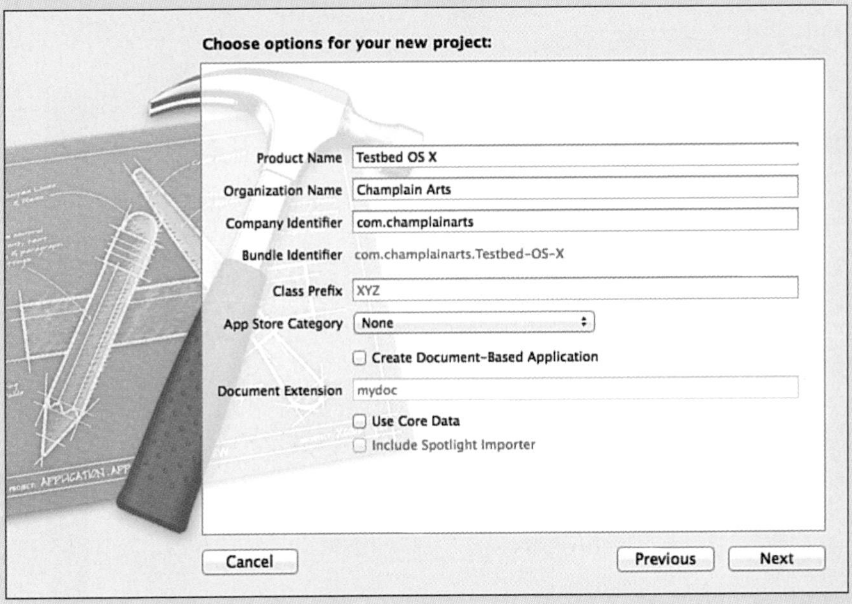

Choose options for your new project:

Product Name	Testbed OS X
Organization Name	Champlain Arts
Company Identifier	com.champlainarts
Bundle Identifier	com.champlainarts.Testbed-OS-X
Class Prefix	XYZ
App Store Category	None ⬍
	☐ Create Document-Based Application
Document Extension	mydoc
	☐ Use Core Data
	☐ Include Spotlight Importer

Cancel   Previous   Next

FIGURE 6.3
Create the Testbed OS X project.

3. Save the project wherever you want. Make certain you create a local Git repository by checking the check box on the Save sheet.

4. Test the project. Click Run at the top left of the Xcode window to build and run the project. You should have a blank window and a default menu bar, as shown in Figure 6.4.

FIGURE 6.4
Test the app.

Adding a Text Field and Connecting It to Your Code

The first testbed experiment you'll conduct involves coloring the text in a text field. To do so, you need to create a text field in the interface and connect it to your code. The techniques are comparable but slightly different on iOS and OS X. The text field is a type of view on both iOS and OS X. All that you need to know at this point is that views are contained within windows. There are really two parts to an interface element such as a text field:

▶ There is a graphical representation of the text field in the interface that you can move around with the graphical Interface Builder editor.

▶ There is a code object that you manipulate with Objective-C code.

Windows and Views in Cocoa and Cocoa Touch

On iOS devices, there is a single window for an app and there is no menu bar. On OS X, you can have multiple windows. In both environments, you can place views inside windows; you also can create a hierarchy of views within views. The topmost view in an OS X view hierarchy is located within a window. The topmost view in an iOS view hierarchy is located within the app's single window. You normally don't deal with the app window in iOS. All this means is that when you start with a blank canvas in either environment, that blank canvas represents the app's single window on iOS or one of the several possible windows on OS X. You then add views to the window. It's really very much the same in both environments, but on iOS the window is generally not mentioned because there is only one.

Adding the Text Field

The first task is to add the text field on iOS and/or OS X.

▼ TRY IT YOURSELF

Add a Text Field to the Window on iOS

These steps let you add a text field to the window on iOS:

1. Show the project navigator if necessary and select Main_iPhone.storyboard, as shown in Figure 6.5. You might have to do some opening and closing of disclosure triangles.

NOTE

You can also use Main_iPad.storyboard, but because the iPhone is smaller, the screenshots reproduce better in this book.

The canvas in the center of the editor shows an outline of an iPhone; note the battery indicator at the top right. This whole area in the center of the editor is the *canvas* where you draw your interface. The outline of the iPhone is a *view controller*. You will probably have a number of view controllers in your app.

2. Show the document outline at the left of the editor, as shown in Figure 6.6 by clicking the control at the lower-left of the canvas. In the center of the window, you have the editor with the document outline at the left and the *canvas* in the center. It contains a view controller scene. You can open the disclosure triangles in the document outline to see the structure. Show or hide the document outline with the small disclosure triangle at the bottom.

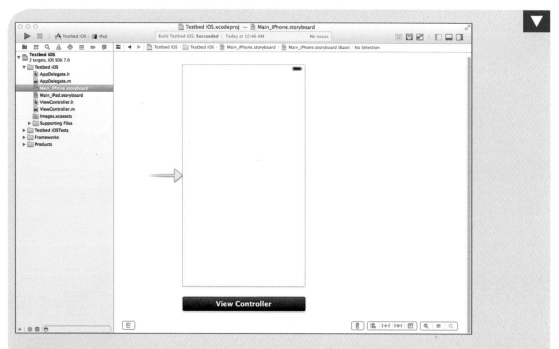

FIGURE 6.5
Select the Main_iPhone.storyboard.

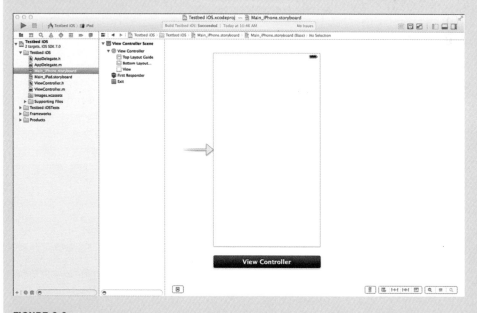

FIGURE 6.6
You can show or hide the document outline. It is shown here.

▼

3. If necessary, show the utility area at the right of the workspace window (see Figure 6.7). Locate the text field in the object library at the bottom of the utility area. The object library is the third button from the left at the top of the library. You can search for it or scroll down the list of objects.

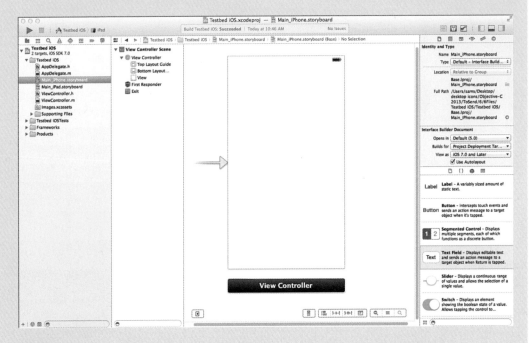

FIGURE 6.7
Show the utility area for the iOS project.

4. Drag the text field from the library into the view controller, as shown in Figure 6.8. It does not matter where you put it.

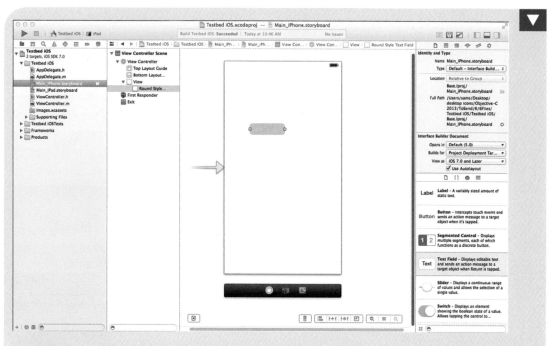

FIGURE 6.8
Add a text field to the window for the iOS project.

Add a Text Field to the Window on OS X

These steps let you add a text field to the window on OS X. Instead of storyboards, you have
`.nib` files (spelled `.xib` for historical reasons). Despite the differences, the work that you do to
draw the interface is much the same.

1. Show the project navigator if necessary and select MainMenu.xib, as shown in Figure 6.9.
   You might have to do some opening and closing of disclosure triangles.

2. In the Interface Builder editor, locate the window, which might be scrolled out of view. You
   also might need to show or hide the document outline depending on how you like to work.
   As long as the window is visible, you are able to continue in either way. Figure 6.10 shows
   the document outline hidden. With the document outline shown, you can click on the
   Testbed window to show it.

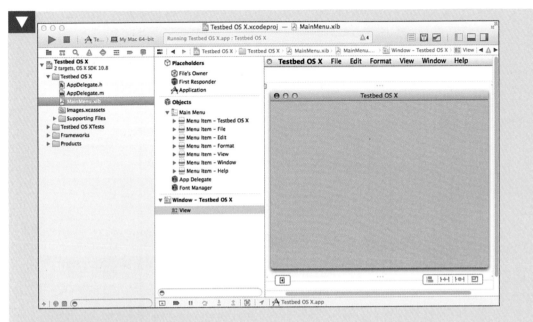

FIGURE 6.9
Select MainMenu.xib.

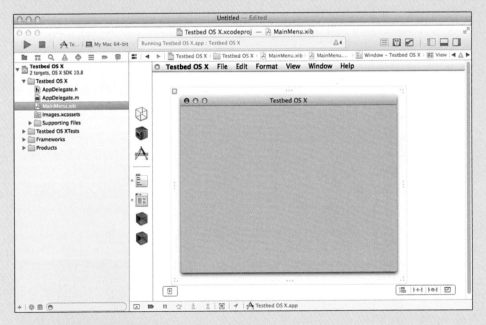

FIGURE 6.10
You can show or hide the document outline. It is hidden here.

3. If necessary, show the utility area at the right of the workspace window (see Figure 6.11).

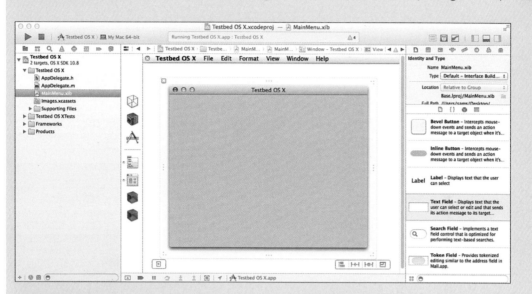

FIGURE 6.11
Show the utility area for the OS X project.

4. Locate the text field in the object library at the bottom of the utility area. The object library is the third button from the left at the top of the library. You can search for it or scroll down the list of objects. Figure 6.11 shows the text field object in the library.

5. Drag the text field from the library into the window, as shown in Figure 6.12. It does not matter where you put it.

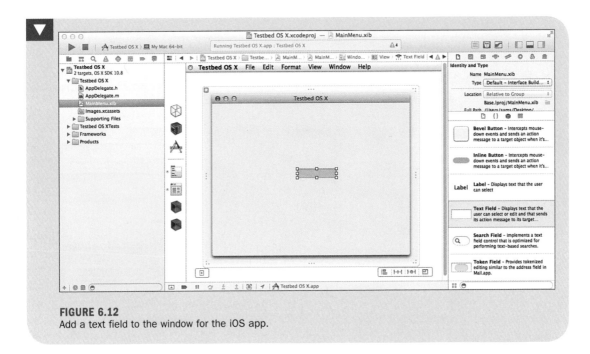

FIGURE 6.12
Add a text field to the window for the iOS app.

Now that you have the text field added to the window, you need a way to reference it in your code. With Xcode 5 and the declared properties that were added to Objective-C 2.0, the process is very simple. Once again, you are not writing code; instead, you are using a graphical editor. But do not worry; as soon as the text field is added to the project, you begin typing away to change the color of the text with your first Objective-C code.

Connecting the Text Field to the Code

The other part of this task is to connect the text field to your Objective-C code.

▼ **TRY IT YOURSELF**

Connect the Text Field to the Code on iOS

The steps in this process are the same whether you are adding a text field, a button, a table view, or any other object to your interface. In file extension terms, it works for `.xib` and `.storyboard` files. The steps in this process connect the interface element to your code so that you can write code to access the interface element:

1. Show the Assistant Editor so you can work with two files at the same time, as shown in Figure 6.13. You can use the button at the top right of the Xcode workspace toolbar, or you can use View, Assistant Editor, Show Assistant Editor.

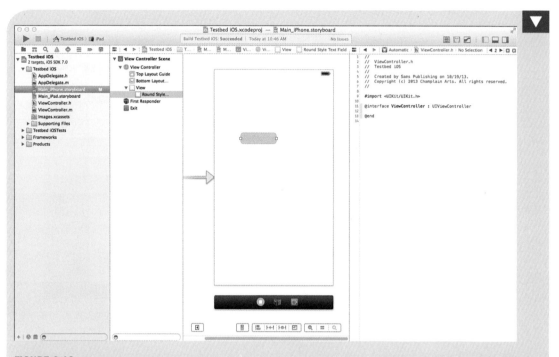

FIGURE 6.13
Use the Assistant Editor.

2. You can configure the two assistant panes using the View, Assistant Editor submenu.

3. Select ViewController.h in the project navigator to open it in one of the panes.

4. Use the jump bar at the top of the other assistant pane to open Main_iPhone. storyboard, as shown in Figure 6.13. It does not matter which file is in which pane. The point of this process is to connect the interface element in Main_iPhone.storyboard to the ViewController.h interface file.

5. Control-drag from the text field in the interface to the declarations in the header file, as shown in Figure 6.14.

6. In the pop-over, name the field `myTextField`, as shown in Figure 6.15. The other settings shown in Figure 6.15 are the defaults, and you do not need to change them. Just name the field.

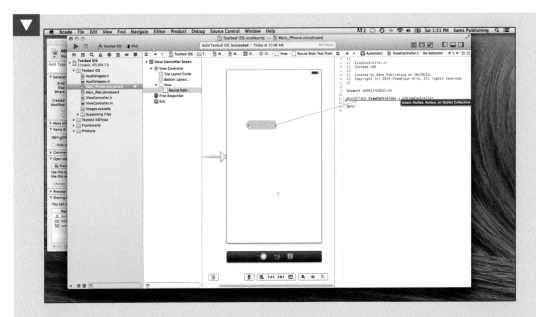

FIGURE 6.14
Start to connect the interface.

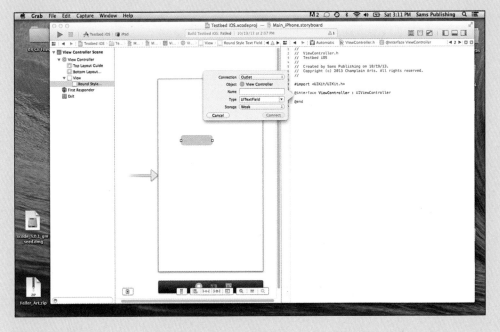

FIGURE 6.15
Name the field.

7. The property declaration is automatically generated, as you see in Figure 6.16. Also note that there's a small dot to the left of the property declaration; it indicates that the property is connected to an interface object (the text field, in this case).

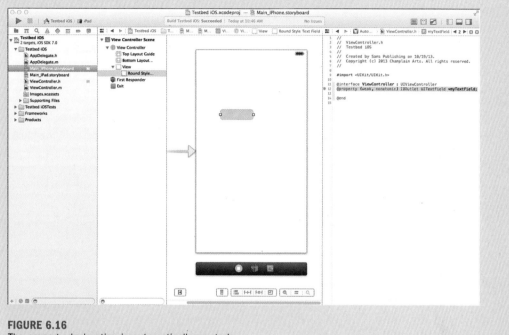

FIGURE 6.16
The property declaration is automatically created.

Connect the Text Field to the Code on OS X

Here is the process on OS X if it is the second connection you make:

1. Show the Assistant Editor so you can work with two files at the same time, as shown previously in Figure 6.13.

2. Select AppDelegate.h in the project navigator to open it in one of the panes.

3. Use the jump bar at the top of the other assistant pane to open MainMenu.xib, as shown previously in Figure 6.13. It does not matter which file is in which pane. The point of this process is to connect the interface element in MainMenu.xib to the AppDelegate.h interface file.

4. Control-drag from the text field in the interface to the property declaration.

Sending a Message to the Text Field

Now that the property `myTextField` is linked to the interface element, you can send a message to it. This might seem like a lot of setup but, in fact, after you have been through the sequence of adding an interface element, connecting it to your code, and automatically generating the property, you will be able to do it in a matter of seconds. After you have the connection made, you can use the property to communicate with the object.

Remember that in Objective-C you are not calling methods of objects; rather you are sending messages to the objects. The structure of the message is basically the following:

```
[receiverName message];
```

You have the first part of the code: `receiverName` is `myTextField`. It is a property of the class in which it is declared, and you need to reference it as `self.myTextField`.

GO TO ▶ Hour 9, "Declaring Properties in an Interface File," p. 127, for more information on working with properties of a class.

The brackets are essential for a message, so the code starts to look like this:

```
[self.myTextField message];
```

Where do you find the messages that can be sent to a text field? Highlight `UITextField` in the property declaration that was created for you. If necessary, show the utility area and choose Quick Help at the top to see the documentation (see Figure 6.17).

From there, you can click on the class reference and see what messages are available to you (see Figure 6.18).

NOTE

As the messages are part of the frameworks, you should explore them on your own because you will need them as you write your code. This is outside the scope of this book, which focuses on the Objective-C language and not the frameworks.

To set the color, you need an `NSColor` (OS X) or `UIColor` (iOS). You can use the class method `blueColor` (or `yellowColor` or `blackColor` and so forth) to get a color. The basic code is as follows:

```
[NSColor blueColor];
```

Remember, that for a class method, the recipient is the class and not an instance of the class. Putting it all together, you can add the line of code shown in Listing 6.1 to ViewController.m for iOS.

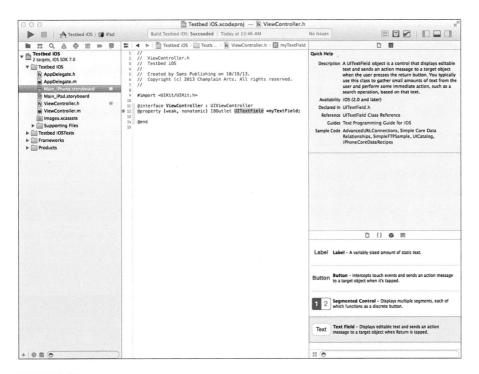

FIGURE 6.17
Show Quick Help for `UITextField`.

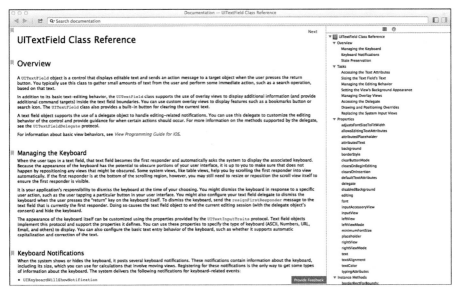

FIGURE 6.18
Browse the available messages.

LISTING 6.1   Set a Color Using a Color from a Class Method on iOS

```
- (void)viewDidLoad
{
    [super viewDidLoad];
  // Do any additional setup after loading the view, typically from a nib.

    [self.myTextField setTextColor: [UIColor blueColor]];
}
```

On OS X, add the code to `AppDelegate.m`, as shown in Listing 6.2.

LISTING 6.2   Set a Color Using a Color from a Class Method

```
- (void)applicationDidFinishLaunching:
    (NSNotification *)aNotification
{
  // Insert code here to initialize your application
  [self.myTextField setTextColor: [NSColor blueColor]];
}
```

Build and test the app, and you see that the text is blue or whatever other color you have chosen.

Reviewing the Message Syntax

Messaging is at the heart of Objective-C, so it is worthwhile to review the syntax involved—the Objective-C syntax as well as the English-language syntax used to discuss it. Here is a quick review of the syntax and what happens:

▶ Messages are enclosed in square brackets. At a minimum, they specify a recipient and a message. The message specifies the method the recipient should perform.

▶ The recipient can be a class or an instance of a class. Methods are declared differently if they are class or instance methods.

▶ Methods can return values. Thus, you can use a class method to return a specific color:

```
myColor = [UIColor textColor];
```

▶ An instance method may return a value; often it is a property:

```
myColor = [self.myTextField textColor];
```

▶ A message may take arguments that are preceded by a colon and identifier:

```
[self.myTextField textColor = myColor;]
```

▶ A message can have multiple arguments. Each is preceded by a colon and an identifier:

```
[self.myTextField insertSubview:myView aboveSubView:baseview];
```

Note that this is actually a method on UIView; because UITextField is a subclass, it inherits this method.

▶ Instead of returning a value, a message can simply perform an action and return nothing:

```
[myTextField myMessage];
```

▶ The selection of a specific method to execute occurs at runtime. It is based on the recipient as well as on the method specified in the message. This enables you to write code such as the following. Because id refers to any type, from the code there is no way of knowing what type of object will be asked to respond to the message:

```
id myObject;
[myObject copy];
```

Because you may not know what type of object will be responding, you should be very careful with syntax like this. At the least, use respondsToSelector: to find out if you will crash. (respondsToSelector: is discussed in Hour 12, "Routing Messages with Selectors.")

Summary

This hour extended the discussion of messaging from Hour 3, "Using Object-Oriented Features in Objective-C." You have built a testbed to use for experiments and testing, and you have built up a very simple message to manipulate an interface element.

Q&A

Q. What is the point of a testbed project?

A. You can create the shell of a project and then do your testing in separate branches, which can be isolated from the rest of the testbed. In other words, you minimize the chances that one of your experiments breaks the whole testbed.

Q. How do you call a method?

A. You send a message to an instance of the class or, in the case of class methods, to the class itself.

Workshop

Quiz

1. When do you use the Assistant Editor?

2. How do you add an interface element to your interface with Interface Builder?

Quiz Answers

1. Use the Assistant Editor when you need to view two files at once. For example, if you need to control-drag from an interface object to a header file, you need both files open at the same time.

2. Find the object you want to add in the object library and drag it onto the Interface Builder canvas.

Activities

If you have not done so already, modify the code in Listing 6.1 to change the text color in the text field. Use Quick Help in the Organizer to review the UITextField class reference and modify the code to change other attributes of the text field.

HOUR 7
Declaring a Class in an Interface File

What You'll Learn in This Hour

▶ Developing classes

▶ Introducing protocols

▶ Looking at class declarations

Letting Xcode Do the Work

In Hour 6, "Exploring Messaging and a Testbed App," you saw how you use messages to tell the object that receives the message what to do. The message itself consists of the name of a method along with zero or more arguments. At runtime, information about the receiver is used to determine what method to invoke to implement the message.

That is the *how* of Objective-C. This hour begins an in-depth look at the *what* of Objective-C—the classes that are instantiated at runtime into instances or into class objects themselves. Within classes, you find the methods that are performed as a result of messages.

Designing Classes

In Hour 6, you saw the use of a simple method that is part of the Cocoa (and Cocoa Touch) framework: It sets the color of text in an NSTextField or UITextField, which is the class that handles text fields in the interface. In many ways, a class such as NSTextField or UITextField can be misleading because you can see the representation of the class (the text field itself), and you can work with it. Many classes are not based on physical objects—they represent abstractions or concepts. As such, those classes might help you understand the basics of working with classes in Objective-C because you are not distracted by the physical object.

For that reason, this hour works with a class that is an abstraction; it is a class that manages currency conversion. You can use it as a model for any computational class—not just for other types of conversions such as length or weight, but also for classes that might, for example, find the factors of a non-prime number.

In reality, many people wind up working with classes that are a combination of representations of the physical world in code and those that are abstractions of processes.

NOTE

The History of the Objective-C Currency Converter

A currency converter is a good process to implement in a class because it is fairly easily understood. For that reason, it has long been used as an example of Objective-C and the Cocoa framework (historically known as the Rhapsody framework from Apple, the OpenStep framework, and the NeXTSTEP framework before that from NeXT). The example used here focuses on the Objective-C code; the Currency Converter example was used to demonstrate the code as well as the frameworks and their support for the user interface. It was published by NeXT Software, Inc., and Apple several times during the period 1993–1997.

Most of the time, each class is written using two files: a header file (.h) with the interface and a .m file containing the implementation. You can put the interface and implementation in the same file, and you can put several classes together. Combining classes in a single file is usually done only for very short utility classes or for private classes that should not be available for use by other classes.

Getting Ready to Create the Class

Before you start to create the class, make certain that you know what it is that you want the class to represent and what you want it to do. A critical part of the design of an object-oriented system is defining the classes. Often, a second, third, or even hundredth pass is needed to refine the class structure. However, at any given moment, you should make certain you know what it is you want to build.

NOTE

As a matter of good design, you also should keep an eye out for other classes in your design that are related to the one you are thinking about. It might be the case that you want to create a class/superclass structure—possibly with an abstract superclass that is never instantiated. The goal is to have the simplest structure with as little repetition and overlap as possible.

After you have decided on what the class is that you want to create, you should name it. Apple's current guidance on naming conventions is that class names should start with a two- or three-letter prefix in capital letters. This typically identifies the framework of which the class is a part. If it is not part of a framework, it might identify the project.

Using a prefix is not required, but it can prevent you from winding up with a collection of unrelated classes with the same or similar names.

Because prefixes are used to help you organize your code, make certain that you do not use Apple's own prefixes such as UI (in Cocoa Touch) and NS (in both Cocoa and Cocoa Touch). Many Apple prefixes are two letters long, so you might want to use three letters for your own prefixes. Also remember that prefixes help you organize your code, but they do not enforce rules: You are free to ignore them and destroy your carefully thought-out organizational scheme.

A class name starts with a capital letter; if it consists of several words, they are separated by internal capital letters rather than underscores or other delimiters. (This technique is often called CamelCase.) Thus, a currency converter class might be called `CurrencyConverter`. If you are writing it as part of a project called Basic Objective-C Programming, you might prefix it to create `BOPCurrencyConverter`.

Because the classes in this book typically are designed for reuse, in most cases they do not have prefixes.

TRY IT YOURSELF ▼

Create a Class with Xcode

You certainly can start by using a text editor to write your class code, but, with Xcode, it is much easier to let Xcode do the work. Except in very unusual circumstances, you do not write a class on its own; you write it in the context of a project. For illustrative purposes, the Testbed iOS project from Hour 6 is used here. You use a series of steps such as the following:

1. If you are using a testbed as described in Hour 6, open it and create a new branch. You might call it Classes.

   Alternatively, create a new app from a template. It really doesn't matter what the project is for the purpose of this hour.

2. Show the project navigator at the left of the workspace window, as shown in Figure 7.1.

3. Select a group in the navigator. You can easily rearrange files and groups later so this is not a life-or-death choice. The overall project group—Testbed iOS, in this case—is a good starting point.

NOTE

Remember: Groups look like file folders, but are not folders or directories on disk.

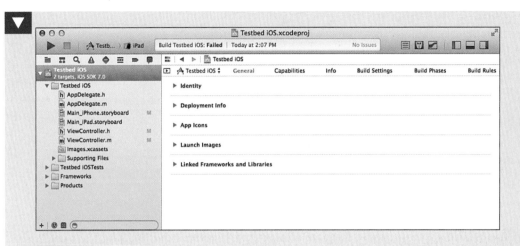

FIGURE 7.1
Show the project navigator.

4. Choose File, New, File, or hold down Control and click the group to bring up the shortcut menu and select New File (see Figure 7.2).

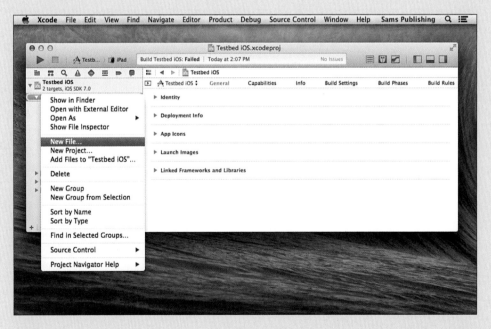

FIGURE 7.2
Start to create a new file.

5. From the file templates in either Cocoa or Cocoa Touch, choose Objective-C class, as shown in Figure 7.3. Make certain that you are in the right OS.

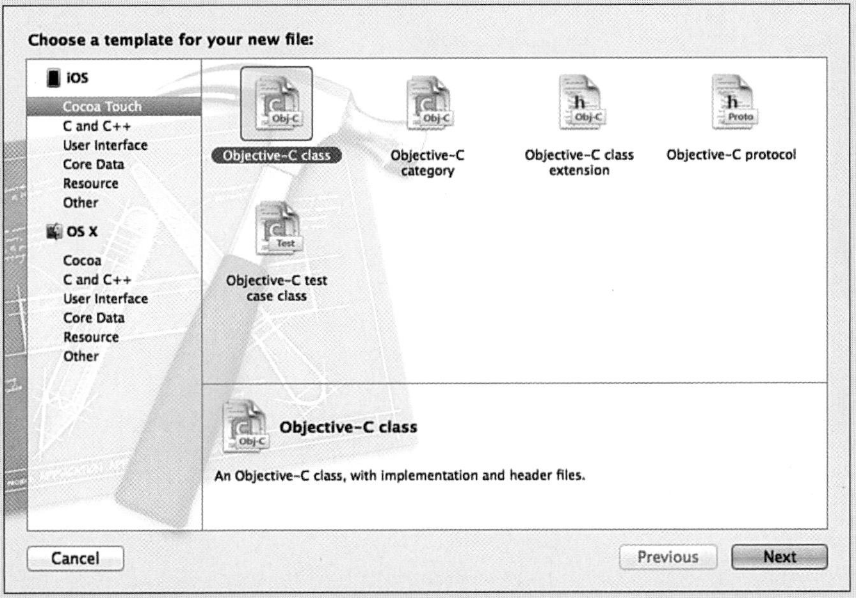

Choose a template for your new file:

iOS				
Cocoa Touch	Objective-C class	Objective-C category	Objective-C class extension	Objective-C protocol
C and C++				
User Interface				
Core Data				
Resource				
Other				

Objective-C test case class

OS X	
Cocoa	
C and C++	
User Interface	
Core Data	
Resource	
Other	

Objective-C class

An Objective-C class, with implementation and header files.

Cancel   Previous   Next

FIGURE 7.3
Choose Objective-C class.

6. Name the class and choose its parent class, as shown in Figure 7.4. Remember to start the class name with a capital letter and do not include spaces or special characters. It should be a subclass of `NSObject`.

If you look at your choices, you can see that none of them is appropriate, so the more general base class is the proper one.

7. Click Next and then save the file, as shown in Figure 7.5. Note that you have a chance here to change the group the file is in.

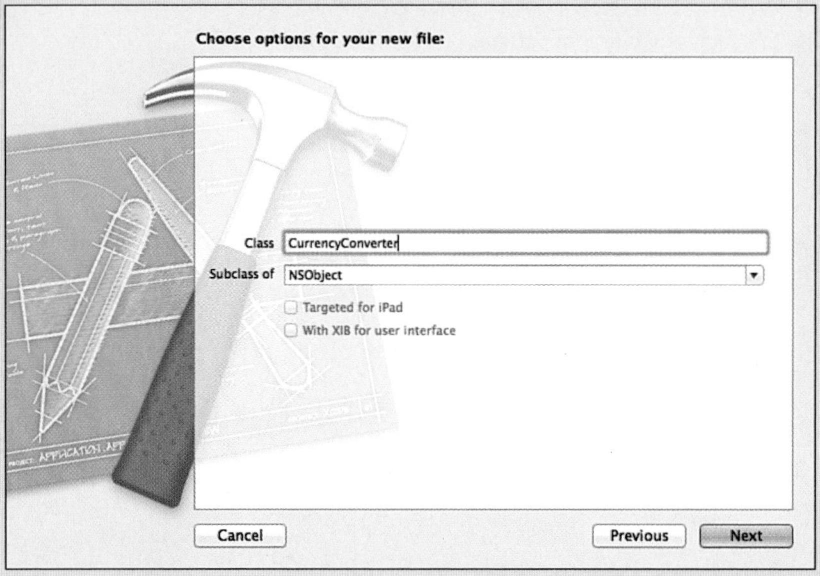

Choose options for your new file:

Class	CurrencyConverter
Subclass of	NSObject

☐ Targeted for iPad
☐ With XIB for user interface

Cancel　　　Previous　　Next

FIGURE 7.4
Select the parent class.

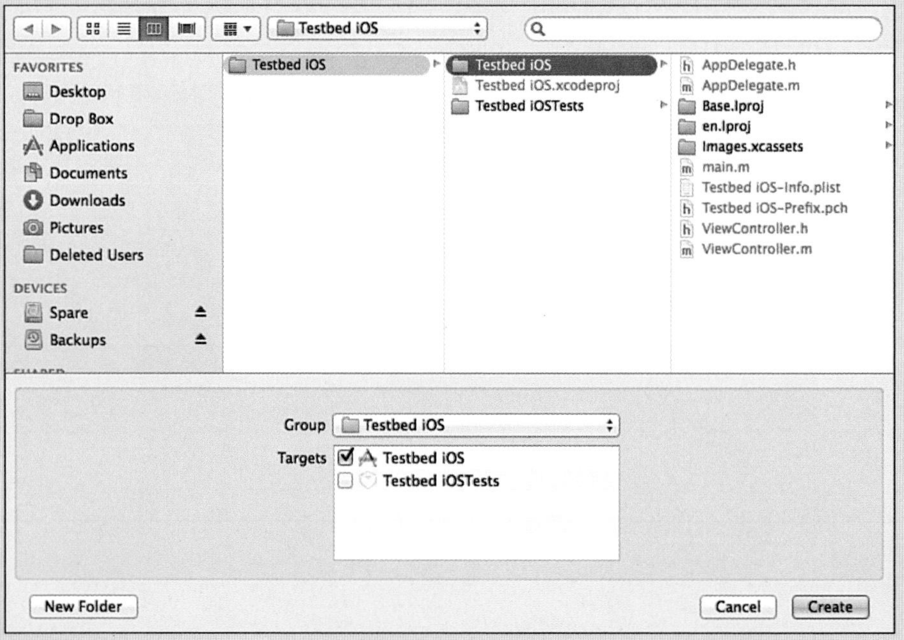

Testbed iOS

FAVORITES
- Desktop
- Drop Box
- Applications
- Documents
- Downloads
- Pictures
- Deleted Users

DEVICES
- Spare
- Backups

Testbed iOS
- Testbed iOS
- Testbed iOS.xcodeproj
- Testbed iOSTests

Testbed iOS
- h AppDelegate.h
- m AppDelegate.m
- Base.lproj
- en.lproj
- Images.xcassets
- m main.m
- Testbed iOS-Info.plist
- h Testbed iOS-Prefix.pch
- h ViewController.h
- m ViewController.m

Group　Testbed iOS

Targets　☑ Testbed iOS
　　　　　☐ Testbed iOSTests

New Folder　　　　　　　　　　　　Cancel　　Create

FIGURE 7.5
Save the files.

8. As you see in Figure 7.6, two files have been added to your project: CurrrencyConverter.h and CurrencyConverter.m. (Note the A badges next to the names as opposed to the M—modified—badges next to other files.) You might want to commit the project now; the A badges will disappear as the files are added to the repository.

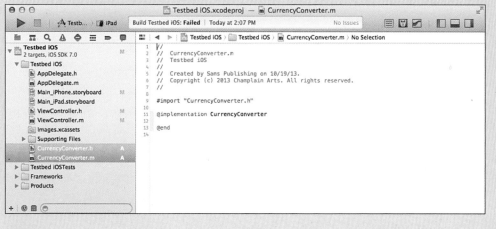

FIGURE 7.6
The files are added to your project.

The files use the same basic structure as the files you have seen in previous hours. These are bare-bones files that are ready for you to implement your class.

The interface file is shown in Listing 7.1.

LISTING 7.1 CurrencyConverter.h

```
//
//  CurrencyConverter.h
//  Testbed
//
//  Created by Jesse Feiler on 11/19/13.
//  Copyright (c) 2013 Champlain Arts Corp. All rights reserved.
//

#import <Foundation/Foundation.h>

@interface CurrencyConverter : NSObject

@end
```

The implementation code is shown in Listing 7.2; the comment at the top has been removed to save space.

LISTING 7.2   CurrencyConverter.m

```
#import "CurrencyConverter.h"

@implementation CurrencyConverter

@end
```

Exploring Class Hierarchies

Except for NSObject, which is the root class in Cocoa, every class has a superclass. You can follow up the hierarchy until you get to NSObject.

Calling Superclass Methods

The methods of each superclass are available to a child class, but only one at a time. For example, consider the imaginary hierarchy shown here:

```
NSObject
UIView
   draw
MyAbstractView
   draw
MyView
   draw
MySpecificView
```

The draw method is implemented in UIView, MyAbstractView, and MyView. If you instantiate MyView, the draw method in MyView is performed when you send a message to the instance of MyView. If you instantiate an instance of UIView, the UIView draw method is performed when you send a draw message to that instance. In terms of the architecture, each of the classes' methods is separate.

However, you can write code that does move up the inheritance chain. To call a method of a superclass, you send a message to super as in

```
[super description];
```

Use `description` for Debugging

`description` is a part of the `NSObject` protocol, so it can be called on any object. It returns an `NSString` description of the object. This is very useful for debugging. As with any method, you can override it to provide more or different information if you want.

You can invoke any method of a superclass subject to some constraints that are set when you declare the method. There are two patterns here. The first is the very specific case of moving up the inheritance structure by calling the superclass method with the same name. In other words, in this example, it would mean writing

```
[super draw];
```

in both `MyAbstractView` and `MyView`. If you are using this structure, the call to `super` is almost always either the first or last line of your method. This means that you can write some setup code in `MyAbstractView` and call it first before you call customized code in `draw` in `MyView`. Using the call to `super` as the last line of a method is done when you want to do your customized code before the general code. In the case of drawing, you typically want the generalized drawing routines to function before you draw your data. In cases such as saving data or disposing of objects, you often want to do your own saving before you let the object save or even dispose of itself.

When you call a method of a superclass with a different name from your own method, that code can be anywhere in your project.

In the case of an instance of a class that does not have a method defined, the message is sent up the class hierarchy until it finds the first class in the hierarchy that defines that method. In the hierarchy shown here, a message `draw` sent to an instance of `MySpecificView` would be passed up the hierarchy because that method is not declared in `MySpecificView`. It would next go to `MyView`, which does implement the method, and that is the code that would be performed. The message would not be passed further up the chain unless `draw` in `MyView` invokes

```
[super draw];
```

It is very common in most object-oriented programming languages to implement *abstract classes*. These are classes that are not meant to be instantiated. They are designed to be subclassed, and it is those subclasses that are instantiated. The methods in an abstract class are called by subclasses using a call to `super`. These methods do not always have the same name as the subclass method. Thus, you could find a subclass method `draw` calling a superclass's `prepareForDraw` method. Abstract classes let you provide an architecture for yourself and others to use in providing detailed concrete subclasses. `UIDocument` is a good example of an abstract class: if you use it, you override it.

Introducing Protocols

Abstract classes are not specific to Objective-C because you can use them in most object-oriented programming languages. However, Objective-C also uses another concept that is somewhat similar to abstract classes and that you will probably use frequently.

Protocols are groups of methods that are not part of a specific class. You define the protocol in some of the same ways that you define a class, but instead of getting to those methods by instantiating a class, you get to those methods when a class adopts a protocol. Adopting a protocol means announcing that your class will implement some of the methods defined for the protocol.

TIP

You can specify which methods are required and which are optional when you declare the protocol.

GO TO ▶ Hour 17, "Extending a Class with Protocols and Delegates," p. 231, for more information on protocols.

When a class adopts a protocol, the methods of that protocol are available to instances of the class. This means that when you invoke a method in an instance of a class, you have access to all of its declared methods and all of the methods in superclasses. The superclass methods are directly available if they are not overridden in the instance in question because you just call a method that is implemented only in a superclass and get right to it. For methods that are overridden, you do have to use `super` to get to them.

In addition to your instance methods and the methods available through superclasses, the methods of adopted protocols are also available. This gives you two paths to finding methods to use. You can go up the standard inheritance structure through superclasses, but you can also jump over to whatever protocols your class might have adopted. This structure was designed in part to handle the issue of multiple inheritance in object-oriented programming in which you sometimes want to inherit parts of various objects. Protocols implement that type of functionality.

Declaring Classes

Class declarations can become complex if they have many methods or instance variables, but the structure is always the same.

Writing a Basic Class Declaration

The class declaration shown previously in Listing 7.1 is the most basic type of declaration possible. It imports the file or framework in which the superclass is declared and then it declares the class and specifies its superclass after a colon:

```
#import <Foundation/Foundation.h>

@interface CurrencyConverter : NSObject
```

The declaration can go on to declare instance variables, properties, methods, and actions. The declaration ends with

```
@end
```

Actions are special types of methods. They are mostly used in conjunction with Interface Builder.

GO TO   For more information on declaring instance variables, properties, methods, and actions, refer to the following hours:

- ▶ Hour 8, "Declaring Instance Variables in an Interface File," p. 111
- ▶ Hour 9, "Declaring Properties in an Interface File," p. 127
- ▶ Hour 10, "Declaring Methods in an Interface File," p. 141
- ▶ Hour 11, "Declaring Actions in an Interface File," p. 149

If you have instance variables to declare, they are placed within brackets. Declared properties, methods, and actions follow the bracketed instance variables. Thus, a declaration might look like this:

```
#import <Foundation/Foundation.h>

@interface CurrencyConverter : NSObject {
  float height; //primitive C instance variable -- not Objective-C object
}

@property (assign) UIView *viewForCurrencyRate; //declared property

- (void)alphabetizeCurrencyNamesInPlace:(NSArray *)names; //method

- (IBAction)done:(id)sender; //action

@end
```

After any instance variables, declared properties, methods, and actions, the declaration finishes with @end.

Using Forward References

In addition to importing the framework or superclass file, you might need to make reference to other classes or protocols in your declaration. For example, if you want to declare an instance variable that contains an instance of one of your own classes, you need to write this:

```
MyClass * anInstance; // instance of MyClass
```

CAUTION

That produces an error because `MyClass` is not declared. You can get rid of the error by importing the file in which `MyClass` is declared (it is likely called MyClass.h).

Although that gets rid of the error, it is not the most elegant way of solving the problem of the forward reference to something not yet declared. You can use the `@class` directive to make it possible to use the class in your declaration without an error. If you do this, your declaration will look like this:

```
#import <Foundation/Foundation.h>

@class MyClass;

@interface CurrencyConverter : NSObject {
  float height; //instance variable
  MyClass * anInstance; // instance of MyClass
}

@property (assign) UIView *viewForCurrencyRate; //declared property

- (void)alphabetizeNamesInPlace:(NSArray *)names; //method

- (IBAction)done:(id)sender; //action

@end
```

You often need to refer to not-yet-declared protocols, and there is a comparable syntax for that purpose:

```
@protocol MyProtocol;
```

NOTE

Be Careful Where You Place #import, @class, and @protocol

Note that the `#import`, `@class`, and `@protocol` directives are placed outside the `@interface` section.

Your forward references as well as imported header files are sufficient for your declaration, but you are going to have to import the corresponding `.m` files when you get around to writing your own implementation that contains the definition of your class file. For this reason, until you add the definitions, do not try to build your project yet.

GO TO ▶ Hour 14, "Defining a Class in an Implementation File," p. 189, for more information.

Summary

This hour showed you the basics of a class declaration. It consists of the class name, its super-class, and space to declare its instance variables, declared properties, methods, and actions. You have seen the ways in which you can access methods that are outside your class declaration by using the class hierarchy as well as protocols.

Q&A

Q. What does the protocol architecture accomplish?

A. It provides a way of specifying related methods that are not part of the inheritance structure.

Q. Why would you use `@class` or `@protocol`?

A. These are forward references that let you compile your declaration without importing the header files. You need to import the implementation files into your own implementation. The forward reference is a much simpler way of being able to use the undeclared class or protocol than importing the header code.

Workshop

Quiz

1. What is a class prefix?

2. What are the rules for naming classes?

Quiz Answers

1. A class prefix consists of two or three capital letters at the beginning of a class name that identifies the framework or project to which it belongs. A class prefix is optional.

2. Start with a capital letter and run together the descriptive words. Do not use special characters to separate the words; instead use interior capitals as in `NSPredicateEditorRowTemplate`. After the prefix, class names usually are nouns.

Activities

Create a new Xcode project (or use a branch of a testbed) and experiment with creating new classes. Watch the errors and warnings that Xcode gives you as you type. If you are using source control, discard your changes when you are done.

Browse the sample code on developer.apple.com. You can download each project, but you can also browse them online. Do not worry about the functionality, but just explore the interface files to see how classes are declared. After you have looked at several of the samples, you should start to see the patterns of class declaration.

Declaring Instance Variables in an Interface File

What You'll Learn in This Hour

▶ Creating an instance variable for a class instance
▶ Using `id`
▶ Working with static typing
▶ Using variable scoping

Declaring Instance Variables and Properties

There are two ways of declaring the data elements that are part of a class. You can declare them as instance variables in the same way that you declare integers and floats. You can also declare them as properties of the class. This hour explores the use of instance variables. In the next hour, Hour 9, "Declaring Properties in an Interface File," you find out how to use properties to accomplish the same results. With declared properties, the compiler actually generates the declarations you see in this hour along with accessors that help to enforce the opacity of objects, which is a hallmark of good object-oriented design.

The use of declared properties is preferred today rather than using instance variables in your code. However, behind your declared properties are the instance variables that are automatically generated when your project is built. For that reason, instance variables are described in this hour and properties are dealt with in the following hour. Just remember that this is background information and that you should be using declared properties in your code. There are a few cases in which you do need to be aware of the instance variables and they are dealt with in these two hours as necessary.

Using the Class

You have created the class inside your project, but it is not instantiated, and there is no way that you can use it in your code until you instantiate it.

TIP

Yes, you can use class methods without instantiation, but for a bare-bones class such as the `CurrencyConverter` class you built in Hour 7, "Declaring a Class in an Interface File," the only class methods are those that are inherited from `NSObject`.

By placing the class files in your project, you have given them a location and context in the world of the code, but now you need to consider where in the runtime world of your app this class would be used. (Of course, in practice this is a discussion that you should have right at the beginning when you are designing the class.)

Placing a Class Instance in Context

Some object in your app will need to instantiate one or more `CurrencyConverter` instances. Depending on your class and your point of view, you may well think that some object (or objects) must instantiate, own, and control the instance(s) of the class. That owner or controller must be in existence before the class is instantiated—a *prime mover* in Aristotle's philosophy.

Eventually, this instance of your class may be passed on to other owners or controllers, but in the normal course of things, some object that survives the instance of your class needs to dispose of it. Today, that is usually done with Automatic Reference Counting (ARC), but although ARC manages the disposal of objects, you still are responsible for managing data. For example, ARC will dispose of a text field that is no longer needed, but it is your responsibility to move data entered into that field to a permanent storage location such as Core Data.

NOTE

This is a high-level conceptual look at instance life cycles. It is not a precise discussion of memory management.

Where Automatic Reference Counting (ARC) Fits In

Before ARC was implemented (in Xcode 4), the object life cycle was implemented in code. You created and initialized an object with this code:

```
myObject = [[MyObject alloc] init];
```

(Note that the previous line of code contains method calls.)

When you were finished with it, you deallocated it with this code:

```
[myObject dealloc];
```

With ARC, the compiler inserts the `dealloc` method call automatically; in fact, when you are using ARC, you are not allowed to use `dealloc` in your own code. The decision of when to deallocate an object is made by the compiler as part of its analysis of the structure of your code. ARC also manages ownership of objects with `retain`, `release`, and `autorelease`, which you also no longer need to use.

It is important to note that ARC was implemented in Xcode 4.2, but that it was an option for your project. There is a great deal of existing code that does not use ARC, so it is important to understand how those apps work. The Edit, Factor, Convert to Objective-C ARC command provides a tool to automatically convert a target to use ARC, so much legacy code has already been converted. With Xcode 5, ARC is no longer an option for new projects: It is on by default.

GO TO ▶ Hour 16, "Managing Memory and Runtime Objects," p. 221, for more information about ARC.

Choosing the Context

Deciding on the owner or controller of an instance is simple in many cases. For a view instance, a descendant of `NSViewController` or `UIViewController` is the most likely candidate to manage the view instance. In a document-based app, it is often a document that brings together many of the class instances in the app—certainly some of the instances related to the document's content. The `CurrencyConverter` class may be written in such a way that it could become part of a view or part of a document—or both.

Looking ahead to see what classes in your app might be users of a class you are considering developing is a good part of the design process. You can write a currency converter class that is designed to fit into a view, one that is designed to fit into a document, or one that can do both.

NOTE

The most significant difference might have to do with the degree of interactivity (if any) that the currency converter supports. A totally internal class might receive its data through arguments and return the results as a method result. Errors can be reported through the method result.

Returning Multiple Result Values from a Method

If you want to return multiple values from a method, you can use one of the collection classes. The most commonly used class for this purpose is `NSDictionary`.

GO TO ▶ Hour 15, "Organizing Data with Collections," p. 205, for more information on returning multiple values from a method.

In other cases, the app itself is responsible for its class instances. (These non-document-based apps are often referred to as *library* or *shoebox* apps. Examples are Address Book and iCal.)

If the app is to own an instance of `CurrencyController`, it needs to have its own instance variable so that it can refer to the instance (and eventually dispose of it). It needs to create an instance of the class and assign it to its own instance variable.

Unlike other object-oriented languages, Objective-C does not extend its base classes in many cases. Certainly, `UIApplication` and `NSApplication` are not subclassed very often. Instead, they have app delegates, and it is those classes that you subclass.

So the next step is to add an instance variable for a class instance to the interface file, to create an instance of the class, and to set the variable to the newly created instance. The next sections of this hour show you three different ways of declaring instance variables to contain instances of classes and compare their functionality. Declarations of noninstance variables are traditional C syntax.

Creating an Instance Variable for `CurrencyConverter` **with** `id`

If you have implemented and imported a `CurrencyConverter` class, you can declare an instance variable using the type `id`, as shown in Figure 8.1.

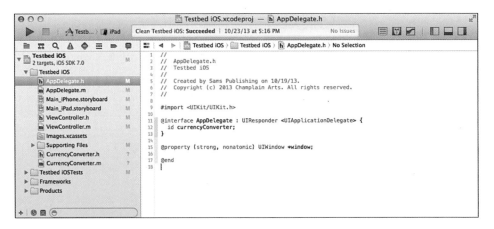

FIGURE 8.1
Declare an instance variable with `id`.

`id` is a basic data type in Objective-C. It can be set to an instance of any class. Because it is part of the Objective-C language, as you see in Figure 8.1, you do not need to import the header file for `CurrencyConverter`. Although `id` will be set to an instance of the class `CurrencyConverter`, in this declaration it is declared as a generic `id`.

The implementation file compiles cleanly and runs without the header file, as shown in Figure 8.2.

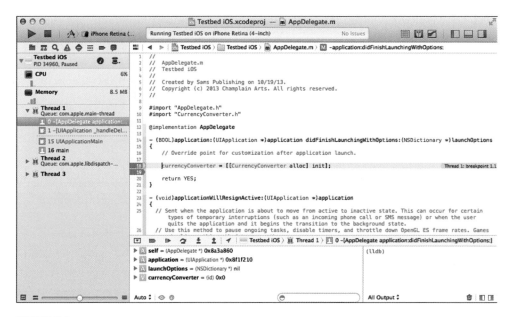

FIGURE 8.2
Use the `id` instance variable in an implementation file.

Note that the only line of code that has been added to this file is line 18. All of the other code was created by Xcode as part of the template.

In Figure 8.2, two breakpoints have been set. You do this by clicking in the gutter on the line of code where you want to break. In this case, execution stops just before line 18, and again just after it. The reason for these breakpoints is so that you can inspect the object that has been created with the debugger.

What Happens When Execution Stops

When you run the app, execution stops at the first breakpoint (notice a small green arrow on the current line just to the right of the breakpoint itself). The debugger can be shown at the bottom of the workspace window with View, Debug Area, Show Debug Area or with the button at the top right of the workspace window. Within the debug area, you can use the buttons at the top right to display the console at the right, variables at the left of the debug area, or both. In Figure 8.2, only the variables are shown.

When execution has stopped, you might need to do a bit of rearranging to see the data shown in Figure 8.2. You almost certainly need to use the disclosure triangle next to `self`; you want to see the variables within the current object, which is an instance of `AppDelegate` as you see in the parentheses. (The asterisk is discussed shortly.) You also see the memory location for the object.

Within the object, you can see the `_window` instance variable that is declared at the top of the implementation file as part of the template. You also see the `currencyConverter` instance variable that you created in the header file shown in Figure 8.1. (`NSObject` is discussed in the following section.)

What is most important in Figure 8.2 is the memory location for `currencyConverter`. It is 0x0—no memory is allocated because the object has not been created. Execution has stopped just before the `alloc` line of code.

Continue to the next breakpoint with the Continue button (second from the left of the debugger controls) or use the Step button to go one step further (third from the left in the control buttons). As you can see in Figure 8.3, there is now a memory location assigned to `currencyConverter`; the object has been created. Also, instead of being identified as of type `id` as it was in Figure 8.2, it is now identified as being of type/class `CurrencyConverter`. (In this context, type and class are interchangeable.)

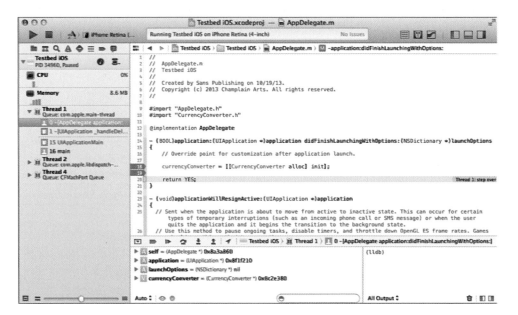

FIGURE 8.3
Step one line further.

Dynamic Binding

`id` is the type of any class instance. As you see in the debugger, at runtime, the type of the instance that is assigned to an `id` variable is known. You can assign an `id` to another `id`, and you can pass them in and out of methods just as you would an integer or other typed variable. You are responsible for making certain that the actual types that are created and stored in an `id` variable are correct.

It is legal to send a message to `id` even if the underlying object cannot respond to it. (In fact, that is necessary.) If the object cannot respond to a message, it simply does not do so. This means that in the code shown here, you can send the display message to `currencyConverter`, which is of type `id`.

This code does not generate either compile or runtime errors:

```
[currencyConverter display];
```

This is an example of *dynamic binding*, one of the key features of Objective-C. This flexibility lets you write very sophisticated code that is put together with the specific objects involved at runtime.

It also enables you to create problems for yourself and others who modify your code. For cases in which you are not certain what you are dealing with, you can call `class` to get an object's class and you can check to see if it responds to specific selectors (method calls).

GO TO ▶ There is more on method calls at "Sending a Message to the Text Field" in Hour 6, "Exploring Messaging and a Testbed App," p. 92.

Creating an Instance Variable for `CurrencyConverter` **with the Class Name**

You can avoid these problems by using *static typing*. Instead of declaring the instance variable as type `id`, you can declare it specifically as type `CurrencyConverter`—the class that you have written and imported.

To declare it that way, you need to either use an `@class` declaration for your `CurrencyConverter` class or import the header file. Many developers consider the `@class` method more elegant. Figure 8.4 shows the interface file.

You do not need to make any changes to the implementation file. However, when you run the app and set a breakpoint before the allocation of the object, notice that although there still is no memory allocated for it, its type is `CurrencyConverter`, as shown in Figure 8.5.

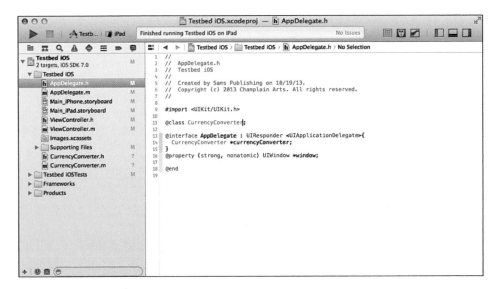

FIGURE 8.4
Use static typing for your instance variable.

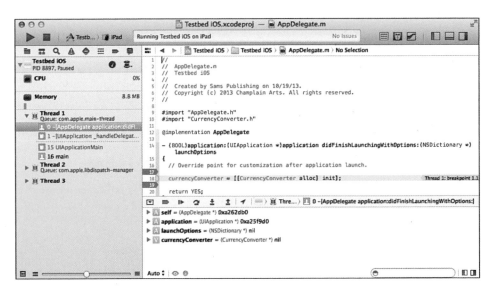

FIGURE 8.5
The variable is typed before it is allocated.

Because you have statically typed the variable, the compiler lets you know that you cannot send the display message to it, as shown in Figure 8.6. When you typed the variable as id, the compiler has no way of knowing if it can respond to a message. At runtime, you may replace the totally flexible `id` variable with an instance that might respond to the message. However, with a statically typed variable, the compiler knows that whatever you may replace it with must be an instance of `CurrencyConverter` or a subclass of it, and `display` is not a legal message.

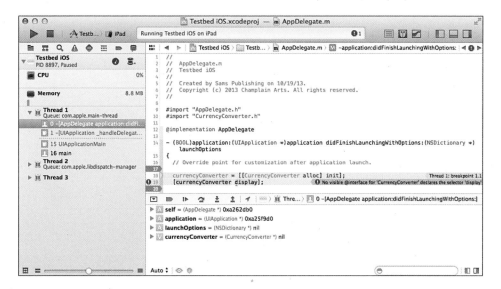

FIGURE 8.6
Use static typing for your instance variable.

NOTE

It is important to note that `id` is a `typedef` (specifically a `typedef` to a pointer to an instance of a class). When you statically type a variable, you provide a pointer to the class, so the declaration looks like

```
CurrencyConverter *currencyConverter;
```

Whether the space comes before or after the asterisk does not matter. It appears that placing the asterisk before the variable identifier rather than after the class name is more common.

Creating an Instance Variable for `CurrencyConverter` with a Superclass Name

There is a variation on the static typing example that you find frequently. In the previous example, the instance variable was statically typed with the class name—`CurrencyConverter`. You can statically type it as a class and then instantiate a subclass of that class. For example, you can declare the instance variable to be of class `NSObject`, as shown in Figure 8.7.

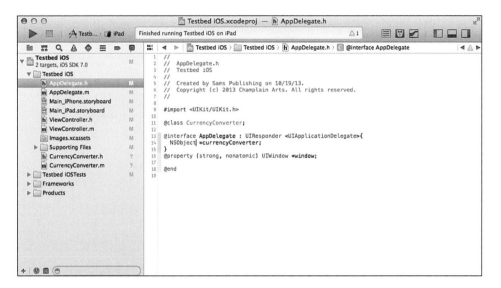

FIGURE 8.7
Declare the instance variable as type `NSObject`.

This means that you still cannot send a display message to it because the compiler knows that display is not a method of `NSObject`, but you can send any of the `NSObject` messages.

You will come across issues like this, particularly in classes with a number of subclasses such as `NSView` and `UIView`. You frequently call methods of the superclass intending either to actually perform those methods or intending to perform code that overrides those methods in subclasses.

In effect, you can write for the class that statically types the instance variable, but at runtime, the class that is actually used may well be a subclass that you have created. The model of typing an instance variable with a superclass is very common.

▼ TRY IT YOURSELF

Create a Static Typed Instance Variable with a Superclass

`NSView` and `UIView` are among the most frequently used static classes for instance variables that, at runtime, are set to a subclass. These steps show you how to make `CurrencyConverter` a subclass of `UIView`, instantiate it, and write code to invoke a method of the superclass. (You saw how to create a subclass in Hour 7.) Then you will change the super-class and cause an error because the superclass does not contain the method you invoked. Note that you do not even have to run the project: These errors are caught in the background as you type.

Here are the steps:

1. If you have been following the code in this hour, set the superclass of `CurrencyConverter` to `UIView` in CurrencyConverter.h (see Figure 8.8).

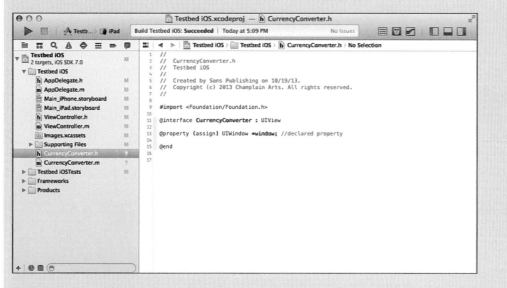

FIGURE 8.8
Start from a subclass of `UIView`.

2. Declare an instance variable of type `CurrencyConverter` in Appdelegate.h. Remember to add the `@class CurrencyConverter` directive.

3. Add a constraints message to AppDelegate.m, as shown in Figure 8.9. All is well for the moment.

4. In CurrencyConverter.h, change the superclass to `NSObject` instead of `UIView`.

5. Clean and build the project. When changing types, it is always a good idea to clean the project. You can use Product, Clean and then Product, Build or Command-Shift-K and then Command-B.

6. You will now have an error on the `constraints` message, as shown in Figure 8.10.

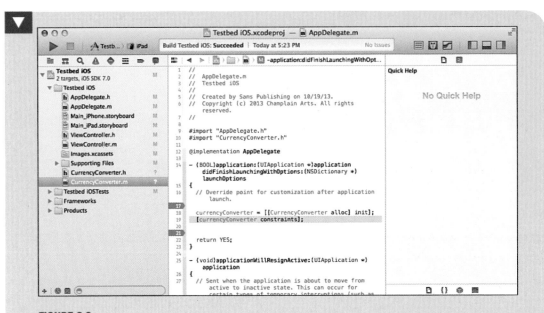

FIGURE 8.9
Add a constraints message.

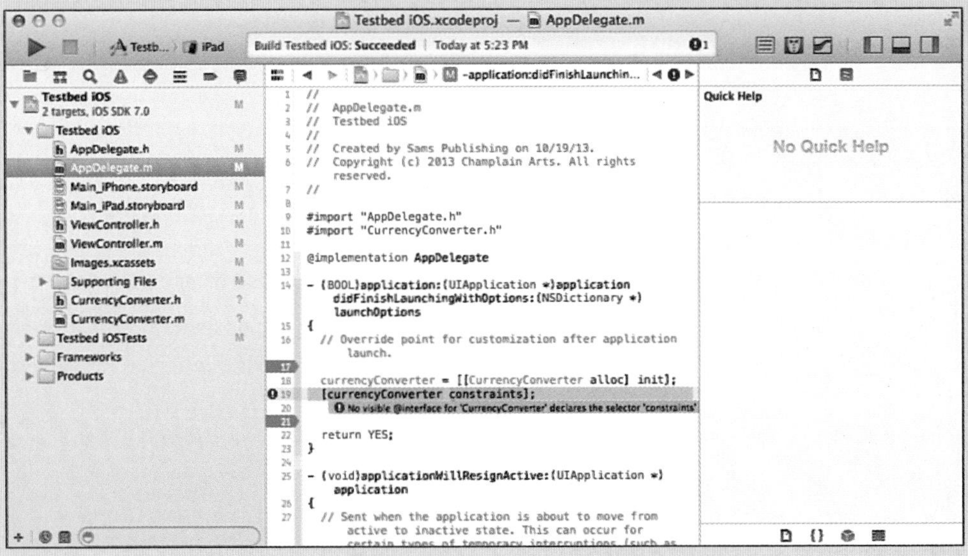

FIGURE 8.10
`constraints` is not a valid message for `NSObject`.

If you are working with an instance that is declared as a superclass (`UIView`, for example) and you know that it is a particular subclass, you can *cast* it to the subclass. For example, if you have instance variables defined as

```
UIView *myView;
UITextView *myTextView;
```

you can cast and assign a `myView` object to `myTextView`, as follows, providing that the actual instance is, indeed, an `UITextView`:

```
myTextView = (UITextView*)myView;
```

Managing Instance Variable Visibility

As is the case in many object-oriented programming languages, you can restrict the visibility of a variable. Your three choices are the following:

▶ **Protected**—The variable is visible to methods of the class in which it is declared as well as to methods in subclasses of that class. This is the default value.

▶ **Private**—The variable is visible only to methods of the class in which it is declared.

▶ **Public**—The variable is visible to all methods. This is very rarely used because it destroys the notion of encapsulation. Anyone could access this method.

Applying these visibility rules, you can have an interface such as the following:

```
@interface CurrencyConverter : NSObject {
  @public
  NSString    *dataSourceCopyrightString;

  @private
  NSDate      *lastDataSourceUpdate;

  @protected
  float       rate;
  float       amount;
  float       result;
}
```

Putting those rules together, you can see that the only variable that is always available is a copyright string. The underlying date of the source is restricted to members of the class. The `floats` that a client might be expected to access are protected. This is not an uncommon strategy.

Summary

In this hour, you have seen how to declare instance variables—variables that are present in each instance of a class. The basic syntax is the same as for any C variable declarations. However, you can use pointers to refer to instances of a class.

Q&A

Q. **What is the difference between static typing and using `id`?**

A. With `id`, variables are typed dynamically at runtime. The class of the instantiated object determines what methods are available. This slightly increases the overhead at runtime. Static typing removes that slight increase in overhead, and it allows error checking to be done by the compiler instead of by the runtime code.

Q. **What is the purpose of casting an instance?**

A. If you have an instance variable that is declared as a superclass of the object you are working with, you can cast the object down to the subclass.

Workshop

Quiz

1. If you change the superclass of a class, what precaution do you take in building the project?

2. When do you use the `@public` visibility rule?

3. How can you tell if an object has been allocated?

Quiz Answers

1. Clean the project.

2. This makes a variable accessible to anyone with access to the class. It is generally not used because it breaks the concept of encapsulation.

3. Using the debugger, set a breakpoint and check to see if memory has been allocated for the object.

Activities

Some of the sample code on developer.apple.com dates back a few years. Download some of the samples with modification dates from 2010 and earlier. Many of them use instance variables rather than properties. Make certain that you can understand their interfaces. Even if you switch over to properties for new projects, you will probably be modifying older code and need to understand the concepts presented in this hour.

HOUR 9
Declaring Properties in an Interface File

What You'll Learn in This Hour

▶ Determining when to use declared properties and when to use instance variables

▶ Exploring attributes for declared properties

▶ Using declared properties to manage memory

▶ Backing declared properties with instance variables

Comparing Interface Variables and Properties

There are two ways of declaring the data elements that are part of a class. You can declare them as instance variables in the same way that you declare integers and floats. You can also declare them as properties of the class. The previous hour, Hour 8, "Declaring Instance Variables in an Interface File," explored the use of interface variables. In this hour, you see how to use properties to accomplish the same results. Behind the scene, Xcode creates the instance variables you saw in Hour 8.

TIP

Another Way of Referring to Instance Variables

Instance variables are often referred to as `ivars`.

The objective in this hour is the same as in the previous one: Be able to use the `CurrencyConverter` class that you created in Hour 7, "Declaring a Class in an Interface File." To be able to use the class, you need to be able to reference it from `AppDelegate` either with an instance variable (Hour 8) or with a declared property (this hour). The goal is the same, but the method of getting there is different.

You have already seen both interface variables and properties in action in the code example. Figure 9.1 shows one of the experiments from Hour 8.

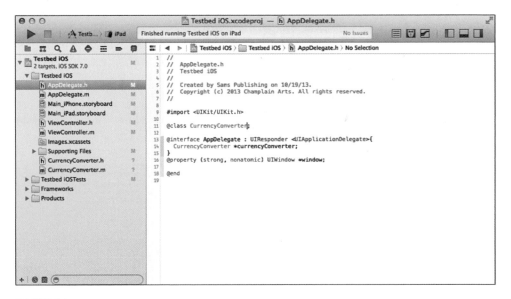

FIGURE 9.1
Variables and properties can be used together.

NOTE

A Word About the Code Chronology

Objective-C has evolved over the years from the initial C-style implementation to declared properties in Objective-C 2.0. In the example code on developer.apple.com, on the web, and in other code you may run across, you will see instance variables (as described in Hour 8) as well as properties (as described in this hour). Both styles exist today, but declared properties are the preferred style moving forward. This hour basically follows the chronological evolution. The advantage of this is that you can follow the different stages of declaration syntax and see what each new stage added to improve the development process. The disadvantage of this sequence is that you see the old and no-longer-recommended styles first. They are marked as no longer recommended, but they are an important part not just of the history but also of the evolving best practices in Objective-C development.

Reviewing Basic Variable Declarations

The most basic variable declaration consists of a type and an identifier as follows:

```
id currencyConverter;
```

NOTE

Using `id`

`id` is used in this section as the most basic type for an object in Objective-C. Static typing (that is, declaring a property or variable as something such as `UIWindow` rather than `id`) is preferred in most cases.

You can expand on a basic declaration by declaring several identifiers that use the same type, as in the following:

```
id currencyConverter, somethingElse;
```

Array declarations can add a bit more complexity, as in the following:

```
id currencyConverter[15], somethingElse[100];
```

But that is about it for variable declarations in C. Because C is valid syntax inside Objective-C code, all of them are usable in Objective-C.

Beyond the declarations, you should consider the basic object-oriented principle of *encapsulation*. Many people believe that the instance variables of a class should not be directly accessible. They prefer to hide the instance variables themselves to enforce the use of accessors—utility methods that get an instance variable's value (*getter*) or set an instance variable's value (*setter*).

Because the use of accessors is an implementation standard in these cases, accessors are designed according to the needs of the project. A very common standard (and one that is used in many Objective-C projects) is to declare accessors such as the following:

```
- (int)value //getter
- (void)setValue: (int)newValue; //setter
```

You can then write the following code:

```
int localValue = [myObject value]; //use the getter
[localObject setValue: localValue]; //use the setter
```

But this use of accessors to achieve the goal of encapsulation is a convention or standard; it is not enforced in any way. You can write all the accessors you want, but if you have an instance variable declared in this way,

```
id currencyConverter;
```

you can use it directly. You can write

```
currencyConverter = nil;
```

or

```
currencyConverter = myObject;
```

TIP

Remember that the declaration uses id, and as a result, any type is compatible.

These lines of code bypass accessors and break the encapsulation concept.

Creating Declared Properties: The Basics

In the simplest view, declared properties enable you to require the use of accessors, thus enforcing encapsulation instead of relying on coding conventions or standards. This section shows you this simplest scenario; the later section, "Working with Attributes for Declared Properties," shows you the variety of advanced features.

▼ TRY IT YOURSELF

Declare and Synthesize a Property

There are two basic components of a declared property: the @property declaration in your interface and a corresponding directive in your implementation that tells the app how the property is created at runtime. You must take steps 1 and 2 in this task to declare the property. Steps 3 and 4 create the corresponding implementation directive and may now be carried out automatically by Xcode as described in this task.

These steps show you how to code them:

1. Declare a currencyConverter property in your interface.

   It consists of the type and identifier as in a standard declaration preceded by an @property directive. (Eventually it will be declared as a CurrencyConverter type.)

   ```
   @property id currencyConverter;
   ```

2. If you want, you can declare several properties and separate them with commas.

   They must have the same type and attributes.

   ```
   @property id currencyConverter, anotherProperty;
   ```

3. Unless Xcode does it for you automatically (see below), use an @synthesize directive in your implementation file.

   ```
   @synthesize currencyConverter;
   ```

4. If you want, you can synthesize several declared properties with one directive.

   ```
   @synthesize currencyConverter, anotherDeclaredProperty, yetAnotherOne;
   ```

Using More Than `@synthesize`

`@synthesize` is one of several ways you can implement declared properties. There are other directives and options that are described later in this hour in "Implementing Properties," but `@synthesize` is the most basic of the directives. That's one of the reasons that Xcode can provide the basic `@synthesize` code for you automatically and behind the scenes. In this section, you start to see how you can create your own `@synthesize` statements that go beyond the basics.

Listing 9.1 shows the declaration from Hour 8 using a traditional instance variable along with getter and setter accessors.

LISTING 9.1   Instance Variable Declarations

```
#import <UIKit/UIKit.h>
#import "CurrencyConverter.h"

@interface AppDelegate : UIResponder <UIApplicationDelegate>{
  CurrencyConverter *currencyConverter;
}

- (CurrencyConverter *)currencyConverter; //getter
- (void)setCurrencyConverter: (CurrencyConverter *)newValue; //setter

@end
```

Listing 9.2 shows the instance variable declaration converted to a declared property. Xcode now has enough information to generate the traditional instance variable declarations as well as the same accessors that you could write for yourself in Listing 9.1. As previously noted, this now happens automatically, so all you have to write is the code in Listing 9.2; but the accessors and instance variable are present behind the scenes.

LISTING 9.2   Instance Declared Properties

```
#import <UIKit/UIKit.h>
#import "CurrencyConverter.h"

@interface AppDelegate : UIResponder <UIApplicationDelegate>

@property CurrencyConverter *currencyConverter;

@end
```

Note that in Listing 9.2 there are no instance variables. The brackets enclosing the instance variables are removed. As you see in the next section, this is not always the case.

Dealing with Memory for Objects

The simplicity of these declarations (type and identifier) can become a weakness when dealing with objects. One of the challenges of developing object-oriented languages and compilers has always been managing memory. If you declare an int in a section of code such as a function or block, when control is passed out of that block, the int is undefined. In most implementations, a location in memory has been assigned to each variable declared in the block; often these variables are stored in a stack. When control passes out of the block, because those variables are undefined, the entire section of the stack that was allocated for the block's variable is deleted.

NOTE

Cut back is a term used particularly in Burroughs large systems—the first major operating system written in a high-level language.

Because you know that your local variables disappear on exit from the block, if you want to preserve their values, you need to somehow preserve them before leaving the block. A common way of doing this is to set a variable that is outside the block to the value of the variable that will be cut back, possibly by passing the value out as a result of a function call.

Objects are not simple variables such as an int or float. Moving them around in memory can require a good deal of manipulation to find space for these often large objects. More important, in most object-oriented languages, objects such as class instances that are declared in a block are not automatically cut back. Thus, in many object-oriented languages, it is not enough just to declare a variable: If it is an object, you also have to create it and delete it.

NOTE

An int that is declared in a block may be initialized to nil or just left undefined depending on the language, operating system, and compiler. But nil or not, it usually takes the same amount of space when it is uninitialized or initialized to a value.

You have seen this code already in calls to alloc and init. If you do not use Automatic Reference Counting (ARC), you would add a call to dealloc to the standard alloc and init calls to handle releasing memory for objects. (Although ARC is the standard today, you may encounter other memory management techniques in legacy code.)

Working with Attributes for Declared Properties

After you start dealing with memory issues, you see one of the weaknesses of traditional declarations: It is not enough just to specify a type and identifier. When dealing with objects, you need to provide additional information such as how they will be managed in memory. The declared property syntax allows for attributes to be placed in parentheses, and you can use them to specify a number of attributes about the property you are declaring.

One property that is used with ARC is `strong`. You see it defined in "Setter Semantics" later in this hour. For now, just use it in your declaration as follows (this avoids a compiler error).

```
@property (strong) CurrencyConverter *currencyConverter;
```

Using Declared Properties

Remember, if you are modifying legacy code, you need to add an `@synthesize` directive in your implementation file. By convention, it is placed at the top of the implementation file right after `@implementation`.

```
@synthesize myCurrencyConverter;
```

TRY IT YOURSELF ▼

Add a Property and a Method to Your Code

You can use declared properties in two ways. To explore those two ways, add a method to `CurrencyCalculator` and two properties to `AppDelegate`, as shown in the following steps:

1. Add a calculate method to CurrencyCalculator.h.

   ```
   @interface CurrencyConverter : NSObject
   - (void)calculate;
   @end
   ```

2. You can add a shell of the method to the implementation in CurrencyCalculator.m.

   ```
   @implementation CurrencyConverter
   - (void)calculate {
   }

   @end
   ```

3. Add an `exchangeRate` property to AppDelegate.h along with a `CurrencyConverter` property.

```
#import <UIKit/UIKit.h>
#import "CurrencyConverter.h"

@interface AppDelegate : UIResponder <UIApplicationDelegate>

@property (strong, nonatomic) UIWindow *window;

@property float exchangeRate;

@property (strong, nonatomic) CurrencyConverter *currencyConverter;

@end
```

NOTE

What Should `calculate` Do?

In practice, this method might return a value. In another scenario, the `calculate` method might do nothing more than calculate (as its name suggests) but not return it. It may perform additional tasks such as notifying other objects that the value has been calculated. If you want to retrieve the calculated value, you might call another method or use the getter for `CurrencyConverter`. This would be a good implementation if the method uses real-time foreign trade conversion values. The getter might return the value as well as the time stamp and source of the conversion value. Your choice depends on the requirements of the app you want to build.

There are two ways to use the declared properties: message syntax and dot syntax.

Accessing the Property with Message Syntax

If you write the code shown in Listing 9.1, you can send a message to the `self` object (the current class) requesting the value of a property. If you have let Xcode create the default getter, here is what you would write to get the value of `exchangeRate`:

```
float f = [self exchangeRate];
```

You can try this out in the `didFinishLaunchingWithOptions:` method of the app delegate. Place it right after the comment indicating the override point.

Accessing the Property with Dot Syntax

Dot syntax uses the standard C syntax used for working with `structs`. When you are working with a declared property, dot syntax uses the accessors that have been created behind the scenes by Xcode. This means that when you use dot syntax and declared properties, as shown in Listing 9.2, you preserve encapsulation and can write:

```
float f = self.exchangeRate;
```

Here is the dot syntax to set a value:

```
float f = 5.0;
self.exchangeRate = f;
```

Preserving encapsulation is not just a matter of design purity or some abstract concept. It means that the accessor can include various types of error checking to prevent accidents from happening.

Given the declared property and its accessor, you can get to the `calculate` method in your implementation by using this code that combines dot and messaging syntaxes:

```
[self.currencyConverter calculate];
```

Using Attributes

As you have seen, the attributes section of declared properties lets you add a variable number of attributes to the basic type and identifier of an instance variable. This section explores those attributes. Most of the attributes consist of a keyword that turns the attribute on or off or to a specific value. Some of them consist of a keyword and a variable. Unless otherwise noted, each of the attributes that follows can have one (or sometimes zero) values in a list of attributes.

Attributes add additional dimensions to properties (and, thus, to variables). Although Objective-C is a dynamic language in which as much as possible is done at runtime rather than at compile time (thus allowing for greater runtime flexibility), some of these attributes allow the compiler to perform more traditional compile-time checking.

NOTE

Striking a Balance Between Runtime and Compile-Time Error Checking

The philosophical differences between compile- and runtime error checking are joined in the practical world by the fact that runtime errors are generally discovered by the user rather than by the developer. The fact that they may be caused by user errors is irrelevant. Developers and users want apps to run successfully despite what a user may do. These issues have been a topic of discussion in the world of dynamic languages for many years. A lot of people feel that the balance achieved in Objective-C 2.0 is appropriate, useful, and beneficial to both users and developers.

Accessor Methods

You can write your own accessor methods rather than having Xcode create them.

You have two choices for writing your own accessors. You can simply implement the accessors that will be looked for using the naming conventions:

```
- (CurrencyConverter *)currencyConverter; //getter
- (void)setCurrencyConverter: (CurrencyConverter *)newValue; //setter
```

You can also create accessors using different names from the naming conventions. If you choose to do so, you use one or both of the following attribute settings. The default is to use the automatically generated getter and setter.

- ▶ getter = getterName—This method must return a result with a type that matches the property type; it must not have any parameters. Beyond these descriptions, you can do anything you want. You can perform calculations to modify the raw result, for example.

- ▶ setter = setterName—This method must return void and take a single parameter that matches the property type. As with getters, you can do any additional processing you want. You get a compiler error if you specify a setter for a readonly attribute (see the following section).

NOTE

Using a Custom Getter for a BOOL

A custom getter is often used for a BOOL property. Consider the following case:

`@property (readwrite) BOOL readyForInput;`

The default getter will let you write code like this:

`[myProperty readyForInput];`

You can improve readability by using a custom getter as in the following:

`@property (readwrite, getter = isReadyForInput) BOOL readyForInput;`

`. . .`

`[myProperty isReadyForInput];`

Writability

Your choices for writability are simple:

- ▶ readwrite [default]—Both a getter and setter are generated by Xcode or you.

- ▶ readonly—You or Xcode must supply a getter. Attempts to use dot syntax to set a value are caught by the compiler.

Setter Semantics

You have your choice of several values that let you handle how references to objects are tracked in a reference-counting environment. Typically, if you take ownership of an object, you need to bump up the reference count when you take it and then bump it down when you are finished. The runtime software watches to see when a reference count hits zero and, at that time, cleans up memory. ARC takes care of this for you.

Here are the two most frequently used values for ARC:

▶ weak (formerly `assign`) [default]—This is the typical assignment paradigm. It simply assigns a value to the property and leaves the reference count untouched. If the object itself disappears (see the next bullet) the value is set to nil.

▶ strong (formerly `retain`)—This calls `retain` on the new value that is being set. It then calls `release` on the previous value, thus bumping its reference count down by one. All of this happens inside the Automatic Reference Counting (ARC) code. When the last strong property is no longer in use, the object itself may be deallocated and weak references to it are set to nil.

Atomicity

It is possible under some circumstances for properties to have partially set values. By making a property atomic, extra instructions are added so that the object is locked before its value is retrieved, and then unlocked afterward. There is a performance penalty for this added security: it is measured in hundredths of a second, but can be significant particularly in loops that execute many times. The default value is to treat properties atomically, but you can specific the non-atomic attribute to eliminate this locking.

GO TO ▶ Hour 22, "Grand Central Dispatch: Using Queues and Threading," p. 283, for more information on this concept.

Using Other Attribute Decorators

You can use any C-style decorators. In addition, you can use `IBOutlet`. These do not appear in the attributes' parentheses. If used, they appear before the type name.

You can use `IBOutlet` to indicate that the property can be used by Interface Builder as an outlet in the interface. This means that the property can be accessed from an interface element such as a button.

Implementing Properties

As noted previously, @synthesize is only one of the implementations you can supply for a declared property. @synthesize and @dynamic are discussed in this section.

Creating Accessors with @synthesize

After you have declared a property, Xcode can generate the appropriate backing variable as well as the getter and setter automatically (getter only for the case of readonly properties). By default, the backing variable is the name of the property preceded by an underscore. Thus, you can also create your own @synthesize directives to customize the process. One of the most frequently used variations of the @synthesize directive is to set the property to an instance value of your own. The default @synthesize statement is effectively

```
@synthesize myProperty = _myProperty;
```

The backing variable is the property name preceded by an underscore. However, you can create any backing variable you want and use it for the property by adding an @synthesize directive like this to the top of your @implementation.

In certain circumstances, you may want to refer directly to the backing variable (most commonly, these are situations such as an init method, and, if you are still using reference counting, a dealloc call). If you do not use a backing variable with a different name from the property, you can reference the instance variable from your code with

```
_myProperty
```

whereas

```
self.myProperty
```

goes through the property to the same instance variable.

NOTE

Legacy Instance Variable Declarations

The ability of the compiler and runtime to dynamically create instance variables is relatively new; it has required changes in the runtime of Objective-C 2.0 as well as more recently in Xcode. If you are dealing with legacy code, you may see instance variable declarations that are used automatically in the @synthesize directive for a property with the same name. You may be tempted to convert all of them to use declared properties and automatic creation of instance variables, but experiment before doing a wholesale conversion. Precisely because of the possibility of confusion between properties and instance variables with the same name as just described, you may break existing code. Going forward, it is a good practice to use properties and backing variables with a different name (such as starting with an underscore).

Promising Data with `@dynamic`

This directive is most often used with `NSManagedObject`. It indicates that the information otherwise provided by `@synthesize` and its getters and setters will be provided dynamically. `@dynamic` is frequently used with Core Data managed objects.

Summary

This hour described the processes you use to declare properties rather than instance variables for your class. The use of properties helps to encapsulate the data for your class by making it accessible only through accessors. In addition, attributes let you specify more features of the data than simply a type as in a traditional declaration.

Q&A

Q. What are the advantages of using declared properties?

A. By automatically creating accessors that you can use with dot syntax, the instance variables are more securely encapsulated. In addition, attributes of declared properties let you set more than just the type of the property; you can control its writability as well as features such as memory management.

Q. What are the advantages of using dot syntax with declared properties?

A. You may have less typing to do because you can use the synthesized accessors. In addition, it can make your code more readable.

Workshop

Quiz

1. What should you do if you are revising an app that uses declared instance variables?

2. Why would you create your own accessors for declared properties?

Quiz Answers

1. For new variables, consider using declared properties. Existing variables may be changed, but be careful that you do not introduce errors. The tighter syntax of declared properties may cause sloppily written code to break.

2. Create your own accessors if you want to do additional processing before or after accessing the backing variable.

Activities

Work through the code samples in this hour. Use the debugger and the techniques described in this hour to track the creating of the properties. Experiment with using declared instance variables and automatically generated ones as you watch the debugger.

Declaring Methods in an Interface File

What You'll Learn in This Hour

▶ Examining the difference between class and instance methods

▶ Naming methods properly

▶ Returning complex data structures as method results

Working with Methods in a Class

As you have seen in the previous hours of this part, you declare classes that can contain instance variables and declared properties in addition to the information in the class declaration itself. The other major component of a class is its *methods*. Methods are the messages to which instances of the class (or, in some cases, the class itself) respond. They provide the functionality for the class.

In this hour, you learn how to declare and define your classes. To help you create useful methods, you also see the basics of how people can use the classes that you create.

Objective-C methods use much the same syntax as do C functions. The major difference is that Objective-C methods use named arguments. Inside the body of a method, the structure is the same as the inside of a C function, although, of course, you can use Objective-C syntax in addition to the standard C syntax. Remember that C code compiles properly under Objective-C, so nothing prevents you from mixing Objective-C and C code; you also can write a method that consists solely of C code.

Because Objective-C methods are so similar to C functions, a good place to start is with the naming conventions for Objective-C and Cocoa methods. The naming conventions provide standards that make your code easier to read (this is valuable even on a one-person project). In addition, the options and standards help you to appreciate the features and options that are available to you as you develop Objective-C methods.

Reviewing Method Syntax

As you have seen, the basic syntax for a method declaration consists of two basic parts followed, as always with a declaration, by a semicolon. The two parts are the instance/class indicator and the method header itself.

Distinguishing Between Class and Instance Methods

The first character indicates if this is a class instance (+) or a method instance (-). Class instances are called using the class name rather than a specific instance. They often are used as factory methods to create new instances of the class. In many cases, these new instances represent a conversion from other classes (or even basic types) to the class.

For example, NSNumber has class methods that return new instances of NSNumber based on values that are passed in. Here is a commonly used method:

```
+ (NSNumber *)numberWithBool:(BOOL)value;
```

You pass in a BOOL and receive a new instance of NSNumber. You perform this method from an implementation file by using the following:

```
NSNumber *myNumber = [NSNumber numberWithBool: YES];
```

A more common invocation would use a variable for the argument:

```
BOOL myBool = YES;
NSNumber *myNumber = [NSNumber numberWithBool: myBool];
```

An instance method is declared with a - at the beginning. Most init methods initialize an already-created instance and set the appropriate values, as follows:

```
- (id)initWithBool:(BOOL)value;
```

The difference between the instance method and the class method is that you must have created the instance first. Thus, you need both of these lines of code:

```
myNumber = [NSNumber alloc];
[myNumber initWithBool: myBool];
```

As shown previously, you can combine these two lines of code into one:

```
myNumber = [[NSNumber alloc] initWithBool: myBool];
```

Copying and Pasting Method Declarations and Implementations

If you have a method declaration such as

```
- (id)initWithBool:(BOOL)value;
```

you can copy and paste it into your implementation. Delete the final semicolon and type a single open brace. When you press Return, Xcode adds a blank line and a closing brace. You can now start to write the code.

```
- (id)initWithBool:(BOOL)value {

}
```

Exploring the Method Declaration

Look closely at a method declaration to understand its three basic components. This is a method declaration that has been used previously in this hour and one that is frequently used by programmers:

```
- (id)numberWithBool:(BOOL)value;
```

After the instance/class indicator, the components are the following:

▶ `Return value`—Just as with C functions, each method can return a result (in fact, all methods return a result, as you see later in this section). The result is a single value, but it can be a collection object such as `NSDictionary` or `NSArray`, which can contain multiple values within the single object.

▶ `Method name`—This is a standard Objective-C identifier. Naming standards for methods are described in this section.

▶ `Arguments`—There can be zero or more of these. As with C functions, you can end the list with an ellipsis (...) to indicate a variable number of arguments (this is called a variadic method or function). That style is rarely used today in Objective-C, and it is not discussed in this book.

Return Value

Every method returns the same type of value: an `id`. This is a pointer to an object—any object. (Note that you don't use an asterisk with the `id` type.) Standard practice is to cast the result of a method to a more specific value using the standard casting syntax. For example, consider this class method:

```
+ (NSNumber *)numberWithBool:(BOOL)value;
```

The returned id (a pointer to an object) is cast to being a pointer to an NSNumber instance. This enables better compile-time checking of the code that you write.

Perhaps the most common casting of a method result is not to a pointer to an object; it is cast to void. You can see this in methods such as the following:

```
- (void)setIdentifier:(NSString *)identifier
```

For methods that return values that are not objects, you can use the standard C types such as float, short, double, and unsigned char.

Method Name

By convention, a method name begins with a lowercase character. If it consists of several words, combine them by starting each word after the first one with a capital letter. Do not use underscores or other special characters.

Method names are often verbs. You may modify them, but somewhere (preferably at the beginning), there should be a verb. You have already seen examples of simple methods that consist only of a verb (init and alloc, for example).

TIP
___
Although "do" is a verb, for the sake of method naming, ignore it. doDuplicate is not a good method name: Simply use duplicate. do adds nothing to the method name.
___

If a method performs several tasks, they should normally be reflected in the method name unless they are clearly part of the main task. As the frequently cited example of alloc and init shows, it can be better to have two separate methods that cooperate by returning a value that is passed into the next one. That way, you know what is happening.

TIP
___
Do Not Hide Method Tasks
The only exception to this guideline is the case in which one or more tasks are subsidiary and are so essential that it is inconceivable that the method's main task could be performed without them. This guidance is particularly important for tasks that create, modify, or change data. If your method is going to create a certain object with a name that is passed into the method, checking to see if the name is a duplicate is pretty clearly part of the basic processing, and there often is no reason to separate the process into two tasks.
___

What is common, however, is to create a composite task that interacts with the user. You might have a task called createNamedObject that returns an NSError object. The composite task createNamedObjectWithError could add user interaction for error handling. Both methods would ultimately do the same thing, but this structure enables you to create a pair of methods that can be used in a variety of circumstances.

Many methods do not perform tasks, and in these cases, verbs are inappropriate. If a method returns a value, the beginning of its method name should be the name of what it is returning; get is as superfluous as do.

Arguments

Methods can accept any number of arguments. A colon precedes each argument. When you are looking at a list of methods (perhaps in a class reference), this fact is important. For example, Listing 10.1 shows the instance methods for working with state information in NSPersistentStore.

LISTING 10.1   State Information Methods in NSPersistentStore

```
- type
- persistentStoreCoordinator
- configurationName
- options
- URL
- setURL:
- identifier
- setIdentifier:
- isReadOnly
- setReadOnly:
```

The colons let you distinguish between the methods that take no arguments and the three methods listed below that take a single argument:

► setURL

► setIdentifier

► setReadOnly

Methods can take more than one argument. Here is a method from NSPersistentStore that takes three arguments:

```
+ setMetadata:forPersistentStoreWithURL:error:
```

As you can see, each argument follows a colon. In all cases except the first argument, the argument has a name. In the case of the first argument, the name of the argument is the name of the method.

Writing the Method Declaration

Particularly when a method has several arguments, the method declaration becomes a meaning-ful phrase and sometimes even a sentence. The method name is frequently a verb, and the argu-ment names often include a preposition as in the example just shown. A good example of the argument is `forPersistentStoreWithURL`. That particular argument has a bonus by having two prepositions. `forPersistentStore` and `WithURL` provide clear indications of how `setMetadata` functions.

Also, the final argument, `error`, illustrates another common aspect of argument naming. Certain arguments such as `error` are so common that it is not necessary to decorate them with a preposition. You could name the final argument `withError`, but the convention of a final argument named `error` is sufficient for most people.

Returning Complex Data Structures from Methods

You can easily return a result from a method. The default return value is `id`, and you can cast it to a pointer to a class instance such as `NSView *` or to the common `void`, which effectively returns nothing from the method.

Because the result is a pointer to a class instance in many cases, it can carry all of the data in that class instance. Many (possibly most) classes have significant amounts of data. The `NSNumber` class is used in this hour precisely because it does not have much data, and you can see how its methods work.

Some classes are specifically designed to manage large amounts of data.

GO TO ▶ Hour 15, "Organizing Data with Collections," p. 205, to learn how to work with dictionaries, sets, and arrays.

Pointers can be dereferenced with `&` so as to get to the underlying data. This is commonly used with `NSError`. Some methods use double indirection in their declaration, as shown here for `outError`:

```
- (BOOL)readFromURL:(NSURL *)url error:(NSError **)outError
```

You can invoke it with code such as the following:

```
NSError *err = nil;
myResult =  [myDocument readFromURL:myURL error: &error];
```

The argument `myURL` is a pointer to the `NSURL` class. `outError` is a pointer to a pointer to the `NSError` class (this is called *double indirection*). If the method makes a change to `myURL`, it affects the object passed in via the argument. With the double indirection of `outError`, the method can change the pointer so that it points to another object. Typically, it is used to change it from its initial value (nil) to another instance of `NSError`. In this way, a method can return a new value not only as its result (BOOL, in this case), but also through a doubly indirected argument.

Biggest Difference in Architectures for Returning Objects

The biggest difference between returning an object as a method result and returning an object using double indirection as described here is that you can only return one method result (although it can contain many elements within the object returned), but with double indirection you can have several arguments that can return results. Before embarking on this architecture, think about whether this is the best structure.

In many cases, if you think you need to return three separate results through arguments, maybe you need to construct a new class or even a `container class` such as `NSDictionary` that can bring those separate results into a single, logical form. Returning several values that are related only by a single method call may indicate that the method is too general or is not focused enough.

The common use of an `NSError` argument that is passed in as nil and may be returned as a value or still as nil is a good design because in most cases, nothing new is returned. If there is no error, nil is passed in and nil is returned. Returning a new `NSError` object (or any other object in other cases) is appropriate when the primary result is returned as the method's result and the other result is returned either in an error condition or another rare and exceptional circumstance.

This all boils down to a matter of programming style and personal preference, but most developers have come to believe that the simplest implementation of any process is best if only because when new developers come along to maintain it, they will understand what it does.

Summary

This hour has shown you how to declare methods in your interface. Methods are of two types: instance and class methods. Class methods are called on the class itself—often they are factory methods that create new instances of the class. Each type of method then has three primary components: a result, a name, and zero or more arguments.

Q&A

Q. What is the purpose of a doubly indirected argument in a method declaration?

A. With a typical argument (single indirection such as `NSError *`), you pass in a pointer to an instance; you may modify it as a result of the method's code. (This is common in the `init` methods.) With double indirection such as `NSError **`, you typically pass in a nil value and return a new object. (In some cases, you pass in one object and return another.)

Q. Why is the ellipsis not used much at the end of a list of method arguments?

A. The code can be clearer if each argument is named. If you need a flexible number of arguments, consider using one of the collection classes such as `NSArray`, `NSSet`, or `NSDictionary`.

Workshop

Quiz

1. What does (`void`) mean at the beginning of a method declaration?

2. What are the basic rules of method declaration naming?

Quiz Answers

1. Nothing is returned.

2. The method itself should be a verb if it does something; if it simply returns a value, it should be the name of the value. Argument names typically end with a prepositional phrase such as `withStyle`.

Activities

How many problems can you find with these declarations?

```
- convertRectToCircle: (NSRect *)aRect;
- doMainProcess;
- (MyUserClass *)getUserIDForName: (NSString*)aName;
```

HOUR 11

Declaring Actions in an Interface File

What You'll Learn in This Hour

▶ Comparing actions and methods

▶ Creating actions with Xcode

▶ Connecting interface elements to actions

Introducing Actions

Hour 10, "Declaring Methods in an Interface File," covered the basics of declaring methods. There is a great deal of flexibility in the Objective-C method declaration structure, and you can use it to make your code easy to read and reuse (not to mention easy for users to use). In this hour, you learn how to create and use actions—a special type of method that is a key part of the Cocoa frameworks. Actions make it possible to connect interface elements such as buttons and menu commands to code that is triggered when the action is invoked by a user. In a very real sense, almost the entire user interface of Cocoa and Cocoa Touch rests on actions.

Without a doubt, actions are part of the Cocoa frameworks; however, they are implemented by writing Objective-C code, and their interactions with interface elements are created in most cases using Xcode. This hour shows you the basics of actions in both the frameworks and in the language contexts.

It might seem a little strange to have both the very flexible structure for building methods you saw in Hour 10 as well as a far more specialized structure to build actions. The reason for this is that by having this highly specialized structure for actions, you gain a great deal of flexibility in developing apps based on Cocoa and Cocoa Touch.

Paradigms and Design Patterns

Objective-C and the Cocoa frameworks take advantage of a range of development technologies that make it easy to share and reuse code as well as what is often the most expensive part of the development process: the analysis and imagination that stand behind the code that is written. These development technologies include model-view-controller, which is the overall concept behind Cocoa, as well as target-action, which is the concept that involves actions.

Concepts such as these are sometimes referred to as paradigms or design patterns. Paradigm is an English word with a long history of use in many fields. Design patterns are a concept first advanced in the late 1970s and refined over time. Some people would say that the design pattern concept fell out of favor and common use at the beginning of the 2000s. In a broader sense, paradigms and design patterns are both conventions. They add nothing to a language or framework other than limiting the ways in which they are used (and those limits can be good things).

They are akin to naming conventions for variables, methods, and classes. As specified in many programming languages, names begin with a letter and then contain letters and numbers but no spaces and, usually, no special characters other than an underscore. Spaces are not allowed. Depending on the language, the case of the letters might or might not matter (it does in Objective-C). A naming convention can limit names to perhaps two or three capital letters that identify the framework to which a class belongs (this is the convention in the Apple frameworks).

Regardless of the status of the terminology, the specific concepts are easy to implement in Objective-C and the Cocoa frameworks, and they are widely used in those contexts.

The easiest way to introduce actions is to demonstrate how you can use them to build an app with a graphical user interface that requires next to no programming. Much of the work is done by dynamic and runtime features of Objective-C as well as by the Cocoa frameworks. A key part of the demonstration involves the target-action paradigm (or design pattern, if you prefer that term).

What Actions Can Do for You

To demonstrate what actions can do for you, the developer, you will see how to build an OS X app and a comparable iOS app with next to no programming. It all relies on actions and Interface Builder in Xcode.

NOTE

Where to Connect Your Actions

In the OS X Cocoa Application template, you connect your actions to AppDelegate. In the iOS Single View Application template, you connect your actions to ViewController. Both of these are shown in the steps that follow. As you explore Cocoa and Cocoa Touch, you will find other objects to which you can connect actions, but that is beyond the scope of this book. The process, however, is exactly the same.

Build an OS X App with an Action

These steps are a classic example of the Xcode development environment. It starts from the Cocoa Application template that gives you an app that displays a window and a menu bar. You see the process of implementing a new menu command and creating an action to respond to the new menu command.

1. Create a new Xcode project from the OS X Cocoa Application template. If you want, you can run it at this point; you have an empty window and a menu bar. The relevant menu commands, such as Quit, work.

2. Select MainMenu.xib in the project navigator. This opens Interface Builder in the editor, as shown in Figure 11.1. At the left side of the editor, you can show or hide the document outline (you can also use Editor, Show/Hide Document Structure).

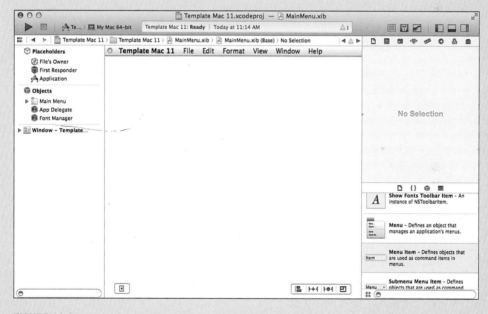

FIGURE 11.1
Locate the Menu Item object.

At the top of the canvas, you see the menu bar that is created as part of the template. Do not confuse this with the Xcode menu bar. The template menu bar consists of Template Mac 11 (the name of the project), File, Edit, Format, View, Window, and Help.

3. If necessary, show the utility area at the right.

4. Locate the Menu and Menu Item objects from the Object library, as shown in Figure 11.1.

Note that Figure 11.1 shows a combination of steps 1–3.

5. Drag the Menu object from the Object library and place it between View and Window on the menu bar.

6. Select the Menu Item. You should see a menu with three menu items within it.

7. Select one of the menu items and change its name in the Attributes inspector to `Experiment`. Delete the other two items. (You can also just double-click the menu item and type the new name in without bothering with the Attributes inspector.)

8. Switch to the Assistant editor. Use the jump bars to set one pane to MainMenu.xib and the other pane to AppDelegate.h.

9. Control-drag from the menu command to the interface of AppDelegate.h. An insertion indicator shows you where the outlet or action will be placed.

10. When you release the mouse button, the small dialog shown in Figure 11.2 displays. Note that this is where the target action paradigm comes into play: Instead of constructing a method as described in Hour 10, you are limited to the choices in the small dialog.

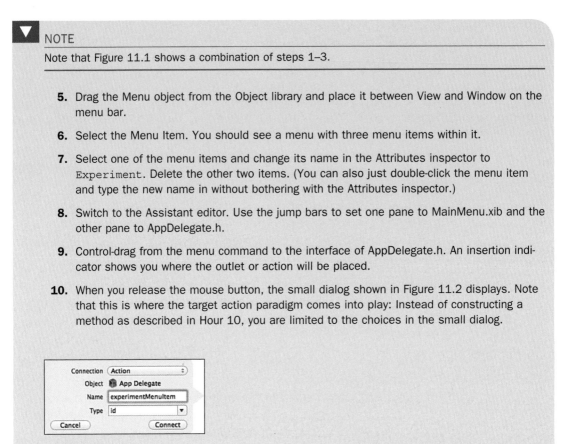

FIGURE 11.2
Name the action.

Select Action (the other choice is Outlet to create a property) and name the action you are creating (`experimentMenuItem` is a good choice). By default, the `AppDelegate` placeholder in Interface Builder is filled in, and the return type of the action (`id`) is filled in.

11. Click Connect.

12. The declaration of the action is created for you, as shown in Figure 11.3.

TIP

One of the reasons Xcode can do this is that the header of an action is specified in the target action paradigm. On OS X, it returns `void`, and it takes one argument, `sender`, which is type `id`.

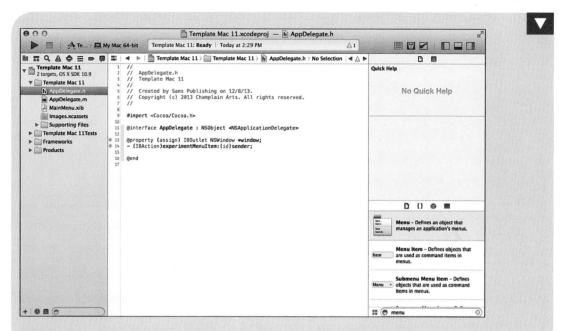

FIGURE 11.3
Xcode creates the action declaration.

NOTE

`IBAction` is handled by the compiler and converted to `void`. While you are using Interface Builder, Xcode uses `IBAction` to indicate action methods, but once the compiler takes over, it is changed to `void`.

The structure is slightly different for iOS, as you will see in the next "Try It Yourself" activity.

13. Show AppDelegate.m either in the Standard or Assistant editor. A shell for the action definition has been created (see Figure 11.4).

14. Set a breakpoint on the action implementation and run the app. Select the Experiment command from the Test menu, and you drop into the debugger, as shown in Figure 11.5. You may want to use the Standard editor and show the debug area to make the window easier to view.

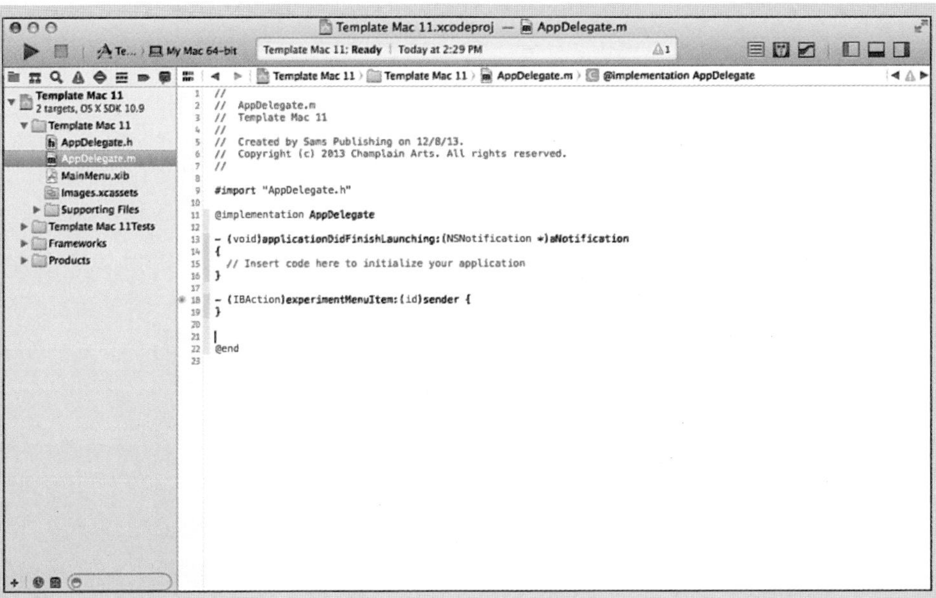

FIGURE 11.4
The definition of the action is started for you.

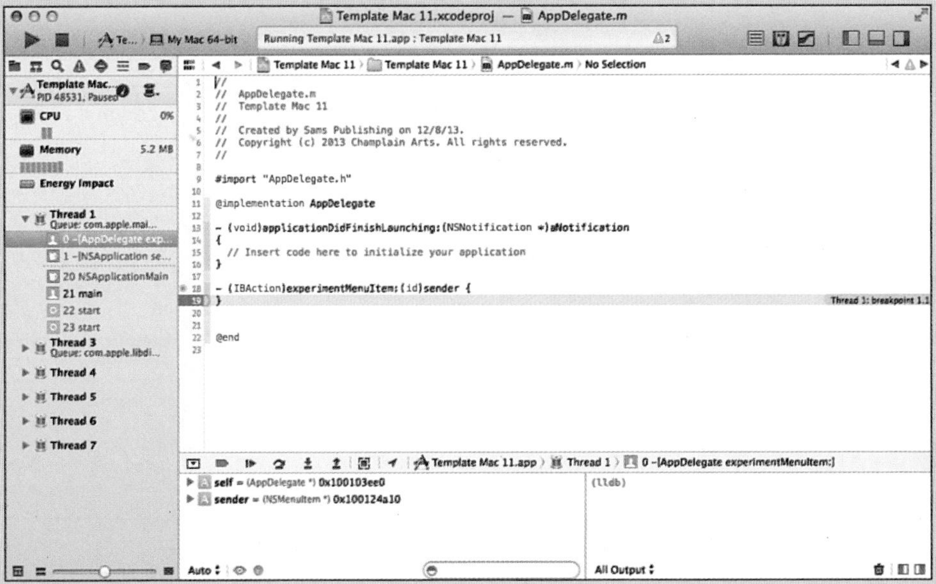

FIGURE 11.5
Run the app.

You have not actually written any code at this point. You have used a totally graphical interface to build your app and its interface. The only code you need to write is the app-specific implementation of the experiment command.

TRY IT YOURSELF ▼

Build an iOS App with an Action

Actions can make it easy to implement a menu command on OS X. The same structure lets you connect interface elements such as buttons to actions on iOS. Here are the steps for the iOS action connection process:

1. Create a new Xcode project from the iOS Single View Application template, as shown in Figure 11.6.

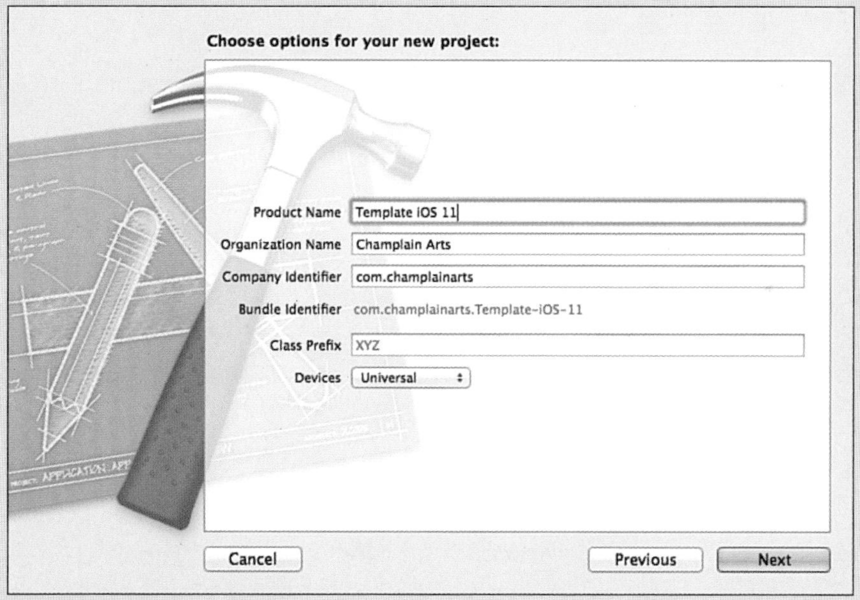

Choose options for your new project:

Product Name | Template iOS 11
Organization Name | Champlain Arts
Company Identifier | com.champlainarts
Bundle Identifier | com.champlainarts.Template-iOS-11
Class Prefix | XYZ
Devices | Universal

Cancel   Previous   Next

FIGURE 11.6
Create a new iOS project.

2. If you want to match the figures in this hour, select Universal or iPhone for Devices as shown in Figure 11.6.

3. When prompted, save the project.

   4. Select MainStoryboard_iPhone.storyboard from the project navigator.

   5. Drag a Button from the Object library into the canvas, as shown in Figure 11.7.

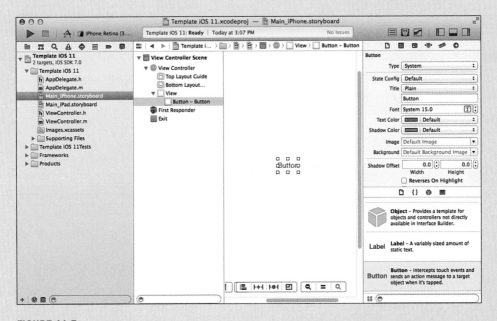

FIGURE 11.7
Add a button.

   6. Using the Assistant editor, show ViewController.h in the other pane.

   7. Control-drag from the button to the interface of ViewController.m (see Figure 11.8), and then release the mouse button.

   8. In the small dialog box, make certain the connection is set to Action and name it `experimentButton`, as shown in Figure 11.9.

   9. Scroll down to the bottom of ViewController.m to see that the definition of the action has been created for you. Set a breakpoint on it (see Figure 11.10).

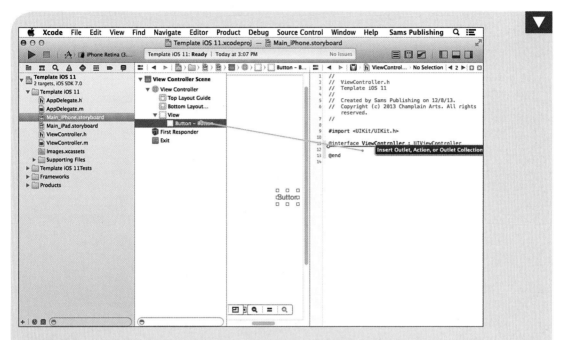

FIGURE 11.8
Start to add the action.

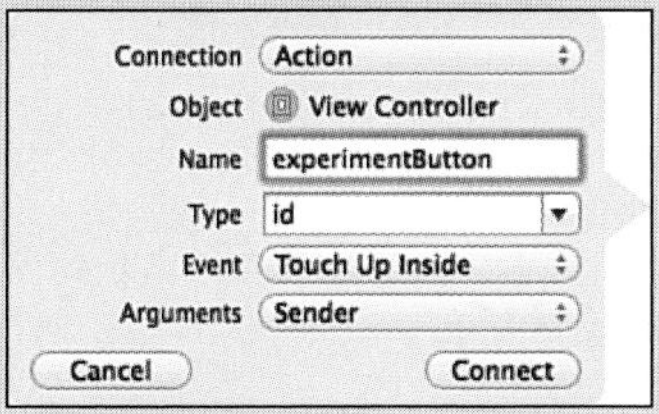

FIGURE 11.9
Create the action declaration.

10. Run the app. When it opens in the simulator, tap the button (you use the mouse in the simulator to click it). The debugger should show you that you have called the action method, as shown in Figure 11.11.

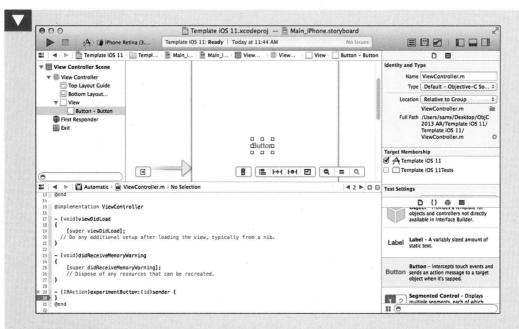

FIGURE 11.10
The action definition shell has been created.

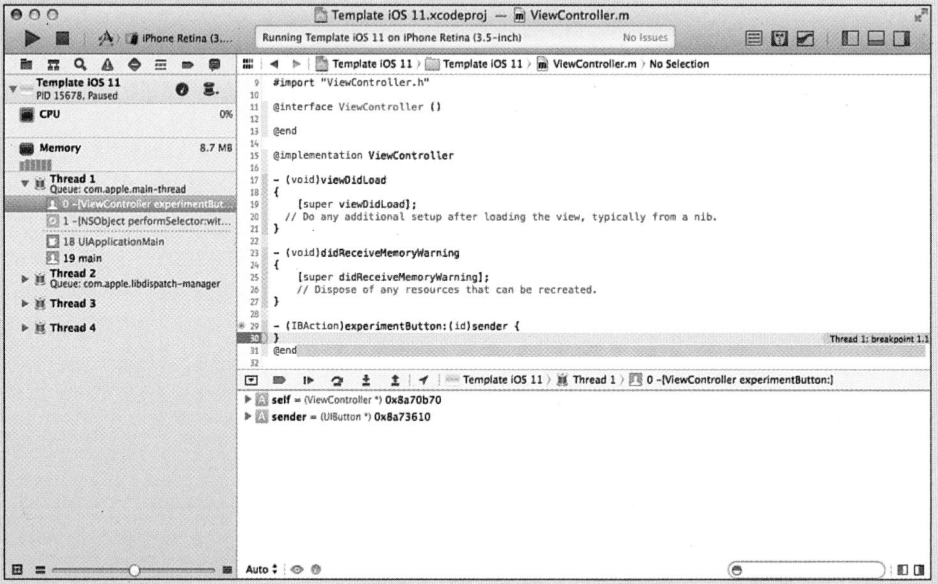

FIGURE 11.11
The debugger shows that the new action method has been called.

Once again, without writing code, you have wired up an interface element to an action. In this case, it is a button rather than a menu command, but the process is the same.

Comparing Actions in OS X and iOS

As you have seen, actions are a specific type of method that are used primarily to implement the consequence of a user's interaction with the user interface—often choosing a menu command or clicking a button or other interface control. Although you are free to name your action what you want, the format of its header is precise, which is one of the reasons it is easy to build the graphical user interface of Interface Builder.

GO TO ▶ Hour 12, "Routing Messages with Selectors," p. 165, to learn more about how actions are dispatched.

The header for an action looks like this in both OS X and iOS:

```
- (IBAction)experimentButton:(id)sender;
```

As you see in the debugger at the bottom of Figure 11.11, although `sender` is typed as `id` (a generic object), when it is passed into the action, the actual type of the object is available (a `UIButton` in this case). This is the standard behavior.

TIP

An `id` can be of any type, but at runtime its actual type is available to you.

As noted previously, `IBAction` is used by Interface Builder to help you build the interface. It signifies an action that can be connected to a control. The compiler defines `IBAction` as `void`, so by compile time this looks like a standard method.

In iOS, there are two variants on action signatures in addition to the one shown previously. You need not pass in a sender, but you can also pass in both a sender and an event as in the following methods:

```
- (IBAction)experimentButton2:(id)sender forEvent:(UIEvent *)event;
- (IBAction)experimentButton3;
```

You choose the type of action you want to create from the small dialog box in which you also name the action. Figure 11.12 provides a close-up view of this dialog box if you follow the previous steps to create a second button and a new action called `experimentButton2`. In this example, both the sender and event are chosen.

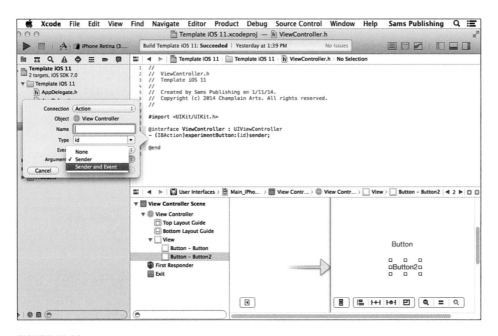

FIGURE 11.12
Add an event to an action signature.

The choices for the Arguments pop-up menu are as follows:

- None

- Sender

- Sender and Event

Set a breakpoint on the new action method and run the app. As you can see in the debugger at the bottom of Figure 11.13, this enables you to see both the object that was acted upon and what the action was. In the case of Figure 11.13, it is the `UIButton` that is the sender, and the event is `UITouchesEvent`. (Those lines in the debugger are highlighted.)

Make your choice, and Xcode does the rest.

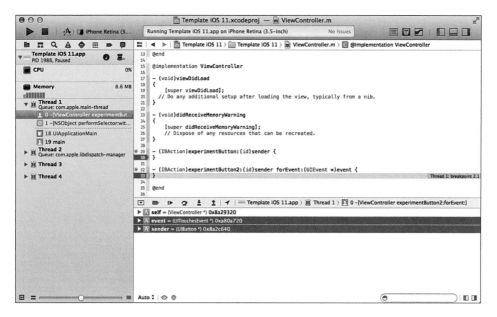

FIGURE 11.13
Review the debugger for the new action.

TIP

If you choose one of the signatures that includes `sender`, you can check `sender` to see which interface element has prompted the action. You can then provide variations within the action.

Disconnecting Actions

You have seen how to connect an interface element to an action that you create in Xcode. Here's how to do the reverse: disconnect an action.

Select the object that is currently connected (it might be a `UIButton`). Open the Connections inspector in the utility area, as shown in Figure 11.14.

You see the connection to your action in Figure 11.14. To its left, there is a small X. Click it to remove the connection. You can now create a new connection to a new or existing action.

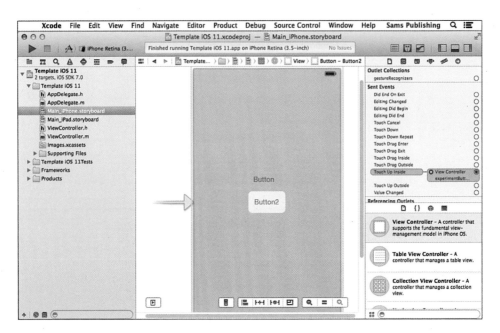

FIGURE 11.14
Remove a connection.

Summary

In this hour, you have seen how to create actions—the special type of methods that provide most of an app's functionality. You've also seen how to connect interface elements such as buttons to those actions.

For many developers, these features (actions, interface elements, and the connections between them) represent the major part of an app's design and development.

Q&A

Q. What makes actions different from methods?

A. Actions use a constrained version of general method syntax. This makes it easy for Xcode to implement automated tools to create actions. It also makes it easier to dispatch varied actions at runtime.

Q. What is one of the reasons why iOS actions can have both a sender and an event?

A. On OS X, user events for controls are primarily mouse clicks. With Cocoa Touch, a wider variety of taps and gestures can be used. The event argument lets you find out more about how an action was triggered.

Workshop

Quiz

1. How many actions should be connected to an interface element?

2. How do you choose a name for an action?

Quiz Answers

1. At least one action should be connected to an interface element if it is enabled. Remember to differentiate enabled from disabled interface elements so that users don't wander around clicking on everything on the screen.

2. Use the standard naming convention for methods that you have adopted for your project. Action names are not subject to additional constraints; it is the arguments that must adhere to specific names and types.

Activities

Use the examples in this hour to build an interface with menus (OS X) or controls such as buttons (iOS). This is a good way to start exploring the Cocoa frameworks with the debugger and, if you want to, with interface elements such as text fields. They all use the same basic pattern: Create an object such as a button or menu command and Control-drag to the interface file. This hour showed you how to create actions. Just choose Outlet instead of Action in the small dialog and you will have created a property that you can use to modify the behavior and appearance of the interface element.

HOUR 12
Routing Messages with Selectors

What You'll Learn in This Hour

▶ Understanding the target-action pattern

▶ Using SEL and `@selector`

▶ Invoking selectors with `NSInvocation`

▶ Managing messages with runtime tools

Getting Inside Objective-C Messages

By now, you should be familiar with Objective-C being described as being a dynamic messaging environment, and you have seen examples of messages in Hour 3, "Using Object-Oriented Features in Objective-C," and in Hour 6, "Exploring Messaging and a Testbed App." This hour looks inside the messages to see how they work. Because this is the heart of Objective-C and also because this is a significant way in which it differs from many other object-oriented programming languages, it is worthwhile to spend some time on the concepts.

In the simple examples shown in Hours 3 and 6, you saw messages that were used somewhat in the way in which functions are used in other languages, although, as noted, messaging is very different from calling functions. The similarity in the examples is that they are sent at a specific place in the code. In Objective-C, you send a message at a certain point in the program's execution, and in other languages at that point you call a function.

However, in Objective-C, you can turn a message into an object that can then be executed directly, but you can also send that object to an object such as an instance of an `NSTimer` that takes care of invoking it at appropriate times. By being able to in effect convert the message to a reusable object, you have a tremendous degree of flexibility. Furthermore, the object contains properties that you can set and reset as the need arises. You see how to do this in the course of this hour.

GO TO ▶ A related use of messages is found in Hour 22, "Grand Central Dispatch: Using Queues and Threading," page 283.

Objective-C's Predecessor: Smalltalk

Smalltalk grew out of a research project led by Alan Kay at Xerox PARC in the 1970s. It was first widely released in 1980, hence the name of the most common variant, Smalltalk-80. It is built on objects and messaging.

Objective-C represents the combination of the Smalltalk style of object-oriented programming with the strategy of making the fewest modifications to C in order to implement an object-oriented language. In fact, Brad J. Cox, who worked with Tom Love to develop Objective-C, wrote in his book, *Object-Oriented Programming: An Evolutionary Approach*, that "Objective-C is a hybrid programming language...formed by grafting the Smalltalk-80 style of object-oriented programming onto a C language rootstock."

That combination was historically important because for many people, Smalltalk had a reputation as being a great concept and teaching tool but not a tool that many people wanted to use for development.

On the other hand, many people found C++ to be too much of an extension to C to the point that it became not so much an extension but a new language. There were (and in some circles still are) fierce arguments over the relative merits of Smalltalk, C++, and Objective-C.

This book deals with the use of Objective-C, so those discussions are beyond its scope. However, it is important to note that messaging is at the heart of Objective-C and that it was implemented in previous languages, most notably Smalltalk. There are a number of books, articles, and web resources about Smalltalk that can help you understand some of the features and design decisions in Objective-C, but remember that this is background and history. Smalltalk syntax is not Objective-C syntax, although there are many similarities.

In Hour 3, you saw simple examples of messages such as the following:

```
myVariable = [myObject init];
```

The high-level description of messaging in Hour 3 identifies the right side of the expression as the message; the result of the message is used in the expression to set the value of `myVariable`.

Receiver and Selector Objects in Messages

Now it is time to look inside the message and to name the two words shown in this example:

▶ *Receiver* is the object to which the message is sent (`myObject`, in this case).

▶ *Selector* is the command sent to the receiver (`init`, in this case).

At runtime, the selector is used to identify the specific method of the object that is to be performed. This distinction between the selector and the method of the receiver that it selects at runtime helps to provide much of the flexibility and dynamism of Objective-C. It is made possible by the Objective-C runtime, which is the topic of the following section.

Getting Inside the Objective-C Runtime

The flexibility described in the previous section is at the heart of many debates, but, as is so often the case, advances in processor speed and memory availability have made many of those arguments much less relevant today. The issue is that when a function call is coded in a statically typed language, the compiler can check to make certain that the object that is asked to perform the function actually has such a function available. With the dynamic messaging environment, the message (specifically the selector) is sent to a receiver, and it is quite possible that the receiver will not be able to perform the method.

In many cases (particularly if the receiver is declared to be of type id, meaning any object), there is no way to perform this check at compile time. At its simplest, the argument has been whether this error checking should be done once at compile time or every time a message is sent at runtime. With the advances on the hardware side and several decades of experience optimizing the dispatching of methods in response to selectors, the flexibility of the messaging model in Objective-C has won out at least in the OS X and iOS environments.

NOTE

The Runtime

The shared library that implements the runtime component of Objective-C programs is commonly referred to simply as the *runtime*.

Here, for example, is the function call that is generated by the compiler on OS X when it encounters a message call in your code:

```
id objc_msg (id theReceiver, SEL theSelector, ...)
```

You can see that it is dynamic: theReceiver is a generic id type, as is the result of the function. theSelector and the SEL type are described in the following section.

Although you rarely use the shared library directly (the most common reason is if you are programming cross-language projects), it is there when your app is running and, at runtime, becomes a part of your app. This does not mean that you can deal with all of your app's bugs by blaming them on the runtime code. In fact, if it is involved with bugs at all, it is most likely an innocent bystander.

Rather, you need to remember that if you are coming from compiler-centric languages, you are gaining a tremendous degree of flexibility with Objective-C and its runtime, but you are also losing a safety net that compilers with strict type checking and compile time can provide.

There are two consequences of this that you should remember:

▶ More than ever before, it is important to catch and correct errors at the earliest possible opportunity. Xcode helps you with its tools to catch syntax errors based on the underlying Objective-C syntax as well as catching some errors that would only be caught at compile time in other environments. Many people are used to writing code and then debugging it in a second step, but today it is common practice to merge those processes into one step. (This is true for other modern programming languages as well as Objective-C.)

▶ You are not at the mercy of what happens at runtime. There are methods you can call to test if a message you are about to send will generate an error or not. They are described later in this hour.

Working with `SEL` and `@selector ()`

Just as there have been concerns about memory management in object-oriented programs, there have also been concerns about performance. As noted, one of the key areas in which performance can be compromised is in the selection and dispatching of methods. Developers of the Objective-C language and its compilers have focused on this area. Method names for a program are stored in a table where they can be looked up as needed. Each is associated with a unique identifier, and it is that unique identifier that is used for dispatching. This avoids handling long strings of characters to identify methods that are (properly) labeled descriptively.

You can gain access to these identifiers indirectly and can not only optimize your code, but also add some additional dynamism to it. To accomplish this, a special type, `SEL`, has been created. You use it to type identifiers just as you would type an identifier as an `int` or `float`.

But what value can you assign to a `SEL`? The answer is simple: You assign to a `SEL` identifier the selector you would use in a message. There are two variations on the way that you do this; they differ in the way they handle arguments to the selector. Both of these mechanisms are described in the sections that follow.

Furthermore, you can use both mechanisms in `NSTimer` methods where you set up a timer to run repeatedly.

TIP

Compiled Versus Computed Selectors

When you write a message such as the following

```
myVariable = [myObject init];
```

you specify the receiver and the selector. As is the case with the other code that you write, the compiler generates the code that runs. The selector is referred to as a *compiled selector*.

By contrast, you can use a selector that is evaluated at runtime from a string that can be generated on the fly. This is referred to as a *computed selector*.

Using `performSelector`

For zero, one, or two arguments, you create a `SEL` that you can subsequently pass into one of the `performSelector` methods. The `performSelector` methods are further limited in that their one or two arguments must be of type `id`. Even with these limitations, they handle many (perhaps most) of the selectors you use in common processing.

Creating a Selector with `@selector ()`

There are several ways of creating a compiled selector. The simplest way is to use the `@selector` compiler directive. If that is the route you take, you just type in the code you would have used in a message. Thus, for a message such as

```
myVariable = [myObject myAction];
```

you can generate a compiled selector with

```
SEL mySelector;
mySelector = @selector(myAction);
```

If you have arguments for the method that you are calling, you supply their keywords but not their values, as follows:

```
mySelector = @selector(myAction: forPurpose:);
```

If there are two arguments, you supply both of them, as follows:

```
mySelector = @selector(myAction: forPurpose: withCondition:);
```

Creating a Selector from a String

Instead of hard-coding the selector in your code, you might want to set it from a variable string at runtime. (These are computed selectors.) There is a utility function for that. The first example in the previous section can be rewritten as the following:

```
NSString * myString;
SEL mySelector;

// set myString from user input, options, a data store, etc.

mySelector = NSSelectorFromString (myString);
```

If you are storing a selector's string for reuse at a later time, you can convert a selector to a string:

```
myString = NSStringFromSelector (myAction: forPurpose:);
```

Using a Selector

After you have a selector, you can perform it with any of these three methods (they are declared in the NSObject protocol so they are available to any Cocoa classes):

```
- (id)performSelector:(SEL)aSelector;

- (id)performSelector:(SEL)aSelector withObject:(id)anObject;

- (id)performSelector:(SEL)aSelector withObject:(id)anObject
  withObject:(id)anotherObject;
```

If you use the second or third version, the selector must take parameters of type id. If you want to use more parameters or if you want to use a selector that does not take id parameters, you use NSInvocation, as described in the following section.

performSelector is used for the selector in a message, as follows:

```
[receiver performSelector:mySelector];
```

If you are using parameters (the second or third version), you pass the id in the objects and the message is put together with the keywords and parameters.

TIP

Just remember the colon before each parameter in the @selector directive. Leaving it out is a very common mistake.

These methods are declared in the NSObject protocol. Related methods are declared directly in NSObject, the root class of Cocoa.

NOTE

The NSObject performSelector methods are listed here so that you can get a sense of the opportunities you have in the Cocoa framework, which itself is beyond the scope of this book.

```
- performSelector:withObject:afterDelay:
- performSelector:withObject:afterDelay:inModes:
- performSelectorOnMainThread:withObject:waitUntilDone:
- performSelectorOnMainThread:withObject:waitUntilDone:modes:
- performSelector:onThread:withObject:waitUntilDone:
- performSelector:onThread:withObject:waitUntilDone:modes:
```

```
- performSelectorInBackground:withObject:
+ cancelPreviousPerformRequestsWithTarget:
+ cancelPreviousPerformRequestsWithTarget:selector:object:
```

In addition, you can use the NSTimer subclass of NSObject to perform selectors.

Using a Selector with Interface Builder

Although this book focuses on the Objective-C language itself, a brief excursion into the application frameworks is relevant here. Selectors lie at the heart of the process by which interface elements, such as menu commands and buttons, perform their actions using the Interface Builder editor in Xcode; you can connect an interface element to an action that is declared as a method in an object.

The object that declares the method, and therefore is responsible for performing the action, can be a specific object such as a document. However, Xcode and the runtime both keep track of whatever object happens to be the first in line to process events such as mouse clicks. This object is the first responder and it constantly changes as the user interacts with the program.

The Interface Builder editor keeps track of all actions of all objects that potentially could become the first responder. You can control-drag from an interface element to the list of these potential first-responder actions. If you Control-Click or Right-Click (depending on your trackpad or mouse settings) on First Responder in the document outline, as shown in Figure 12.1, you see the first responders. You can connect one of them to an interface element such as a button or (on OS X) a menu command.

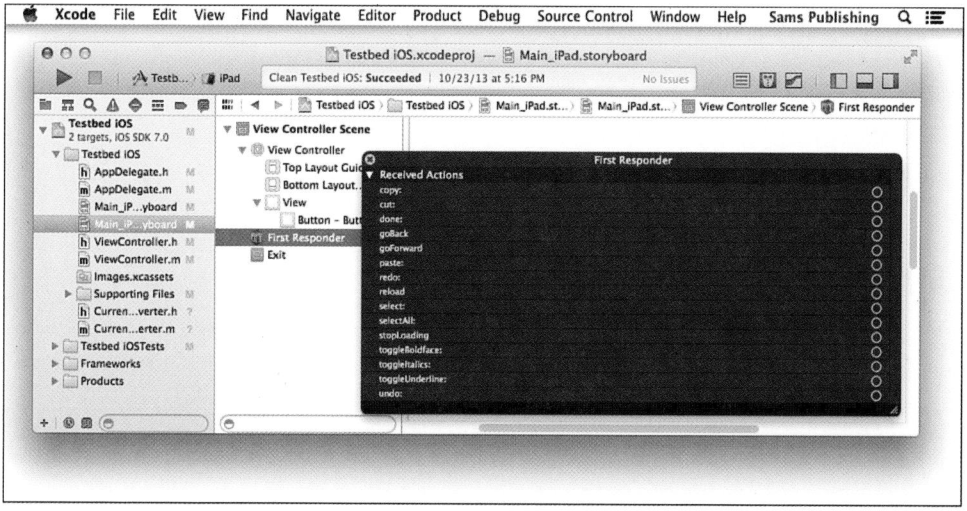

FIGURE 12.1
Connect an interface element to an action.

Using NSInvocation

For three or more arguments, you use an NSInvocation object. In addition to being able to handle more arguments, you are not limited to using arguments of type id as long as they are classes (in other words, no ints or chars). With performSelector, you specify the receiver and action as arguments to performSelector. NSInvocation is a more sophisticated mechanism in which you convert a message to an object. NSInvocation objects have properties that specify the target, selector, arguments, and return value. This flexibility lets you use NSInvocation objects with much more flexibility than when you use performSelector.

There are situations in which a common use of NSInvocation instances is to use and reuse the same selector a number of times in different contexts. You can, for example, set up a selector and vary its target (that is, the receiver of the message). You can also change arguments. However, the one thing you cannot change is the method signature of the selector. That is set when you create the object, and it cannot be varied.

Method Signatures

In Objective-C, a method signature consists of the method name along with parameter names and colons (if needed). Thus, you can have insertObject:atIndex:, which is a method that takes two parameters.

Although NSInvocation objects are more flexible than performSelector, in practice you might not need them very often because the simpler interface of performSelector handles many of the common cases. If you do want to use an NSInvocation object, it is summarized in this section. There are three sets of methods that enable you to do the following:

▶ Create an NSInvocation instance.

▶ Set and get its properties.

▶ Invoke the instance (that is, perform the selector).

Creating an NSInvocation

Although you can change every property of an NSInvocation instance, you cannot change the message signature of the instance you have created. You create it using the class method shown here:

```
+ (NSInvocation *)invocationWithMethodSignature:(NSMethodSignature *)signature
```

Create a Message Signature

As with all class methods, you invoke it from the class itself and not an instance. Here are the steps:

1. Create the message signature. Use the NSObject method instanceMethodSignature-ForSelector for the class and method you want. If you want a message signature for myMethod in MyClass, use this code:

```
NSMethodSignature * mySignature =
    [MyClass instanceMethodSignatureForSelector:@selector(myMethod:)];
```

2. Create the NSInvocation instance, as follows:

```
NSInvocation * myInvocation =
    [NSInvocation invocationWithMethodSignature:mySignature];
```

Using NSInvocation **Properties**

After you have your NSInvocation instance, you set its properties. You can use a newly created instance, or you can reuse an existing one if it is created for the right message signature. This is most commonly done if you want to reinvoke the invocation with a minor modification of its target or arguments or at a different time. The following sections cover the setters you use.

GO TO ▶ Hour 16, "Managing Memory and Runtime Objects," p. 221, for more information on memory aspects of NSInvocation.

Setting the Target

You use setTarget to set the target. Here is the declaration:

```
- (void)setTarget:(id)anObject
```

Following on from the NSInvocation created in the Try It Yourself activity, if you have an instance of MyClass called myInstance, you can write:

```
[myInvocation setTarget:myInstance];
```

The corresponding getter is:

```
- (id)target
```

Setting the Selector

You can set the selector as long as it is compatible with the message signature you used in creating the NSInvocation instance. You use setSelector; here is the declaration:

```
- (void)setSelector:(SEL)selector
```

You frequently see the same selector used here as was used in creating the message signature. That certainly ensures compatibility because they are identical, but as long as they are compatible, you are fine:

```
[myInvocation setSelector:@selector(myMethod:)];
```

The corresponding getter is:

```
- (SEL)selector
```

Setting the Arguments

The arguments for the NSInvocation instance are in a buffer. The zeroth element is the target, and the first is the selector. You use the accessors just described to access those, so you start working with element 2 of the array. Here is the declaration to set an argument:

```
- (void)setArgument:(void *)buffer atIndex:(NSInteger)index
```

When you are setting an argument to an object, remember to pass in a pointer to it, as shown in the following line of code:

```
[myInvocation setArgument:&myObjectForArgument atIndex:2];
```

The corresponding getter is:

```
- (void)getArgument:(void *)buffer atIndex:(NSInteger)index
```

Remember that you pass in a pointer so that to retrieve the same argument set in the previous code, you write:

```
[myInvocation getArgument:&anArray atIndex:2];
```

Getting the Result

When you send a message in your code, you receive the result back and can assign it to a variable, or you can use it in an expression. When you are invoking a message at some time in the future, you have to retrieve the result from the invocation. Here is the getter:

```
- (void)getReturnValue:(void *)buffer
```

You have two ways of using this getter: one for objects and another one for C variables other than pointers and objects.

In the case of an object, you declare it in the code where you want to access the result just as you normally would. You then get it from the NSInvocation and pass in a pointer to your variable as in this code:

```
[myInvocation getReturnValue:&myLocallyDeclaredVariable];
```

If the result is not an object, you allocate a buffer of the right size and pass that in. You can get the size of the returned value by asking the method signature. And, because you used the method signature in creating your NSInvocation instance, you can ask that instance for the signature. Here is an example:

```
NSUInteger length = [[myInvocation methodSignature] methodReturnLength];
buffer = (void *)malloc(length);
[myInvocation getReturnValue:buffer];
```

Invoking an NSInvocation

After you have your instance of NSInvocation and have set its target, selector, and arguments, you can invoke it with the following:

```
- (void)invoke
```

You simply write:

```
[myInvocation invoke];
```

You can short-circuit the process by using the following:

```
- (void)invokeWithTarget:(id)anObject
```

This means you can write:

```
[myInvocation invokeWithTarget: myInstance];
```

In this case, you need to set the selector and the arguments, but you do not need to set the target separately.

In addition to these methods, you can use the NSTimer subclass of NSObject to invoke NSInvocation instances.

Testing Whether an Instance Can Respond to a Selector

As noted previously, the messaging structure in Objective-C is implemented in large part in the runtime. This provides a great deal of flexibility, but it also means that you can generate errors at runtime that, in other languages, would have been caught at compile time. This is not merely a matter of the error appearing at a different time. It means in most cases that the error is seen by the end user rather than by the developer.

To avoid such circumstances, you can check to see if a class can respond to a selector. Here is the declaration:

```
- (BOOL) respondsToSelector: (SEL) aSelector
```

You can write:

```
BOOL myBool = [self.myCurrencyConverter respondsToSelector:@selector (calculate);
```

or

```
BOOL myBool = [self.myCurrencyConverter respondsToSelector: mySelector];
```

This is declared in the NSObject protocol, so it is available for all instances of all classes.

A companion class method lets you test a class:

```
+ (BOOL) instancesRespondToSelector: (SEL) aSelector
```

Summary

Messages are at the core of Objective-C and represent one of the biggest differences between it and some other object-oriented programming languages. In this hour, you have examined how messages are constructed as well as how you can construct them yourself in code. You have also seen how you can perform and invoke them not only when you need to, but also as prepackaged messages that can be sent as the need arises.

Q&A

Q. How do you choose between using `performSelector` and using `NSInvocation`?

A. `performSelector` works for messages with zero, one, or two arguments. Also, they must be of type `id` and must be objects.

Q. What is the runtime?

A. It is the data structures and functions that implement the runtime dynamic features of Objective-C. It is not optional, but it's there for you and you rarely need to worry about it. It is written mostly in C and Assembler. It provides the underpinnings of Objective-C but is written in previous languages.

Workshop

Quiz

1. How do you make certain that a message you are sending is valid?

2. `NSInvocation` converts an Objective-C message to what?

Quiz Answers

1. Package it in a selector and test it against the receiver with `respondsToSelector`.

2. `NSInvocation` converts an Objective-C message to an object.

Activities

Explore the sample code on developer.apple.com to see how you can use selectors. Good choices are the following:

▶ Use any of the Xcode storyboard templates on iOS and search for the code that implements bar button items. (Often it is in `viewDidLoad`.) You'll see how selectors are attached to these buttons.

▶ Look at the `MenuMadness` sample code to see how selectors are attached to menu commands on OS X.

Building on the Foundation

What You'll Learn in This Hour

▶ Exploring the frameworks that extend Objective-C

▶ Understanding Foundation policies and paradigms

▶ Working with mutable classes

▶ Using class clusters

▶ Handling notifications

Exploring the Foundation Framework

This book is about the Objective-C language; the Cocoa and Cocoa Touch frameworks are out-side the scope of the book. However, the Foundation framework is relevant. The earliest guide to Objective-C, *Object Oriented Programming: An Evolutionary Approach* by Brad J. Cox (who code-veloped the language with Tom Love) was published in 1986. It describes Objective-C before the NeXT extensions and before the later extensions at Apple that culminated in OS X and iOS. The objects and methods listed in this book for the most part are still part of the language today. They were organized into *collections* in 1986; today they are organized into *frameworks*, a some-what different structure, but still an organizing tool for objects.

These classes and methods are part of the language itself: Today, they are part of the Foundation framework (sometimes referred to simply as Foundation). They include the root class, NSObject. The performSelector method discussed at length in Hour 12, "Routing Messages with Selectors," for example, is a method of NSObject in the Cox book. Today, it has moved from NSObject itself to the NSObject protocol, but that is a relatively minor change.

The major Cocoa and Cocoa Touch frameworks are AppKit (OS X) and UIKit (iOS). These differ from the Foundation framework in that Foundation has nothing to do with the user interface. Thus, windows, views, and controls are not found anywhere in Foundation. There are a number of other Cocoa frameworks such as Core Data, Address Book, WebKit (only public in OS X), iAd (iOS only), and Preference Panes (OS X only). These are also beyond the scope of this book.

The complete *Foundation Framework Reference* is available on developer.apple.com as well as in Xcode (it is 2,000 pages long). This hour and others that follow provide a high-level road map and introduction.

There is a companion to the Foundation framework: the Core Foundation framework. They have similar structures and functionality, but Foundation is written in Objective-C, whereas Core Foundation is written in C. This was done in part to support the Carbon development environment that was a critical part of the transition from the C and C++ world of the Macintosh operating system to the Objective-C world of OS X. (By way of comparison, the *Core Foundation Framework Reference* is a mere 800 pages long.)

Foundation Classes

Foundation contains the classes that you use and subclass in your apps. There are two root classes along with a variety of other classes that are divided into groups.

Root Classes

NSObject has been referred to as the root class for all other classes. In fact, it is one of two root classes—the other is NSProxy, which is used with distributed objects. As the name suggests, it stands in for an object that may be distant or even may not be created yet. NSProxy is a relatively recent addition to the world of Objective-C, and its addition caused a restructuring that has been alluded to previously.

The NSObject protocol contains methods that formerly were part of the NSObject class itself. By pulling a number of them out into the NSObject protocol, all the root objects (that is, both of them) can share the functionality of the protocol.

Turning Part of a Class into a Protocol

This restructuring is something you might want to do in similar circumstances. If you were starting from scratch, you might design an abstract object (perhaps RootClass) and subclass it into NSProxy and NSObject. In your own development, you can easily come across a situation in which you want to insert a new abstract object so that two existing objects can subclass it and share its functionality. That can entail quite a bit of restructuring, so using the technique of taking the common methods out into a protocol adopted by your original object, and also by the new object, can be less work. It also means that if your original object adopts the new protocol, you can leave all of its code intact with perhaps a slight adjustment to the protocol declarations in the source code.

The NSObject root class and its proxy implement methods in the following areas. Note that this is not a complete list of the methods in each area; it is designed to give you a general idea of what is included.

▶ **Allocation, initialization, and duplication**—You have already seen some of the commonly used methods in this area, such as `alloc` and `init`.

▶ **Introspection and comparison**—You have seen `respondsToSelector:` and `instances-RespondToSelector:` as well as `description` in other hours. Additional methods in this area include `isEqual:` for testing two objects as well as the introspection methods `class` and `superclass`, which return the appropriate values as class objects (not strings).

▶ **Encoding and decoding**—The methods in this area are used in archiving and unarchiving objects—converting them from objects in memory to byte streams that can be transmitted or written to files (and vice versa).

▶ **Message forwarding**—This allows an object to forward a message it has received to another object.

▶ **Message dispatch**—This includes the `performSelector` methods described in Hour 12.

▶ **Object retention and disposal**—Methods such as `retain`, `release`, `autorelease`, `retainCount`, and `dealloc` let you manage memory for your objects.

GO TO ▶ Hour 16, "Managing Memory and Runtime Objects," p. 221, for more on this topic as well as a discussion of Automatic Reference Counting (ARC), which eliminates the need for much manual memory management in object retention and disposal.

Other Classes

Beyond the root classes and their shared protocol, the other Foundation classes are divided into a number of groups. They provide object-oriented support for common programming tasks. The groups are the following:

▶ **Value objects**—These include numbers, dates, and general data types.

▶ **XML support**—These methods help you parse XML documents.

▶ **Strings**—These methods include string classes themselves as well as support classes such as `NSFormatter`.

▶ **Collections**—These include arrays, dictionaries, and sets.

GO TO ▶ Hour 15, "Organizing Data with Collections," p. 205, for more on collections.

▶ **Predicates**—These methods help you construct predicates for use in selecting data.

▶ **Operating system services**—Here, you find everything from spell checking to timers and `NSError`.

▶ **File system**—These routines manage files, metadata, and streams.

▶ **URL**—These are the methods to connect to and download files by URL. They also include methods to handle cookies.

▶ **Interprocess communication**—IPC has been a built-in component of Objective-C and Cocoa for many years. These methods implement pipes and ports among others.

▶ **Locking/threading**—These methods let you manage multiple threads in your apps.

▶ **Notifications**—The notification methods let you use the Objective-C messaging structure to keep track of events as they occur.

▶ **Objective-C language services**—These include methods such as NSMethodSignature, which was discussed in Hour 12 in the context of invocations.

▶ **Scripting**—These are the methods to handle Apple events and script commands. They are implemented only on OS X.

▶ **Distributed objects**—These methods are also only implemented on OS X. They are supported by NSProxy, which is what led to the restructuring of NSObject.

Foundation Paradigms and Policies

The common underpinnings of Foundation include implementation of policies and paradigms that are implemented across the other frameworks and in the code that you write. There are four sections of these paradigms and policies:

▶ Mutability

▶ Class clusters

▶ Notifications

▶ Garbage collection

GO TO ▶ Hour 16, "Managing Memory and Runtime Objects," p. 221, for a discussion of garbage collection.

Mutability

Many Foundation classes, such as NSArray, NSSet, NSString, and NSData, have mutable and immutable variants. Typically, the mutable variant is a subclass of the immutable one; the mutable subclass is identified by its name. For example, NSMutableArray is the mutable variant of NSArray. As you can imagine, this can make it possible for the compiler and runtime to optimize performance for the immutable variants.

If your changes to a mutable class are isolated to one or two methods (and that is often a good design), that can enable you to take advantage of the efficiencies of working with immutable variants. You can work with an immutable array or other class and, when you need to modify it, use `mutableCopy` to make a mutable copy, modify it, and then use `copy` to turn it back into an immutable object. (That is the default behavior for `copy`.) You can then continue with the immutable copy.

TIP

Whether this type of switching between mutable and immutable variants is worthwhile or not depends on how much modifying you need to carry out compared with how much time it takes to copy the object in question.

Class Clusters

Foundation makes use of class clusters that group hidden subclasses behind an abstract superclass with which you interact. The most commonly cited example of a class cluster is `NSNumber`. There are hidden subclasses of the abstract `NSNumber` class that are used for `ints`, `longlongs`, `chars`, and so forth. The `init` methods of the abstract superclass dispatch the appropriate factory methods to create the appropriate hidden subclass as in the following code:

```
NSNumber *myInteger = [NSNumber numberWithInt: 1234];
```

Inside the abstract superclass `NSNumber`, `numberWithInt` creates a specific and hidden subclass that is an `int`. You only see an `NSNumber`, but it hides the various subclasses from you.

TIP

You can use this design pattern in your own code. It is an excellent way of implementing a variety of subclasses without revealing that they are separate subclasses.

TRY IT YOURSELF ▼

Explore a Class Cluster

In this activity, you can peek inside a class cluster at a hidden subclass. It also shows you some useful debugging techniques.

1. Create a new project. It can be an OS X Cocoa Application or one of the iOS templates such as the iOS Empty Application. You probably do not want to add this test to a Git repository.

2. Add a new `myID` property to the interface of AppDelegate.h:

   ```
   @property (retain) id myID;
   ```

▼

3. At the end of `applicationDidFinishLaunching` in AppDelegate.m, create a new `NSNumber` and set `myID` to it. Use `numberWithInt` to create a private subclass of `NSNumber`:

   ```
   self.myID = [NSNumber numberWithInt: 17];
   ```

4. Use `NSLog` to write out the string value of `myID`. `stringValue` is a method of `NSNumber`.

   ```
   NSLog(@"%@", [(NSNumber*)self.myID stringValue]);
   ```

5. You should see the result shown here. The value should be the value you set in step 4.

   ```
   2013-11-27 11:19:39.986 iSA Demo[4685:707] 17
   ```

6. Use the `NSObject` method class to obtain the class of `myID`. Then use the `NSObject` method description to obtain the description of the class, and write it out to the log:

   ```
   NSLog(@"%@", [[self.myID class] description]);
   ```

7. You should see the result shown here:

   ```
   2013-11-27 11:19:39.985 iSA Demo[4685:707] __NSCFNumber
   ```

The description of the class is its name. In this case, it is the private __NSCFNumber subclass of `NSNumber`.

Notifications

Notifications provide a broadcast type of communication. Observers register to watch a certain event, and objects within your app post notifications. This is handled by a notification center that is part of each process.

Notifications are a very efficient low-level form of communicating information throughout your app. In many cases, they are an alternative to polling inside a loop to test whether or not something has happened. You just register to receive notifications about the event in which you are interested, and, assuming that you properly broadcast a notification when the event occurs, you find out that the event has occurred. There is no need for a polling loop to repeatedly check on what has or has not happened.

Notifications are subclasses of `NSNotification`. There are three basic values, and you can add others if you need them. However, the basic `NSNotification` structure is simple and very efficient.

Every notification has these three values:

▶ **name**—This should be a unique name within the notifications for your app. Observers need to know it so that they can register for the type of notifications in which they are interested. This is an NSString.

▶ **object**—Typically, this is the object that posts the notification, but it need not be. It can even be nil. This is an id.

▶ **userInfo**—This is a dictionary containing data relevant to the notification. It is up to you to define it and to let your observers know what is in it. This is an NSDictionary.

It is important to note that the notification center for a process is the clearinghouse for notifications. Your process does not need to track observers. You just post notifications as necessary, and observers will receive them. You get the notification center for your process with the following snippet of code:

```
[NSNotificationCenter defaultCenter];
```

This snippet typically is used as part of a line of code that carries out a notification task, as you see in the following sections.

Posting a Notification

To create a new notification, you can use any of the two NSNotification class methods:

```
+ (instancetype)notificationWithName:(NSString *)aName object:(id)anObject
+ (instancetype)notificationWithName:(NSString *)aName object:(id)anObject
    userInfo:(NSDictionary *)userInfo
```

Your choice between them depends on whether you want simply to pass on a notification that something has happened (the first version) or a notification along with some relevant data (the second version) with the userInfo dictionary.

More commonly, you use NSNotificationCenter methods to create and post notifications in one step. Here are the three variations:

```
- (void)postNotification:(NSNotification *)notification
- (void)postNotificationName:(NSString *)notificationName
    object:(id)notificationSender
- (void)postNotificationName:(NSString *)notificationName
    object:(id)notificationSender userInfo:(NSDictionary *)userInfo
```

You need the notification center to use these methods, so a typical use of the first one might be:

```
[[NSNotificationCenter defaultCenter]
  postNotificationName:(NSString *)notificationName];
```

Registering to Receive Notifications

You register to receive specific notifications (that is, to become an observer of the notification) with one of these `NSNotificationCenter` methods.

This is the simplest way to add an observer. You specify the object to be notified, as well as the selector that is sent to that object. You further specify the name of the notification and, optionally, the sender of the notification. Either or both of `notificationName` and `notification-Sender` can be nil; in those cases, notifications are delivered regardless of name and/or sender.

```
- (void)addObserver:(id)notificationObserver selector:(SEL)notificationSelector
    name:(NSString *)notificationName object:(id)notificationSender
```

A typical example of registering to receive a notification would be:

```
[[NSNotificationCenter defaultCenter]
  addObserver: myObserver selector: (SEL)mynotificationAction
  name: nil notificationSender: nil];
```

GO TO ▶ Hour 20, "Working with Blocks," p. 259, for more information on blocks.

Instead of using a selector, you can specify a queue and a block to add to it. The block takes one argument, which is the notification.

```
- (id)addObserverForName:(NSString *)name object:(id)obj queue:(NSOperationQueue
 *)queue
    usingBlock:(void (^)(NSNotification *))block
```

Removing Observers

When you no longer want to receive notifications, just remove the appropriate observer with one of these `NSNotificationCenter` methods:

```
- (void)removeObserver:(id)notificationObserver
- (void)removeObserver:(id)notificationObserver name:
    (NSString *)notificationName object:(id)notificationSender
```

A typical use would be:

```
[[NSNotificationCenter defaultCenter]
  removeObserver: myObserver];
```

Summary

This hour has shown you the parts of the Objective-C language that are implemented in the Foundation framework. They include NSObject (both the class and the protocol) as well as key functionalities, such as shared paradigms and policies. You have also seen key components of Foundation such as class clusters and their hidden subclasses as well as notifications.

Q&A

Q. What do notifications accomplish?

A. They let you send messages to observers via a dispatch center. You post messages to the dispatch center, and it posts to the observers. You do not need a direct communication link to the observers.

Q. What is the purpose of class clusters?

A. These are related classes that frequently share a common abstract superclass. Developers use the methods of the abstract superclass, but in reality they are often manipulating the hidden internal subclasses. The abstract class's initWith methods frequently take care of creating the specific subclasses.

Workshop

Quiz

1. How many notification centers are there for each app?
2. What is the purpose of mutable and immutable classes?

Quiz Answers

1. There is one notification center for each app.
2. They can let you create optimized code for objects that will not be modified.

Activities

Explore the sample code for Core Recipes (OS X) and Core Data Books (iOS) to see notifications in action. Look at DocInteraction (iOS) to see how to receive process notifications when the files in a folder change.

HOUR 14
Defining a Class in an Implementation File

What You'll Learn in This Hour

▶ Cleaning up the Converter app

▶ Adding debugging code

▶ Refining the method

Working with a New Project

So far in this part of the book, you have explored many of the Objective-C basics—messaging and selectors; declarations of classes, instance variables, properties, methods, and actions; and building on Foundation. In this hour, you pull those concepts together as you define classes in their implementation files. After all, the definition of classes consists of the executable code rather than the declarations that set up the app's structure.

In the two hours that remain in this part of the book, you will see how to work with the collection classes and how to manage memory. For now, though, it is time to pull the threads together to get an app running. The app that you create does not focus on the user interface frameworks, but it shows you how to use the features of the Objective-C language in a prototype of a real-world app.

This hour is somewhat different from most of the other hours in this book. It does give you details of Objective-C syntax as well as tips for implementation. However, in addition, it walks you through a realistic process for building a class. That process starts with a simple idea for a class and steps through the iterations that occur as the idea evolves into a usable and reusable class.

NOTE

Currency Converter History

The basic idea for this app has been used to demonstrate Cocoa app development for many years. Each iteration by each author has emphasized different aspects of the code and the frameworks.

Reconsidering Dynamic Typing

In Hour 6, "Exploring Messaging and a Testbed App," you first explored the concept of a Testbed app that has been used to experiment with the Objective-C basics. Over the course of the hours between Hour 6 and this one, you have seen how various Objective-C features refine and extend the basic concepts. As an example, in "Reviewing the Message Syntax" at the end of Hour 6, you used dynamic typing in declaring

```
id myObject;
```

Dynamic typing provides a great deal of flexibility, which carries with it a trade-off with type checking at compile time (rather than at runtime). There have been many discussions about this trade-off, but today consensus has formed around the use of static typing, in part so that errors are caught by the compiler and presented to the developer rather than being caught by the runtime and presented to the end user.

NOTE

The Static Versus Dynamic Typing Discussion

This is still an ongoing conversation with regard to many programming languages as you can discover in this article: http://en.wikipedia.org/wiki/Type_system#Static_and_dynamic_type_checking_in_practice on Wikipedia.

The flexibility of dynamic typing makes it easier to use in some cases, and one of those cases is in simplified demonstration code such as that used in the previous chapters as the Objective-C concepts have been introduced. Before moving on, it is appropriate to clean up the code that you have been experimenting with in the Testbed app.

This new app has an app delegate created automatically as part of the template. You add a currency converter class to it. The currency converter is stored in an instance variable of the app delegate.

Designing the (Currency) Converter

Designing software is a linear process at each step of the way, but the lines are not continuous. For example, when you send a message to a method (or call a function in another programming language), control passes to the beginning of the method and continues sequentially through each subsequent line until the end of the method is reached or some other event (perhaps a `return` statement or even an error) interrupts it. After the method has completed, you move on to another set of linear steps. This means that you have to simultaneously jump back and forth to figure out how your app will work.

The heart of the app is the `CurrencyConverter` class, and the heart of that class is a method that converts currency. Putting together what you have learned in previous hours such as Hour 10, "Declaring Methods in an Interface File," you can jump ahead and start planning what this critical method looks like. (Not only can you do this, you should get in the habit of doing so.)

Implementing the Method

This critical method returns the computed value. It needs to work with the exchange rate and the number of units of currency to be converted. To make the most flexible method, you can pass the number of units and the exchange rate in as parameters. That structure enables you to call this method from a user interface in which the user enters the rate and the number of units. It also enables you to create an interface in which the user enters the number of units and the type of currency; an intermediate method can look up the current exchange rate and pass it along with the number of units into the method. In that way, your conversion method does double duty for an interactive interface as well as for one with an online database access for the exchange rate. The heart of the computation is the same in both cases.

Take another step and think about what the method looks like. It returns the computed value and accepts two parameters—the units of currency to convert and the exchange rate to use. In Objective-C, each parameter has a keyword, so you may start thinking about what they are. Because exchange rates are rarely integers, you may think that your return value is a float. This would give you a method header such as this:

```
- (float) convertCurrency: (float)units withRate: (float)exchangeRate;
```

NOTE

Floats, Decimals, and Currencies

Calculations on currencies other than simple addition and subtraction need to take into account the issues involved with rounding fractions particularly when multiplication and division are involved. As you will see, Objective-C can help you out further.

That is a good start, and it is one that many people would use. This means that the code inside the method practically writes itself:

```
return units * exchangeRate;
```

But remember that in Objective-C it is often preferable to use the Objective-C classes rather than raw C types. A better method header might be the following:

```
- (NSNumber *) convertCurrency: (NSNumber *)units
    withRate: (NSNumber *)exchangeRate;
```

The difference between the first version in which the arguments and return value are all float types and the second in which they are NSNumber objects is that that the latter is more generalized. NSNumber objects can be creavted from and returned as a multitude of different types. Here are the getters for NSNumber:

- ▶ boolValue
- ▶ charValue
- ▶ decimalValue
- ▶ doubleValue
- ▶ floatValue
- ▶ intValue
- ▶ integerValue
- ▶ longLongValue
- ▶ longValue
- ▶ shortValue
- ▶ unsignedCharValue
- ▶ unsignedIntegerValue
- ▶ unsignedIntValue
- ▶ unsignedLongLongValue
- ▶ unsignedLongValue
- ▶ unsignedShortValue

This allows any necessary conversions to happen internally to the NSNumber arguments. You can use and reuse the method. If some types of values are going to be problematic, you can manage them inside the conversion method where they are used.

That said, there is a certain overhead for using the objects as opposed to the scalar values. In many cases, you wind up using both because some of the framework methods you use as well as others that you write might have been written in one form or the other. The efficiency issue tends to be minimal in a large number of cases. Yes, it may take a dozen operations to access a value from an object rather than a single operation, but if you actually do careful analysis of the impact on the user experience and on the overall device performance, it may not matter.

NOTE

The sample code in this chapter uses `NSNumber` objects and converts them to floats as needed. This has the benefit of introducing you to how to function in a heterogeneous environment of objects and scalars.

While you are thinking of generalizing the method, consider the fact that the name is more specific than needed. As implemented at this point, the method works for currency conversion as well as conversions of units of measure. Why limit its usefulness only to currency conversion if it is not necessary? You can always come back later and change the generalized method to a more specific one. Going in the other direction can be a bit more work.

TIP

Balancing Generality and Specificity

You always have to strike a balance between writing generalizable code and code that is specific to the task at hand. What may be most productive is to keep a mental eye out for issues such as this one (the fact that this is a generalized conversion method and not just one for currencies). If making methods more generalized does not involve additional coding, it often is useful to take that route so that you have code that is more easily reused. If writing a generalized method entails extra effort or complexity that future developers have to understand, it might not be worth pursuing.

Recapping the New Method Terminology

If you walk through a design process such as this, you can see that generalizing the method does not require extra work and might make it easier to reuse in the future. Incorporating these changes means that the method header now looks like this:

```
- (NSNumber *) convertUnits: (NSNumber *)units
    withFactor: (NSNumber *)factor;
```

A method such as this is now referred to as

```
convertUnits:withFactor:
```

The colons indicate that there are two arguments, and the keyword as well as the method name help to form a meaningful phrase.

Creating a New App

Now that you have thought about the naming of methods, you can create a new app from scratch using standard techniques as shown in this section.

▼ TRY IT YOURSELF

Build an iOS App with Best Practices

The following steps summarize and review the creation of a Testbed app for iOS using the concepts that have been introduced in the last few hours and in the previous sections of this hour:

1. Create a new Xcode project from the iOS Single View Application template, as shown in Figure 14.1.

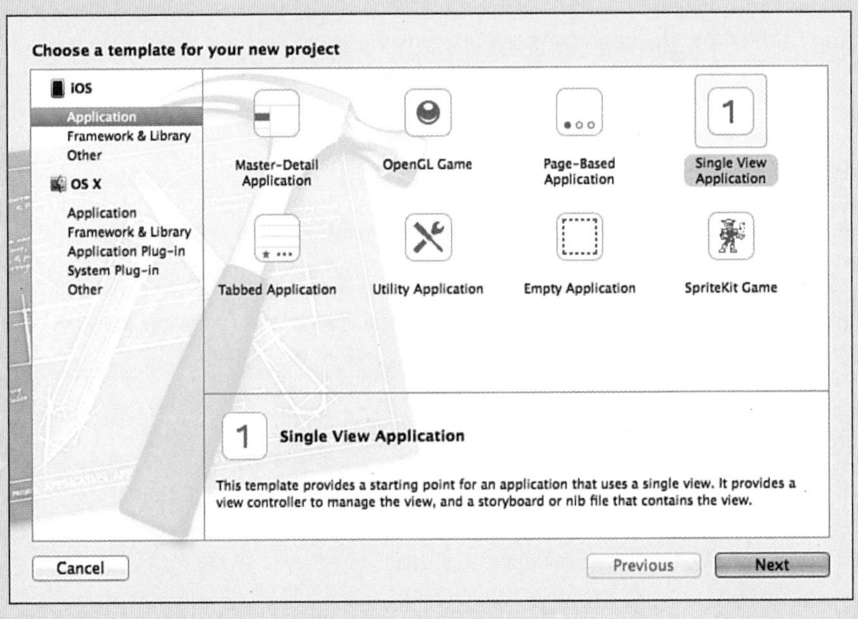

FIGURE 14.1
Create a new project.

2. Name it Testbed in the project options as shown in Figure 14.2.

3. Open AppDelegate.h and add a forward `@class` declaration for `Converter`. (It goes just before the `@interface` line.)

4. Add an instance declared property for the converter:

```
@property (strong) Converter *converter;
```

AppDelegate.h should look like Figure 14.3 at this point.

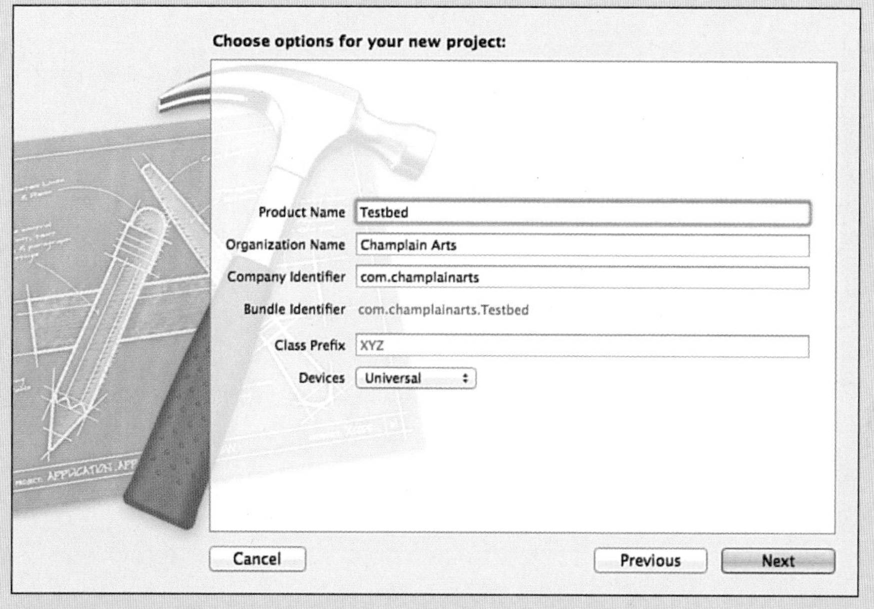

FIGURE 14.2
Set the project options.

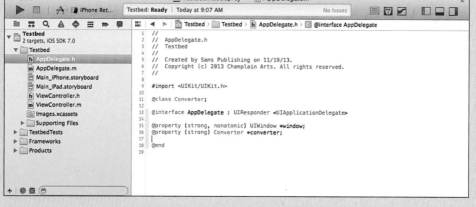

FIGURE 14.3
Finish the AppDelegate interface.

▼ **GO TO** ▶ The `strong` attribute is explained in Hour 16, "Managing Memory and Runtime Objects," p. 221.

TIP

Note that you may have a warning until after you complete the following step.

5. Create the `Converter` class. Use File, New, File, Objective-C Class and make it a subclass of `NSObject`, as shown in Figure 14.4. Save it in your project's folder.

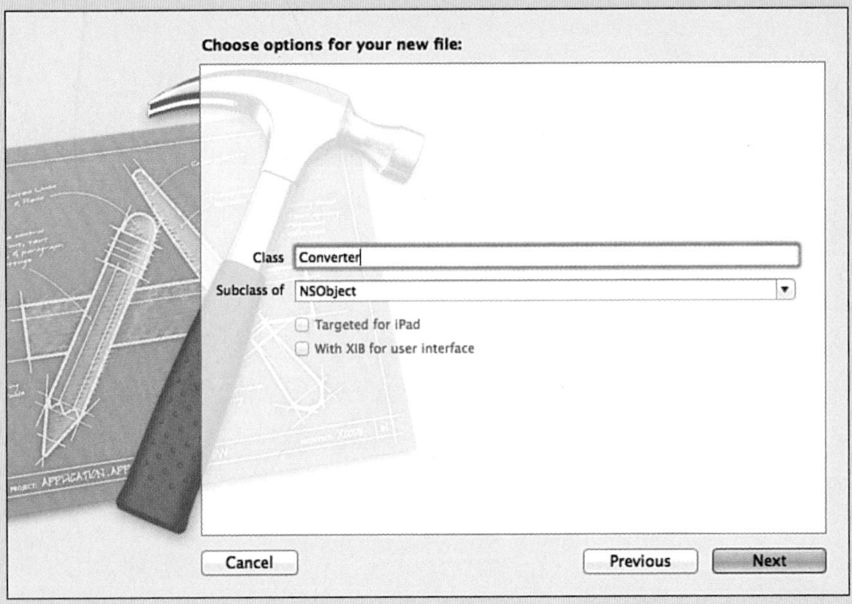

FIGURE 14.4
Create the `Converter` class.

6. Create a `Converter` instance and assign it to the `converter` property in AppDelegate.m with this code. Place it in `applicationDidFinishLaunchingWithOptions:` just before the `return` statement.

```
_converter = [[Converter alloc] init ];
```

7. You must import Converter.h into AppDelegate.m. So add the `#import` statement to the top of the file.

8. Set a breakpoint on the assignment statement created in step 6, and run the app on any of the simulators you have installed. You should see that converter is not allocated when the breakpoint is reached; if you step over that line, you should see that it is now created, as shown in Figure 14.5.

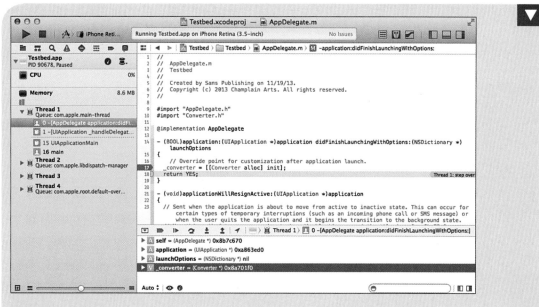

FIGURE 14.5
Check to see that the instance is created.

Implementing a Method

The `Converter` class can create an instance, as you have just seen, but it cannot do much of anything except perform the instance methods specified in the `NSObject` class and protocol. You need to implement a converter method to make it useful.

If you have gone through a process of analysis and design similar to "Working with a New Project" at the beginning of this hour, you know what you have to do inside the `convertUnits:withFactor:` method: Multiply units by factor.

In this section, you see two ways of doing this. The first method is a detailed step-by-step method that shows you how to manage the conversion to and from `NSNumber` objects and arithmetic float values. The second method is a concise one-line compression of the step-by-step method.

TIP
_____

As you work through code such as this, you might want to use a step-by-step method until you are familiar with the various type and class conversion routines.

▼ TRY IT YOURSELF

Build a Step-by-Step Conversion Routine

Here is the detailed conversion routine. These steps provide the full details for a debugging view of what is happening:

1. Declare the `convertUnits` method in Converter.h. When you add the declaration, the file looks like this:

```
@interface Converter: NSObject
- (NSNumber *) convertUnits: (NSNumber *)units withFactor: (NSNumber *)factor;
@end
```

2. Add the definition to Converter.m. Add the method header and brackets to begin. You can copy the declaration from the interface file and just change the semicolon at the end to brackets. When you have added the method header to the interface file, the file should look like this:

```
#import "Converter.h"
@implementation Converter
- (NSNumber *) convertUnits: (NSNumber *)units withFactor: (NSNumber *)factor{
}
@end
```

3. For debugging, declare float variables inside the `convertUnits:withFactor:` method and set them to the arguments:

```
float f1 = [units floatValue];
float f2 = [factor floatValue];
```

4. Do the arithmetic and return the result as an `NSNumber`:

```
return [NSNumber numberWithFloat:  (f1 * f2) ];
```

5. In AppDelegate.m, locate `applicationDidFinishLaunchingWithOptions:`. Before allocating the `Converter` (step 5 in "Build an iOS App with Best Practices"), create local `NSNumber` variables to use as the arguments to the new method. Set them to any test values you want to use:

```
NSNumber * myUnits = [NSNumber numberWithFloat:5];
NSNumber * myFactor = [NSNumber numberWithFloat:10];
_converter = [[Converter alloc] init ];
```

6. You may still have a breakpoint set on the line that allocates the `Converter` instance. If not, set one there.

7. Add the invocation of `convertUnits:withFactor:` to `applicationDidFinish-LaunchingWithOptions:`. It should now look like Figure 14.6.

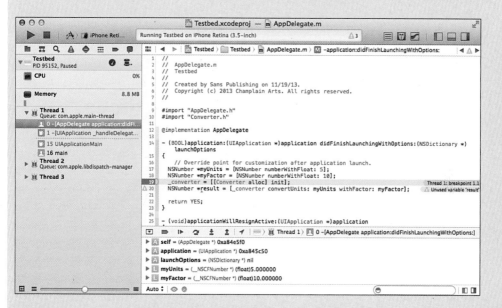

FIGURE 14.6
Invoke `convertUnits:withFactor:`.

TIP

In step 7, you will have a warning because `result` is not used.

GO TO ▶ Hour 23, "Working with the Debugger," p. 293, explains how to use `NSLog` to write a value to the log rather than storing it in a variable that you declare only for the purpose of debugging.

8. Set a breakpoint on the invocation of `convertUnits:withFactor:` and run it. When execution stops, you should be able to see your debugging variables set properly. Use the controls as shown in the debug pane at the bottom of the workspace window in Figure 14.6 to step into `convertUnits:withFactor:`.

9. Monitor the variables you created in step 3 to make certain that the arguments are passed in properly. You can create temporary variables for them to view in the debugger.

GO TO ▶ Hour 23, "Working with the Debugger," p. 293, for techniques to write variables to `NSLog`.

10. Eliminate any debugging code, and you're done.

Remember that this process is painstakingly slow and pedantic to show you how you can use the debugger and temporary variables to track the app's execution. Many people find that this step-by-step process is the only way to track down certain types of bugs that are caused by careless typing. Xcode is very good at catching mistakes as you make them, but some types of errors slip past. And, because the eye and brain work together to help you process what you see, you (and perhaps several colleagues) can look at code with a dash instead of a minus sign and never notice that the symbol is a fraction of an inch too big for a minus sign.

Expanding the Class with `init` Methods

This is an example of how you can develop a method in a real-life project. The method started as a currency converter, and it performs the conversion task well; you just pass in the units to convert and the conversion factor.

Some conversions do not require a conversion factor to be passed in each time. Feet to meters, for example, can be done with a constant. Even currency conversion is often done with a relatively constant value such as the real-time value from the close of yesterday's foreign exchange trading.

NOTE

For currency conversion for a specific business, the conversion factor is often set periodically to a value that reflects both the real-time value on foreign exchange markets as well as a markup for the business.

Just as you refined the syntax of the method in order to create `convertUnits:withFactor`, you can also refine the functionality so that you can store the conversion factor inside the `Converter` instance. That requires three changes:

▶ Add a declared property for the factor.

▶ Create an `init` method that takes the factor as an argument and sets the property.

▶ Add a new method that uses the declared property for the factor. It is `units:` because it already has the factor.

You also need accessors for the factor (both a getter and a setter), but they come for free with the synthesis of a declared property.

Add a Declared Property for the Conversion Factor

This type of restructuring and modification of a class and a method is common during the development process. You have already seen the use of multiple `init` methods, and all of the syntax needed to implement this new functionality has already been described. The following steps needed to improve the `Converter` class thus provide a handy review:

1. Add a property to Converter.h for the factor:

```
@property (strong) NSNumber *exchangeFactor;
```

2. Add an `initWithFactor:` method and a `convertUnits:` method to the existing `convertUnits:withFactor:` method. Remember that `init` methods return id.

```
- (id) initWithFactor: (NSNumber *)factor;
- (NSNumber *) convertUnits: (NSNumber *)units;
- (NSNumber *) convertUnits: (NSNumber *)units withFactor: (NSNumber *)factor;
```

3. Implement `initWithFactor:` in Converter.m. Remember the call to `[super init]` comes at the start of the subclass's implementation. The following boilerplate code is Apple's suggestion for code that returns `nil` if the superclass `init` fails:

```
- (id) initWithFactor: (NSNumber *)factor{
  if (self = [super init]) { // equivalent to "self does not equal nil"
    self.exchangeFactor = factor;
  }
  return self;
}
```

4. Implement `convertUnits:` in Converter.m.

```
- (NSNumber *) convertUnits: (NSNumber *)units
{
  return [NSNumber numberWithFloat:
    [units floatValue] * [self.exchangeFactor floatValue]];
}
```

5. Modify `applicationDidFinishLaunchingWithOptions:` to use the new initializer and method. You may want to add a debugging variable at the end to be able to check the result. Also, note that by using the class method `alloc`, you do not have to coerce the returned result to the `Converter` class:

```
- (void)applicationDidFinishLaunchingWithOptions:(NSNotification *)
      notification
{
  // Override point for customization after application launch
  NSNumber * myFactor = [NSNumber numberWithFloat:8];
```

```
    _converter = [[Converter alloc] initWithFactor:myFactor];
    NSNumber * myUnits = [NSNumber numberWithFloat:5];

    NSNumber *result = [self.converter convertUnits:myUnits];
}
```

Summary

This hour has shown you how to define a class and its methods in an implementation (.m) file. It has walked you through the details of typical debugging of new code as well as a real-life example of how your classes and methods can evolve as you work on them.

Q&A

Q. Why is it important to consider and reconsider the keywords and method names in your method headers?

A. You want them to be clear and understandable. In addition, as you and others use your new class and its methods, you are creating brief phrases that are able to be self-documenting to a large extent. You want to avoid method and keywords that give a false impression of the method and what it does. Implying that it does more or less than what it does can lead to confusion and mistakes down the line.

Q. Can you find a potential runtime error in both `convertUnits:withFactor:` and `units:`?

A. If a value for `exchangeFactor` is not passed in or has not been set with the `initWithFactor:` method, the result is undefined.

Workshop

Quiz

1. Where does `[super init]` go in your override?

2. What do you do about warnings regarding the `debug` variable?

Quiz Answers

1. `[super init]` goes at the beginning of your override.

2. Ignore them.

Activities

How would you deal with the problem identified in the second question (errors if the conversion factor is not defined)? Remember that this code is designed to function without user interaction, so you cannot put up a dialog box.

HOUR 15
Organizing Data with Collections

What You'll Learn in This Hour

- ▶ Working with collection objects
- ▶ Reviewing property lists
- ▶ Creating a collection
- ▶ Enumerating a collection
- ▶ Testing membership in a collection
- ▶ Accessing a collection member

Collecting Objects

Objective-C adds objects to C itself with as few additions to that language as possible. This contrasts with other languages that dramatically change and expand C as well as object-oriented languages that are not built on C (Smalltalk, one of the most important influences on the development of Objective-C, comes to mind).

C types (often referred to as *primitive types*) such as `int`, `float`, and the like are available for use in Objective-C. However, as part of its classes, Objective-C declares objects that are frequently used instead of the primitive types. Many of these objects are declared and implemented in the Foundation frameworks of Cocoa and Cocoa Touch.

One of the advantages of using Objective-C objects instead of primitive types is that the objects contain much of the functionality that you implement (and reimplement and reimplement) with code to manipulate the primitive types. For example, how many times have you iterated through an array in C by writing the code shown in Listing 15.1?

LISTING 15.1   Iterating Through a C Array

```
int counter = 0;
int limit = 100;
float myCArray [limit];
// fill the array

  for (counter = 0; counter < limit; counter++ )
{
  //do something with myCArray [counter]
}
```

Even if the array consists of objects (for example, `NSString *s[100]`), you still need to write the code to iterate through the array.

Collection objects incorporate both the ability to store and organize data just as a C array does along with the most common functionality for which you would otherwise have to write code (that you have probably written over and over). In the case of `NSArray`, the array object can create an instance of `NSEnumerator`, which can convert the code just shown into the code in Listing 15.2.

LISTING 15.2   Iterating Through an `NSArray`

```
NSArray *myArray;
// initialize the array
myArray = @[@"Obj1", "Obj2", "Obj3", "Obj4"];

NSEnumerator *enumerator = [myArray objectEnumerator];
id anObject;
myArray = [NSArray array];
while (anObject = [enumerator nextObject]) {
  //do something with anObject
}
```

GO TO ▶ Hour 19, "Using Associative References and Fast Enumeration," p. 249, to find out about a more concise way of iterating through collections.

The code is roughly comparable, but you do not have to worry about setting the counter and limit: They are automatically set when the `NSArray` object creates its `NSEnumerator` object. Also, note that the code in the Objective-C version has to be passed by the compiler. If you type **enkmerator** instead of **enumerator**, the compiler objects, but if you set the limit in the C language version to 1000 instead of to 100, the compiler has no problem with that.

This is definitely a small point, but the efficiencies and safeguards that derive from objects handling their own routine operations make your code less error-prone and more maintainable.

GO TO ▶ Hour 16, "Managing Memory and Runtime Objects," p. 221, for discussion of the implications of adding objects to collections.

Collections are Foundation framework classes: NSSet, NSArray, and NSDictionary. They share common functionalities:

▶ **Enumeration**—Collections can enumerate their objects. Some people prefer the term iteration. In both cases, the process results in the objects in a collection being returned one by one based on certain rules.

▶ **Membership**—A collection can quickly determine if a given object is in the collection.

▶ **Access**—A collection can return one of its objects based on criteria.

Collections come in pairs, one of which is mutable. In the case of a mutable collection, you can add and remove objects to and from it. Some people come to the concept of collections with experience primarily using arrays in other languages. In many languages, the concept of mutable and immutable collections does not exist, so you may find yourself gravitating to the use of mutable collections to the exclusion of the other collections. Explore all of the collections because you will find that the built-in functionality can reduce the amount of code that you write and, perhaps more important, improve your app's functionality.

NOTE

Immutable collections have significant performance advantages over mutable ones in most cases.

Collections: NSSet, NSArray, and NSDictionary

In this hour, you see how to use the collection classes. Before exploring them, it is important to note that there is no NSCollection class. The collection classes themselves are immediate descendants of NSObject and are not related to one another in the Cocoa class hierarchy. However, they share the basic functionalities described here. Also, as noted, each one of them comes in both mutable and immutable variations (the mutable variation is a subclass of the immutable base class).

Getting Familiar with Property Lists

Property lists are used throughout Cocoa and Cocoa Touch. You have seen property list files (with extension .plist) in your projects, and you have viewed property lists in your project, as shown in Figure 15.1.

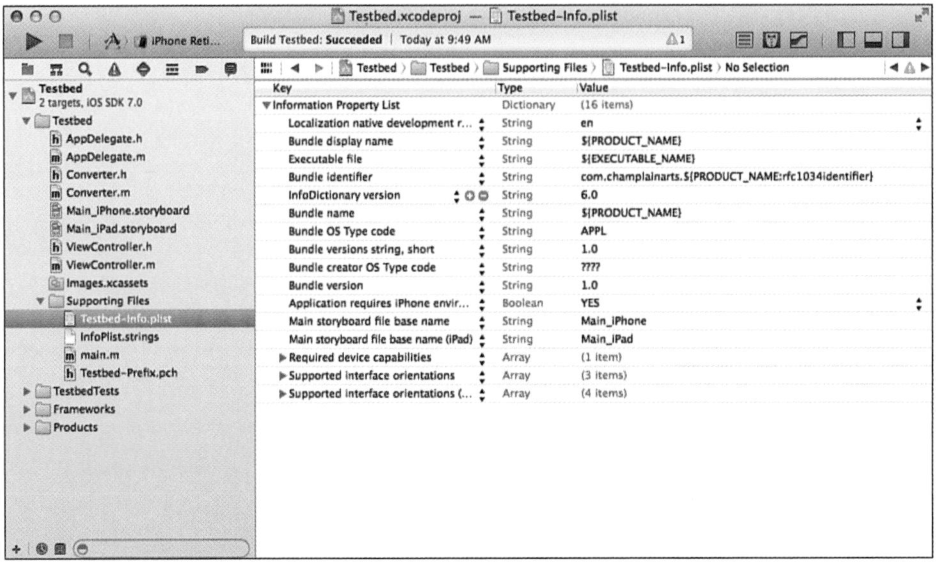

FIGURE 15.1
Property lists store project settings.

Property lists are one of the places where the boundary between the Objective-C language and the Cocoa and Cocoa Touch frameworks warrants your attention. Property lists are clearly framework objects; however, getting the most out of them requires you to not only be familiar with basic Objective-C types, but also be familiar with the collection objects that are the topic of this hour.

Property lists interact with collections in two ways. They are described in the following sections.

Using Collections in Property Lists

First, a property is a set of key-value pairs. For example, if you look closely at Figure 15.1, you can see that the main storyboard file base name (iPad) key (toward the bottom of the list) has the value `Main_iPad`.

In addition to the key and the value, each entry in a property list has a type. The supported scalar types are the following:

▶ NSDate

▶ NSNumber (through the `intValue` accessor)

▶ NSNumber (through the `boolValue` accessor)

▶ NSNumber (through the `floatValue` accessor)

In addition, two collections and a composite structure are supported:

▶ NSArray

▶ NSDictionary

▶ NSString

Xcode Labels for Collection Types

Xcode uses simple labels for the various types: Array, Dictionary, Boolean, Data, Date, Number, and String.

Property lists can be read and written as binary streams or as XML documents. (An older ASCII format is supported today only for reading.) Because support for property lists is built into Cocoa, property lists are widely used for storing relatively small amounts of data. Often, as shown previously in Figure 15.1, they are strings. But by using collections, more complex data structures can be stored in a simple property list.

Building Collections from Property Lists at Runtime

You can use property lists to initialize collection instances using utility methods. This is part of the generalized framework support for property lists. By making it simple to move from a property list to an in-memory collection instance, all of the collection management tools (enumeration, membership, and access) can quickly be brought to bear on property lists.

Comparing the Collection Classes

As noted previously, there are six collection classes: immutable and mutable versions of NSArray, NSSet, and NSDictionary. The three basic classes need little introduction because they are based on standard programming concepts. All of the classes contain objects, but other than being objects, they need no other characteristics.

NOTE

Of course, you can enforce your own rules so that, for example, you can have an NSArray consisting only of MySpecialObject instances.

Other than the mutable/immutable variation, the most significant difference among the three basic classes has to do with the way in which their elements are arranged:

▶ Arrays are ordered. Each object has an index number that can be used to access it. This is the standard behavior of arrays in most programming languages.

▶ Dictionaries are arranged by keys, which are usually strings but can be any object (an id). When the keys are strings, access is implemented using a hash function. The keys are unique, so there are no duplicate objects in a dictionary.

▶ Sets are not arranged. With the exception of NSCountedSet, there are no duplicate objects in a set.

Each of the collection classes has its strengths and weaknesses. For example, it is easy to test for membership in a collection, but that test is generally fastest in a set. Inserting an object in the middle of an array takes varying amounts of time; accessing the first and last elements takes constant amounts of time as does accessing elements of sets and of dictionaries (this last point is true for good hash functions).

You can use enumerators to loop through any of the collection classes, and there are a variety of methods you can use to find subsets of any collection and then enumerate through the subset. Using tools such as these, you can easily take all or part of a collection and turn it into a new collection of a different type.

Creating a Collection

Although each collection class has its own characteristics, all of them implement the basic functionalities (enumeration, membership, and access). The methods that they use for these implementations are parallel and sometimes identical, but there are minor variations that reflect the difference in the classes. In this and the sections that follow, the main functions of collections are shown and compared.

The first thing you need to do with a collection is to create it. Class factory methods let you do this easily. You can start with an empty collection and then add to it as well as delete and rearrange it, or you can start with a populated collection. The difference is that in the first case, you need to create a mutable collection so that you can do your manipulation of the collection's objects. In the second case, you just create and populate it in one step. If you are using a mutable collection, you can create and populate it in one step and then continue to manipulate the collection as you want.

Collections Are Highly Optimized

Remember the fact that you can also take an immutable collection and use it as the basis of another collection that might or might not be mutable. This process of building a new collection from all or part of an existing collection can let you work with immutable collections as if they were mutable in many ways. Whether or not you choose this structure depends on what you are doing with the data and, of course, how big your collection is.

Keep in mind that the code that implements collections in Cocoa and Cocoa Touch is some of the oldest code in the frameworks. It has been optimized extensively over time, and it is used all through the operating systems and various software products. Sometimes, engineers are cautious about using tools such as collections because they understand the complexity of the operations that are performed behind the scenes, and they might fear that the convenience of using a tool such as a collection is counterbalanced by performance issues. If you are worried about the performance of collections, create a small testbed app and test it. In most cases, you will find that your fears are exaggerated. And, if you do find that collections are not giving you the performance that you want (this is sometimes the case with very large collections), take a look at Core Data, which might be just what you need.

Using the Common Collection Creation Methods

These methods are implemented by all three collection classes; the only difference is in the name of the method.

You can create a collection instance using a class factory method like this (there are similar ones for other collections):

```
+ (instancetype)array
```

There also are factory methods that convert data from other collections and even files into the newly created collection as in this method:

```
+ (instancetype)arrayWithArray:(NSArray *)anArray:
```

Unless you are creating mutable versions of collections, you almost always create them with a method such as this one that populates the collection. However with an immutable instance, you do get one chance to modify it with an `init` method if you have created it using `alloc` rather than the simple factory method such as `array`. The `init` methods parallel the factory methods. Thus, just as there is an `arrayWithArray:` factory method, there is an `initWithArray:`.

You can create a collection instance using an existing collection:

```
+ (instancetype)arrayWithArray:(NSArray *)anArray
+ (instancetype)setWithSet:(NSSet *)set
+ (instancetype)dictionaryWithDictionary:(NSDictionary *)otherDictionary
```

There are more of these in the documentation for each collection class.

There is a trio of methods that enable you to create a set or array with a single object, with a comma-delimited list of objects that ends with `nil`, or with a C array of objects (in this case, you specify the count of objects to be used).

```
+ (instancetype)arrayWithObject:(id)anObject
+ (instancetype)arrayWithObjects:(id)firstObj, ...
+ (instancetype)arrayWithObjects:(const id [])objects count:(NSUInteger)count
```

Those three methods differ slightly for dictionaries because a dictionary consists of key-value pairs. In addition, the second and third methods use an NSArray of objects rather than a comma-delimited or C-style list. Also, note that although dictionaries typically use strings for the keys, the key arguments in these methods are of type id:

```
+ (instancetype)dictionaryWithObject:(id)anObject forKey:(id<NSCopying>) aKey
+ (instancetype)dictionaryWithObjects:(NSArray *)objects forKeys:(NSArray *)keys
+ (instancetype)dictionaryWithObjects:(const id [])objects forKeys:(const
  id<NSCopying> [])keys count:(NSUInteger)count
```

NOTE

nil-Terminate init Lists

The methods that take lists such as initWithObjects typically take comma-separated lists that must be terminated with a final value of nil. See the following section on Objective-C literal syntax for a simpler and more modern way of specifying lists.

In addition to these generic methods, there are some specific creation methods for the specific types of collections. They are described in the following sections.

Using Objective-C Literal Syntax

In recent versions of Xcode, you have the ability to create collections using literals rather than the methods shown in the previous section.

For example, instead of using arrayWithObjects:, you can use the following code:

```
myArray = @[ a, b, c];
```

a, b, and c are assumed to be NSObject instances (or instances of a subclass).

In addition, you can construct a dictionary with key-value pairs using syntax such as the following:

```
myDictionary = @{key1: value1, key2: value2};
```

You also can use literal subscripts for both arrays and dictionaries. These replace objectAtIndex: and objectForKey:.

```
anArrayElement = myArray [counter];
aValue = myDictionary {@"key"};
```

Reading and Writing Arrays

Foundation frequently lets you refer to files both with a file path in an NSString and with a URL in an NSURL instance. Methods let you use both references to read and write arrays. In both cases, you have a pair of methods. In chronological order, they are a method to write out an array and then a method to read in an array.

Working with File Paths

Given an NSArray instance in memory, here is how you can write it out to a file:

```
- (BOOL)writeToFile:(NSString *)path atomically:(BOOL)flag
```

The atomically argument provides a degree of protection in case of failure. If it is YES, a scratch copy of the file is written out and saved. Then, the name is changed. If it is NO, the file is simply written out, and if there is a hardware or other failure during the process, you might lose data.

The companion method is a class method; it reads in a file written by an instance:

```
+ (id)arrayWithContentsOfFile:(NSString *)aPath
```

Working with URLs

If you are using URLs, here is the instance method to write out an NSArray:

```
- (BOOL)writeToURL:(NSURL *)aURL atomically:(BOOL)flag
```

The companion method is the following:

```
+ (id)arrayWithContentsOfURL:(NSURL *)aURL
```

Reading and Writing Dictionaries

Dictionaries are read and written like arrays in the sense that you can use either a file path or a URL. The main difference is in the format that is used: The read and write methods use property lists for their format, which means that the content of the dictionary must conform to the data types for a property list (NSData, NSDate, NSNumber, NSString, NSArray, or NSDictionary).

Working with File Paths

Here is the instance method to write out a dictionary as a property list:

```
- (BOOL)writeToFile:(NSString *)path atomically:(BOOL)flag
```

To create a new dictionary from a file path, here is the method. Note that this is a class method, not an instance method.

```
+ (id)dictionaryWithContentsOfFile:(NSString *)path
```

Working with URLs

Here is the instance method to write out a dictionary:

```
- (BOOL)writeToURL:(NSURL *)aURL atomically:(BOOL)flag
```

This is the companion class method to create a dictionary from a URL:

```
+ (id)dictionaryWithContentsOfURL:(NSURL *)aURL
```

Creating Sets

There are some additional methods to create sets. For example, you can create a set from an array. Sets are not ordered, so the order of an array is lost, but sometimes that does not matter.

```
+ (instancetype)setWithArray:(NSArray *)array
```

You also have the ability to create a new set from an existing one by adding a single object, an array, or a set to the existing set. The result is a new set. Here are the three relevant methods:

```
- (NSSet *)setByAddingObject:(id)anObject
- (NSSet *)setByAddingObjectsFromArray:(NSArray *)other
- (NSSet *)setByAddingObjectsFromSet:(NSSet *)other
```

Enumerating a Collection

Enumerators (class NSEnumerator) enable you to step through a collection. A collection instance can return an NSEnumerator that is configured properly for that instance. Enumerators have only two methods: nextObject and allObjects.

Examining NSEnumerator Methods

This enumerator method takes you to the next object in the collection. If you have just created the enumerator, the next object is the first object.

```
- (id)nextObject
```

NOTE

Getting Specific Objects

Ordered collections let you get specific objects such as the first and last, as you will see in the "Accessing an Object in a Collection" section later in this hour.

This enumerator method returns an array of all not-yet-enumerated objects:

- (NSArray *)allObjects

Creating NSEnumerator **Instances for Collections**

With all three types of collections, you can create an NSEnumerator by using the method objectEnumerator:

- (NSEnumerator *)objectEnumerator

For an NSArray instance, you can also create a reverse enumerator:

- (NSEnumerator *)reverseObjectEnumerator

For an NSDictionary, you can enumerate the keys as well as the objects (values):

- (NSEnumerator *)keyEnumerator

Remember that sets are not ordered, so the suggestion that nextObject implies sequence does not apply to NSSet instances.

GO TO ▶ Hour 19, "Using Associative References and Fast Enumeration," p. 249, for more on enumerating.

TRY IT YOURSELF ▼

Create an NSArray and Enumerate Through It

You can put together some of the code from "Creating a Collection" and this section on enumerators as an example. Follow these steps to create an NSArray with several objects and then to work with an NSEnumerator:

1. Use a testbed project. Either create a new one as described in Hour 6, "Exploring Messaging and a Testbed App," or modify an existing one. If you are using Git, you can also create a branch in an existing project.

2. Locate applicationDidFinishLaunchingWithOptions:. If necessary, delete existing code to get back to the basic method.

```
- (BOOL)application:(UIApplication *)applicationdidFinishLaunching:
(NSNotification *)aNotification
{
    // Insert code here to initialize your application
}
```

3. Create an `NSString` and set its value:

```
NSString *myString = @"Test String";
```

4. Create an `NSNumber` and use a class method to set its value:

```
NSNumber *myNumber = [NSNumber numberWithInt:1234];
```

5. Create an `NSDate` and use a class method to set its value to the current date:

```
NSDate *myDate = [NSDate date];
```

6. Create an `NSArray` from the three objects you have created:

```
NSArray *myArray = @[myString, myNumber, myDate];
```

7. Verify the `NSArray` with a log message:

```
NSLog(@"myArray:%@\n",[myArray description]);
```

8. You should see this message when you run the code. (The spacing may be different.)

```
2013-12-11 15:31:25.650 Testbed[15808:707] myArray:(
    "Test String",
    1234,
    "2013-12-11 20:31:23 +0000"
)
```

9. Create an `NSEnumerator` on the `NSArray`:

```
NSEnumerator *myEnumerator = [myArray objectEnumerator];
```

10. Declare an object to use in the enumerator loop:

```
id anObject;
```

11. Use the enumerator to loop through each object and log its description:

```
while ((anObject = [myEnumerator nextObject])) {
    NSLog(@"anObject:%@\n",[anObject description]);
}
```

12. You should see these results in the debugger:

```
2013-12-11 15:51:12.317 Testbed[16636:707] anObject:Test String
2013-12-11 15:51:15.594 Testbed[16636:707] anObject:1234
2013-12-11 15:51:18.085 Testbed[16636:707] anObject:2013-12-11 20:51:08
•+0000
```

Testing Membership in a Collection

Each collection class has its own way of testing for membership. You can add code after the last step in the previous Try It Yourself activity to test for membership. Listing 15.3 shows how you can add your objects to a set. You can then test to see if one of the objects is in that set using the `member` method. It will return the object or nil if the object is not in the collection.

```
- (id)member:(id)object
```

The code snippet is shown in Listing 15.3.

LISTING 15.3 **Testing for Membership in a Set**

```
NSSet *mySet = [NSSet setWithObjects: myString, myNumber, myDate, nil];
NSLog (@"mySet:%@\n", [mySet description]);

anObject = [mySet member:myDate];
NSLog(@"member:%@\n",[anObject description]);
```

Experiment with adding other objects (and not adding objects) to watch the results. You can also simply ask if an object is a member of a collection (the result is YES or NO rather than the object itself).

For NSArray and NSSet instances, the code is

```
(BOOL)containsObject:(id)anObject
```

For NSDictionary instances, you check for the key and receive an object back if it is in the dictionary:

```
- (id)objectForKey:(id)aKey
```

The class references for the collection classes show additional methods for testing membership.

Accessing an Object in a Collection

As with memberships, accessing objects differs across the collection classes, and the class references are the fundamental guides. For `NSDictionary` instances, `objectForKey`, which was just shown, is a good place to start.

For `NSSet`, in addition to `member`, there is an interesting access method. It returns any object in the set, not a randomly chosen object, but, according to the class reference, "The object returned is chosen at the set's convenience." For example, if you construct a set of transactions for the last customer served, you can choose any of those transaction objects to get the name of the last customer served.

```
- (id)anyObject
```

For `NSArray` instances, the subscript is the commonly used means of access:

```
- (id)objectAtIndex:(NSUInteger)index
```

It is worthwhile to look through the class references for collections to see what other access and membership methods there are. You can access objects not only in the ways described here, but also based on conditions. The speed of the collection classes is impressive.

Summary

Collection classes not only let you manage arrays, sets, and dictionaries, but they also incorporate sophisticated, powerful, and remarkably efficient functionality that manages the data for you. In fact, the methods of the collection classes pretty much incorporate the bulk of an introductory programming course with algorithms that you no longer have to write for yourself.

Q&A

Q. What is the relationship between dictionaries and property lists?

A. Property lists can contain dictionaries. Also, dictionaries are read and written as property lists.

Q. What do the collection classes do?

A. They store arrays, sets, and dictionaries. They also incorporate the basic functionality for accessing, enumerating, and managing membership for the collections.

Workshop

Quiz

1. If you use an immutable collection, can you ever make a change to it?

2. Why can you create a set from an array but you cannot create an array from a set?

Quiz Answers

1. No. You can populate it with one of the `init` methods if you have created it with `alloc`, but that is the extent of the "modifications" you can make.

2. Arrays are ordered, and sets are unordered. Converting an array (ordered) to an unordered set means ignoring a piece of data. Doing the reverse would require you to create the order. You can use the `NSSet allObjects` method to convert the set to an array and then use `arrayWithArray` to create an array, but `allObjects` presents the data in an undefined order (which is set behavior).

Activities

Create a collection with half a dozen objects in it. Use one of the immutable classes. Now write code to extract three of the objects into a new collection. To become even more familiar with collections, extract objects based on some characteristic. This helps you become familiar with additional methods of the collection classes.

HOUR 16
Managing Memory and Runtime Objects

What You'll Learn in This Hour

▶ Reviewing memory management for objects

▶ Using manual reference counting

▶ Using Automatic Reference Counting

Managing Objects in Memory

One of the most significant ways in which object-oriented programs and their languages differ from traditional programming is in their use of memory. In older styles of programming, variables were declared in blocks and could be used throughout the block in which they were declared. (Sometimes the entire program was one block.) Variables were placed on the stack when control entered into a block, and when control left the block, the stack was cut back so that the variables were no longer accessible, and their memory was restored to the operating system.

With objects, there is a different pattern of use. It is not the mere declaration of a variable in a block that allocates memory; rather, it is the creation of the object that takes up memory. At the end of the object's life cycle, the deletion of the object releases its memory.

It is no longer a question of the scope of variables that determines their existence and memory usage but rather the programmer's creation and destruction of the object. It is true that there are some cases in which an object is created and destroyed in a single block, but often an object is created in one place in a program and destroyed in another.

Objective-C and the Cocoa frameworks have addressed the issue of managing memory for objects in two ways:

▶ **Reference counting**—Objects carry with them a reference count that represents the number of parties interested in the object. As long as the reference count is greater than zero, the object is deemed to be in use and cannot be deleted. When an interested party is no longer interested in the object, the reference count is decremented by one. When it reaches zero, that signifies that there is no interest in the object and it can be safely deleted.

▶ **Garbage collection**—At runtime, the interested parties are tracked without the use of reference counters. Periodically, a garbage collection process deletes objects that are no longer needed. Although the code can be highly optimized, it nevertheless adds to the burden on the computer's resources.

NOTE

Garbage collection has never been implemented on iOS, and it is now deprecated on OS X. However, you still find references to it in various documents and in old code.

The biggest distinction between these two methods is when they are performed. Reference counting is coded by the developer as the app is being written. Garbage collection happens at runtime, but the developer does not have to worry about managing reference counts.

This is no small consideration because implementing the reference counting code is not particularly complex in the way that managing a multidimensional array can be, but it is remarkably unforgiving. One reference count decrement in the wrong place can let the OS know that it is safe to delete an object when it is not. On the other hand, one reference count increment too many can prevent an object from ever being deleted, and you and your users will have to contend with memory leaks.

With the advent of Mac OS X 10.7 (Lion) and iOS 5, *Automatic Reference Counting* (ARC) entered the picture. (ARC is pronounced just as the arc of a circle is pronounced.) ARC imposes no runtime burden on the app because it is implemented in the compiler and optimizer. It relies on Cocoa naming conventions to actually generate the code that you had to hand-code in the past to manage reference counting.

Today, reference counting is the basis of memory management for Objective-C. In older apps, it is implemented explicitly using methods of NSObject and the NSObject protocol. In modern code, it is implemented with ARC. Accordingly, this hour focuses on reference counting techniques.

Managing Reference Counts Manually

ARC implements reference counting in the compiler and optimizer, but you still should understand what it is doing for you. If you are working on older code, you definitely need to understand manual reference counting because that is what you see in your code. Even with new code, not every developer is able to switch over to using ARC, so that is yet another reason for understanding the process.

Because ARC is implementing reference counting behind the scenes, in the unlikely event that something goes wrong, understanding reference counting may help you troubleshoot the problems. However, if you are working only on new code, you can postpone learning about reference counting and just focus on ARC (as described in the following section).

TRY IT YOURSELF ▼

Manage Memory with Reference Counting for Created Objects

The steps that follow provide a basic overview of an object's life cycle in a reference counted environment:

1. Create, retain, and initialize an object (`alloc` does the `retain` behind the scenes):

   ```
   id myObject = [[SomeObject alloc] init];
   ```

2. Use it in your code.

3. When you are finished with it, release it.

   ```
   [myObject release];
   ```

4. The runtime calls the object's `dealloc` method to release its memory after it is no longer needed. The runtime does the work after you have released the object; you don't have to do anything.

Looking at Memory Management Before ARC

In Hour 14, "Defining a Class in an Implementation File," you saw how to build a small converter. In Hour 14, you built it with ARC. If you were writing this code in the past (that is, before iOS 5 or Lion), you probably would have written it differently. In the listings that follow, you see comments on the lines that would have been written differently in older versions of the operating systems.

Xcode has turned on ARC starting in the Apple LLVM Compiler 3.0. The settings are in Apple LLVM 5.0 – Language – Objective-C under Build Settings for your project once you have selected your project in the project navigator—and, if necessary, scrolled down to that section. You can also manually adjust the various ARC warnings, as shown in Figure 16.1. There are additional options in Apple LLVM 5.0 – Warnings – Objective C and ARC.

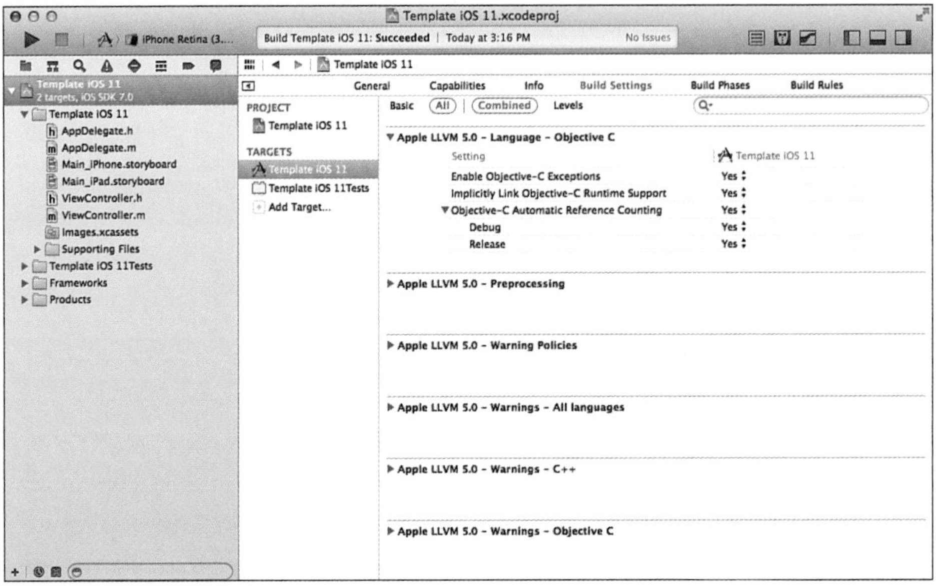

FIGURE 16.1
Adjust ARC warnings.

Listing 16.1 shows the interface file as it would have been written before ARC. (Compare this to Figure 14.3 in Chapter 14.) Remember, you should not be writing new code this way. It is presented here because there is still so much pre-ARC code around that you might have to understand, debug, and even modify it.

LISTING 16.1   AppDelegate.h

```
#import <UIKit/UIKit.h>

@class Converter;

@interface AppDelegate : NSObject <UIApplicationDelegate>

  @property (assign) IBOutlet NSWindow *window; //pre-ARC
  @property (retain) Converter *currencyConverter; //pre-ARC
@end
```

The setter attributes of the property declarations in the pre-ARC world can now be described. The property for the IBOutlet window is set to assign. This means that a simple assignment statement is used to set the property. The object itself is created at runtime based on your settings in Interface Builder, so it is not an object that your code creates.

When `currencyConverter` is set, a `retain` message is sent to the object as it is assigned. As described previously, each `retain` message must be balanced with a `release` message so that the reference count is properly adjusted. The property declaration as shown here provides the `retain`.

Summarizing Memory Management

There is a great deal of material on developer.apple.com covering memory management. In particular, you will find examples and discussion of retain cycles. The most common case of a retain cycle is that in which two objects each retain the other.

"Advanced Memory Management Programming Guide" on developer.apple.com provides a thorough guide to what happens. It summarizes what you need to know in three points:

▶ "You own any object you create [...] using a method whose name starts with `alloc`, `new`, `copy`, or `mutableCopy`." You do not need to retain these objects because you already own them.

▶ "You can take ownership of an object using retain." The object will not be deleted as long as you continue to own it, and that leads to the final point...

▶ "You must release any object when you no longer need it. If you do not, it will not be deallocated and its memory will continue to be held in use. Note that you release an object when you no longer need it. Releasing it in no way suggests that no one else needs it— other parties release it when they are done with it."

Managing memory in this way is not very complicated conceptually. However, as you will see from the volume of information and discussion on developer.apple.com, this form of memory management is labor and detail intensive. Automatic Reference Counting addresses those issues.

Managing Reference Counts with ARC

When ARC is turned on, the compiler and optimizer implement the needed `retain`, `release`, and `dealloc` code. In fact, you are not allowed to use them. For pre-ARC projects, you can turn ARC on; however, that can break existing code.

You might not notice it at first, but as soon as you clean a project where you have turned on ARC and built it again, you have errors. For this reason, you are safer using the Edit, Refactor, Convert to Objective-C ARC command for legacy projects. You will have a chance to compare the before and after versions of changed files, and Xcode will normally take care of problems.

TIP

Note, however, that there are a few circumstances in which Xcode cannot do the ARC conversion. At least in this author's experience, Xcode handles most conversions well; and if it can't do the conversion, it advises you. There are few if any reports of faulty conversions to ARC.

Using Cocoa Coding Conventions to Take Advantage of ARC

ARC relies on the Cocoa coding conventions—particularly the convention that a method name begins with a verb. The following verbs cause ARC to retain the object that is returned: `alloc`, `init`, `new`, and `copy`. Thus, a method called `prepareMyObjectAndCopy` does not trigger an ARC `retain` (and it also is a bad method name for other reasons).

Using Declared Property Attributes

There is another issue for you to confront when you are using ARC and iOS 5 or later along with Mac OS X 10.7 (Lion) or later. There are some modifications to declared property attributes. Property attributes before these versions included the following types and values:

▶ **Accessor method names**—You can specify methods to use for getter and setter if you want to write your own accessors. If you do not use your own accessors, they are created for you with the default names.

▶ **Writeability**—The values are `readwrite` and `readonly`.

▶ **Setter semantics**—These determine what happens when the property is set. Until iOS 5 and Mac OS X 10.7, the only values were `assign`, `retain`, and `copy`. There are additional values that are described in the following section.

▶ **Atomicity**—If your accessors are nonatomic, you can use the `nonatomic` keyword. (There is not a comparable atomic setting; it is the default.)

The setter semantic values make sense in the world of ARC, and they remain available to you. This avoids breaking existing code, but it means that you have to think about the memory management and reference counting that the compiler now implements for you. Two new keywords listed below are available to let you avoid thinking about the details of reference counting:

▶ **strong**—A synonym for `retain`. It describes the link to the object rather than the action to take when setting the property. Do not worry: It is a true synonym and a `retain` message is going to be generated, but when you think about `strong`, you are thinking about the link to the object and letting the compiler handle the mechanics of implementing it.

▶ **weak**—Similar to `assign`, but it also focuses on the nature of the link to the object rather than on the mechanics of implementation. It is not exactly the same as `assign` because it implements a significant additional feature.

NOTE

In pre-ARC days, it was very common to wind up with dangling pointers to objects. If you have a property that points to an object, and if that object is deallocated, the property still points to where the object was.

The best practice was to set the property to `nil` immediately after releasing it so that the pointer was safe. Remember that sending a message to a `nil` object is not an error.

With the `weak` keyword, if the object that the property points to is deallocated, the property is automatically set to nil. This saves a great deal of time that previously was spent debugging crashes. It also might prevent some memory leaks that were caused by people being hesitant to release objects. This was never a good programming practice, but it was definitely used in many cases.

CAUTION

An additional keyword, `unsafe_unretained`, implements exactly the old `assign` functionality. However, its use is discouraged because you might wind up with a dangling pointer.

`strong` and `weak` are not required for ARC; you can continue using `assign` and `retain`. However, over time, `assign` and `retain` will probably wind up requiring more explanation than `strong` and `weak` as the details of manual reference counting for memory management slip into the past. Using `strong` and `weak` makes the code more readable.

Variable Qualifiers

If you are using variables directly (as opposed to properties), you can attach qualifiers to them. In most cases, you do not need to use them because the default (__strong) is correct in most cases. These are the variable qualifiers available with ARC. Note that each one starts with two underscore characters.

► __strong—This is the default value for variables, so you do not need to specify it.

► __weak—This is used for a reference to an object that may disappear—exactly as is the case with the setter semantic for declared properties. If the object disappears, the variable is set to `nil`.

► __unsafe_unretained—This self-explanatory qualifier is used to reference objects that might not be zeroed out with `nil` when the object disappears.

► __autoreleasing—This is a part of a new implementation of `autoreleasing` that is described in the next section.

Autoreleasing **Variables**

The `retain` message is processed immediately when it is sent. Until you send a `release` message, you own the object you have retained, and you can rely on it being present.

TIP

Your ownership might not be unique because there may be other owners. Each one is guaranteed that the object will be there until the owner releases it. It might be there longer if other owners still own it, but once you have released your ownership, you don't care.

As you saw in Listing 16.1, it is common to release a number of objects at the same time when you are finished with them. In many cases, your `retain` messages are scattered through your code as you encounter the need for them, but you may release them at a known location (such as a `dealloc` method). The `NSAutoreleasePool` class lets you add to-be-released objects to a pool from which they are all released at the same time. This is particularly useful in tight loops where the objects are being retained and released in rapid succession.

Before ARC, this was implemented with a class. Your code would look like this:

```
NSAutoreleasePool *pool = [[NSAutoreleasePool alloc] init;
  // code in which you retain objects
  [pool release];
```

Once you have a pool, you add objects to it as you create them. `NSObject` protocol has an `autorelease` method that adds that object to the current `autorelease` pool. It's typically used in this way:

```
[[[SomeObject alloc] init] autorelease]
```

You no longer have to deal with `autorelease` pools directly. You use a compiler directive that is similar to a `try` block to delimit the pool. The syntax is quite simple: Use the `@autoreleasepool` directive and place the code for the objects to be `autoreleased` in brackets. Here is how the previous code is now written:

```
@autoreleasepool {
  // code in which you retain objects
}
```

A frequent use of an `@autoreleasepool` block is to delimit code in which a large number of objects are created. On exit from the block, they are released. ARC would get around to doing so, but this can speed up the process and reduce the memory footprint.

Summary

Before ARC, you had to manually take care of memory management for the objects you created. In this chapter, you find a brief overiew of how memory management is implemented with reference counting as well as a discussion of how ARC automates that process for you.

Q&A

Q. What are the most common problems that result from manual reference counting?

A. Memory leaks and app crashes are the most common problems that result from manual reference counting. Be thankful for ARC!

Q. Why should you think twice about converting existing code to ARC?

A. Because constructs such as `retain`, `release`, and `dealloc` are not allowed under ARC, you may break existing code.

Workshop

Quiz

1. Why are the Cocoa coding conventions so important with ARC?

2. What is the difference between garbage collection and reference counting?

Quiz Answers

1. The initial verb in a method name (`alloc`, `init`, `new`, or `copy`) triggers ARC to retain an object.

2. Garbage collection is a process that runs at runtime. Reference counting is implemented when the code is written and compiled. Its effects are seen at runtime.

Activities

Adding ARC to an existing Xcode project can break it, as pointed out in this hour. However, it is worth your time to experiment with an old project to see how much damage is done. There are projects that have little damage by adopting ARC. These can be projects that you (or someone else) might have written when you were first starting out. If a project totally ignores memory management, it might leak like a sieve, but for some small projects that doesn't matter. In a case such as that, moving to ARC plugs the leaks with minimal effort on your part. Just remember: When you switch the ARC settings, clean your project before rebuilding it. And, of course, work in a copy of the code.

Extending a Class with Protocols and Delegates

What You'll Learn in This Hour

▶ Comparing subclassing with Objective-C techniques

▶ Using a protocol

▶ Understanding delegates

▶ Exploring documentation and header files

Exploring the Pros and Cons of Subclassing

In general, this book focuses on Objective-C itself and leaves detailed comparisons with other object-oriented languages to other sources. Even though it has been a quarter-century since the rapid rise of object-oriented programming languages, some of the battles among partisans of those languages remain vivid and even bitter.

One of the purposes of object-oriented languages is to enable people to work with objects that can be similar to one another in a way that lets developers write only the code involved in the difference. If you have a bank account class, it could display the account owner's name and address as well as other information that is relevant to all types of bank accounts.

If you subclass the bank account class, you can create a savings account. The code to display the owner's name and address can be inherited from the basic bank account class, but for the calculation of daily interest, the savings account class might have to have its own code just as a checking account class might also have its own code. This object-oriented structure holds great promise for being able to make modifications that are confined in their effect (changing or creating a savings account class should not affect a checking account class). Code that has been written and tested in the context of a superclass can be invoked by subclasses with a fair degree of confidence the superclass will continue to function properly. The hope is that only the new code needs detailed testing.

Partisans of Objective-C point out that subclassing is in many ways a blunt instrument, and it is not the precise answer in many cases. Because your primary tool for differentiating related objects from one another is subclassing, you wind up constructing hierarchies that frequently are many layers deep. With Objective-C, a variety of techniques have been implemented that enable you to write code for a variation on an existing object without subclassing it. These are techniques in which structured sections of code can be written and managed without placing them into a class.

Introducing the Example

As an example, the Master-Detail Application template can be modified to use a protocol and delegate. Consider the possibility of editing data in a detail view controller. If you were to do so, you would need to save it when the user navigates away or taps a Save button. In the Master-Detail Application template, it is the master view controller that reads and writes data. It presents the list of detail items to the user, so it is the master view controller that sets up the appropriate detail view controller. Because it sets up the detail view controller, it knows when the detail item changes and can save any changes that have been made to it.

If there is a Save button, it would be in the Detail View Controller. So it seems that both master and detail view controllers need access to the code to save data.

The master view controller does have a reference to the detail view controller, but there isn't a reverse reference. It is possible to locate the master view controller from the detail view controller, but many people would argue that this kind of circular referencing is poor style. A protocol and delegate can work together to solve the problem.

TIP

Although this is a simple issue that could be solved in other ways, it's a good example of how a protocol can work without tangling up references and dependencies among classes. Another way to accomplish this goal is to use a notification. In this case, the detail view controller would not call the method on its delegate; instead, the detail view controller would notify any object that is listening for the notification that it should save the data.

Working with Protocols

Protocols can be described as a set of methods that are not part of a class. They can also be considered methods of an anonymous class because you know nothing about the class to which they may actually belong.

How can you have methods that are not part of a class? They would be methods that respond to messages (or perform operations) that are defined conceptually but not in specific terms for a class.

These methods are defined as part of a protocol rather than as part of a class. Classes can then adopt the protocol; they are expected to implement the methods declared in the protocol (subject to the fact that some of them are optional). Classes can adopt many protocols, but in practice the number is not much more than five with the exception of some of the framework classes.

Unlike classes, protocols do not let you declare instance variables, so it is only the methods and properties that are part of the protocol.

Working with Delegates

A *delegate* is an object to which a class instance hands off certain messages. The delegate is expected to handle those messages for the instance and take appropriate actions. The messages that the delegate handles are declared in a protocol. Both the protocol and the delegate need access to the protocol declaration, but only the implementer of the protocol needs access to the protocol definition and code. Thus, two objects that are linked by a protocol/delegate connection have access to the same functionality, but only one (the implementer) has access to the detailed definition.

NOTE

This is where the optional and required methods can become very useful. Thinking through what is optional and what is required can help you to focus a protocol. Some people believe that protocols with a fairly limited focus and with methods that are predominantly (or all) optional or required improves reusability.

Putting Protocols and Delegates Together

This section explains how you can use a protocol and delegate for the scenario described in the example. Putting it all together, here's what you get:

1. The class that will implement the protocol declares it in most cases. You can declare it in other places and include it, but most commonly it is declared in the implementer. Figure 17.1 shows MasterViewController.h, which declares the protocol and then indicates that it will implement it the protocol with `<DetailDelegateProtocol>`.

2. The class that adopts the protocol (which means that it promises to implement it) must do so. Figure 17.2 shows the implementation in MasterViewController.m.

FIGURE 17.1
Declare the protocol and adopt it.

FIGURE 17.2
Implement the protocol.

3. The class that will use the protocol declares a delegate. As you can see in Figure 17.3, this delegate is often named delegate (but it doesn't have to be), it is commonly typed as `id` (but, again, doesn't have to be), and its declaration indicates that it must implement the required methods of the protocol (this does have to be). Note the forward `@protocol` statement. This keeps the code clean by not needing to import MasterViewController.h here in DetailViewController.h.

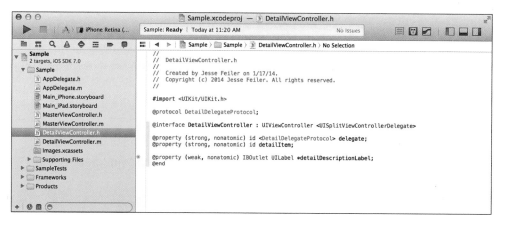

FIGURE 17.3
Declare a delegate that will use the protocol.

4. A class that knows about the protocol and the instance that will use it must set the delegate of that class. In the example, MasterViewController implements the protocol. It also has a reference to the detail view controller. It therefore can set the delegate with this line of code:

```
self.detailViewController.delegate = self;
```

5. In DetailViewController.m, import MasterViewController.h and then use the protocol methods as shown in the highlighted code in Figure 17.4.

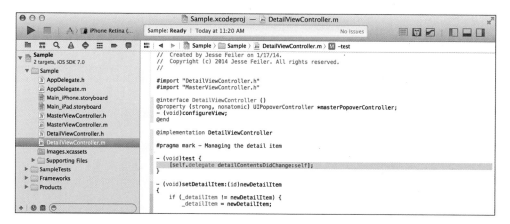

FIGURE 17.4
The delegate can now use the protocol's methods.

Looking Deeper Inside Protocols

As mentioned previously, a protocol's methods can be optional. This is a relatively recent change to Objective-C. As a result, you will see code that might appear unclear. What is absolutely certain is that any methods declared in a protocol preceded by `@optional` are, indeed, optional. You cannot rely on their being implemented by classes that adopt the protocol.

Classes that are preceded by `@required` can safely be considered required. However, classes within a protocol that are preceded by neither are construed as being required. The reason is that until the addition of optional methods, all protocol methods were required. To avoid breaking code, that is the default interpretation for the compiler.

When working with optional methods, it is essential to check if they are implemented. The code for that is

```
if ([self.detailDelegate respondsToSelector:
  @selector(detailContentsDidChange:)])
  {...}
```

Going forward, it is better to specify which methods or properties are optional and which are required.

Summary

This hour has introduced protocols and delegates. Together, they let you assemble code that enhances the code that you write and that is inherited by your superclass. The structure can make for a simpler pattern than relying on subclassing objects.

Q&A

Q. How do you use a protocol to add properties to a class?

A. Declare the property in the protocol and add an `@synthesize` directive in the protocol adopter.

Q. What is a delegate and how is it related to protocols?

A. A delegate is a part of many Cocoa classes. It is designed to be implemented by a class that you create and assign to the delegate property of the class. Your class must respond to the messages that can be sent to the delegate. Those are usually specified in a protocol for that delegate.

Workshop

Quiz

1. If a protocol method is not marked as required or optional, how is it interpreted?

2. How many protocols can a class adopt?

Quiz Answers

1. If a protocol method is not marked as required or optional, it is interpreted as required.

2. There is no specified limit.

Activities

`UITableView` has both a delegate and a data source. Each has a protocol that it must implement. Why are they separate, particularly when you consider that frequently a subclass of `UITableView` is its own delegate and data source?

Hint: Look at the names of the methods in the two protocols. One manages the data and the other manages the appearance of the data in the interface.

The protocol would be declared and implemented in the master view controller, and it would contain the code to save the data. If a master view controller adopts that protocol, it will be expected to execute the code to manage the save when the detail view controller requests it via the protocol. This eliminates the need for the detail view controller to have a reference to the master view controller.

What it does have is a delegate that adopts the protocol. Via that delegate, it can request the save to occur. It doesn't need to know what object is implementing the protocol because the delegate is set by the master view controller when it sets up the detail view controller. The detail view controller only knows that something implements the protocol.

Here are the steps to implement this scenario. It's worth reviewing because the pattern is so common in Objective-C. (Note that although the steps are numbered, they can be implemented in any order. Until the last step—whatever it might be in your sequence of steps—one or more errors or warnings may appear.)

1. In the header of the class that will implement the protocol, declare it. In this case, you would add code such as that shown in Listing 17.1 at the top of MasterViewController.h before the `@interface` section.

LISTING 17.1   `DetailDelegateProtocol` Declaration

```
@protocol DetailDelegateProtocol <NSObject>
@required
- (void)detailContentsDidChange:(id)item;
@end
```

2. Specify that the master view controller will adopt the protocol with this code:

   ```
   @interface MasterViewController : UITableViewController
   <DetailDelegateProtocol>
   ```

3. Implement the protocol code in MasterViewController.m

4. Set the delegate of the object that will call the protocol to the master view controller itself. For example, in the `viewDidLoad` method of MasterViewController, you could use this line of code.

   ```
   self.detailViewController.delegate = self;
   ```

5. In DetailViewController.h, declare a forward reference to the protocol like this:

   ```
   @protocol DetailDelegateProtocol;
   ```

6. Declare the delegate in the interface of DetailViewController.h:

   ```
   @property (strong, nonatomic) id <DetailDelegateProtocol> delegate;
   ```

7. In DetailViewController.m, you can now use the protocol. For example, you could write this code:

   ```
   [self.delegate detailContentsDidChange:self];
   ```

Extending a Class with Categories and Extensions

What You'll Learn in This Hour

▶ Differentiating categories and protocols

▶ Choosing when to use a category

▶ Comparing categories and subclasses

▶ Building and testing a category

Comparing Categories and Protocols

In Hour 17, "Extending a Class with Protocols and Delegates," you saw how to specify a set of methods for a protocol that can be adopted by any class. How the class that adopts the protocol implements it is up to that class: The protocol merely defines the required methods that must be (somehow) implemented by the class. Accordingly, when a class adopts a protocol, it can assume that it can call the required methods in that protocol. It will need to check to see if the optional methods are implemented.

Categories are somewhat similar to protocols. However, instead of being able to be adopted by any class, they are tied to a specific class. A category consists of an `@interface` as well as an `@implementation` just like a class. A category is added to the specific class at runtime rather than during the build process. Once added, the class and category together behave as a class does. Like protocols, categories declare methods. They do not declare variables or properties in their interface. You can declare private instance variables inside the method implementation.

You will find categories for some of the Cocoa frameworks classes on the web and in other resources. They are a good way to extend a framework class relatively safely (provided, of course, that the category code works properly).

Choosing When to Use a Category

Categories can be used to structure large projects. A base class can be designed with one or more categories, each of which adds specific types of functionality to the base class. Different individuals or teams can work on each category without running into too many conflicts. In addition, because the categories are assembled into the class at runtime, the people working on the categories do not need access to the source code of the class to which they are adding categories. They do need access to the interface, but the details of the coding can be kept confidential. This can help manage large projects in which parts of the project are confidential for one reason or another. At runtime, as categories are added to the primary class, any methods with the same signature as methods in the primary class are replaced with same-signature methods from a category.

NOTE

Multiple Method Replacements

If you replace a method in a class with more than one same-signature method in more than one category, the results are undefined.

These are among the purposes of categories as described in the documentation from Apple (and before that from NeXT—categories are an original part of Objective-C).

Comparing Other Techniques with Categories

Today, there are more tools available for managing source code and handling changes, so the issue of managing and structuring large, monolithic projects is often not the issue it was in the past. In addition, for many people, the rise of open source code has in some cases broken down the traditional confidentiality and even secrecy of code. The trade-off between the benefits of many eyes looking at the code as compared with confidentiality often tips toward a bit more openness of code as compared with the practices a few decades ago.

NOTE

That said, critical pieces of proprietary code, such as the Facebook algorithm for generating the news stream, remain as carefully guarded as the legendary formula for Coca-Cola.

In Cocoa and Cocoa Touch as well as many third-party apps, categories are commonly used for another purpose; they help you avoid subclassing in some cases.

Comparing Categories with Subclasses

Categories can help you manage one of the issues that often arises with subclassing objects. Many projects evolve over time as hardware, software, and user expectations change. Periodically, a major overhaul and restructuring of the code might take place. (In the world of Apple, this has happened on a grand scale with the move from Mac OS to OS X and, on a lesser scale, with the moves from Motorola chips to PowerPC chips and then to Intel chips.) Even with large-scale changes such as these, it is not always possible to substantially reconfigure an object hierarchy. (You'll find an example in the following section.)

Modifying a Class Hierarchy

Adding a subclass at the bottom of the object hierarchy is not usually very difficult, but when you realize that you really need to insert an intermediate object at the top of the hierarchy, you might encounter problems. The evolution of AppleScript in OS X provides a case in point.

AppleScript is the scripting language used on OS X and, before that, on Mac OS. Today, it is one of several scripting languages that are available on the Mac. It has been integrated into workflows (often involving Automator from Apple), and for organizations that rely on AppleScript and Automator, their investment in these tools can be enormous. The issues involved in integrating AppleScript are not specific to AppleScript. The steps described here occur in many cases where the object hierarchy needs revision.

NOTE

AppleScript is used extensively in various publishing scenarios. QuarkXPress was one of the early mainstays of scripting, and InDesign likewise supports AppleScript as one of its scripting tools.

To fully integrate AppleScript with the frameworks, support code is needed at a very basic level. Modifying `NSObject` to provide scripting support would be simple in one sense, but it would burden `NSObject` with scripting code that many (perhaps most) users would never need. Another way to integrate scripting is to add new classes, and perhaps a protocol, that are only invoked when needed. In fact, that is the strategy implemented with `NSScriptObjectSpecifier`.

That works for many AppleScript purposes, but in order to implement certain behaviors, it is necessary to add app-specific functionality to the application object itself. This is not practical for a number of reasons that are beyond the scope of this book.

For now, just note that this is a situation in which you want to extend `NSApplication` for your specific app. There are other cases in which you need to add some functionality to `NSObject` itself. Obviously, making these changes in the frameworks themselves is not feasible:

By definition, these are changes needed for specific apps. If the source code for `NSObject` or `NSApplication` was readily available, users could modify it for their specific purposes and thereby fragment the platform.

Confining Modifications to Categories

Adding the needed code in a category at runtime accomplishes the goal of modifying a class that is widely used and possibly subclassed but with an assurance that those modifications will have limited dangerous consequences. The fact that the category is compiled on its own limits potential harmful side effects. If it needs to be backed out, you do not have to make modifications in source code that was developed for other purposes. The category can be removed from the project without harm, although you have to remove any invocations of methods created in the new category.

GO TO ▶ Hour 4, "Using Xcode 5," p. 41, to see how to use a branch of your project to experiment with code such as a category and then back it out.

Working with Categories

Category declarations specify the class on which they are placed. They do not specify a superclass because it is the superclass of the class on which they are placed.

Here is a typical category declaration:

```
@interface NSApplication (SampleCategory)
- (void)testCategory;
@end
```

The category name is entered in parentheses after the name of the class on which this category is placed. (The common terminology is "placing a category on a class.")

By convention, the filenames for a category combine the class and the category name with a plus sign as in NSApplication+SampleCategory.h.

▼ **TRY IT YOURSELF**

Create and Use a Category

You do not have to remember the naming conventions for the category files or the format of declarations. As you see in the following steps, Xcode handles this all for you:

1. Create a new project in Xcode. Alternatively, take an existing project and create a new branch to experiment with. In the figures of this chapter, the iOS testbed application based on the Single View Application template is used.

2. Choose File, New, File or Control-click (or right-click) in the project navigator. The sheet shown in Figure 18.1 opens.

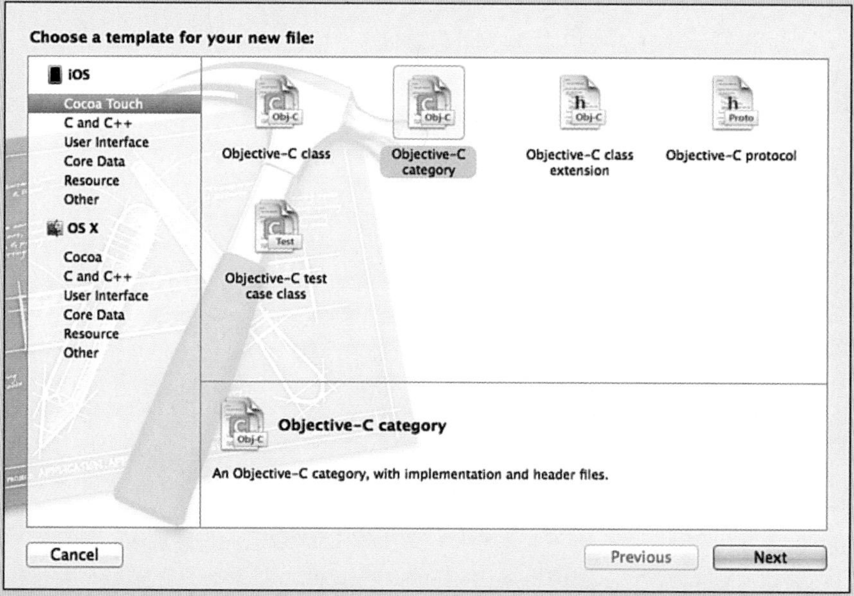

Choose a template for your new file:

iOS
- Cocoa Touch
- C and C++
- User Interface
- Core Data
- Resource
- Other

OS X
- Cocoa
- C and C++
- User Interface
- Core Data
- Resource
- Other

Objective-C class   Objective-C category   Objective-C class extension   Objective-C protocol

Objective-C test case class

Objective-C category

An Objective-C category, with implementation and header files.

Cancel   Previous   Next

FIGURE 18.1
Create a new category.

3. Choose Objective-C category.

4. Name your category and enter the name of the class on which it is to be placed, as shown in Figure 18.2.

5. When prompted, save the file. The default settings for location and name (UIApplication+SampleCategory) are fine to use.

6. Open the .h file. The following code should be in the file:

```
#import <UIKit/UIKit.h>

@interface UIApplication (SampleCategory)

@end
```

7. Enter a method declaration such as the following test:

```
- (void)testCategory;
```

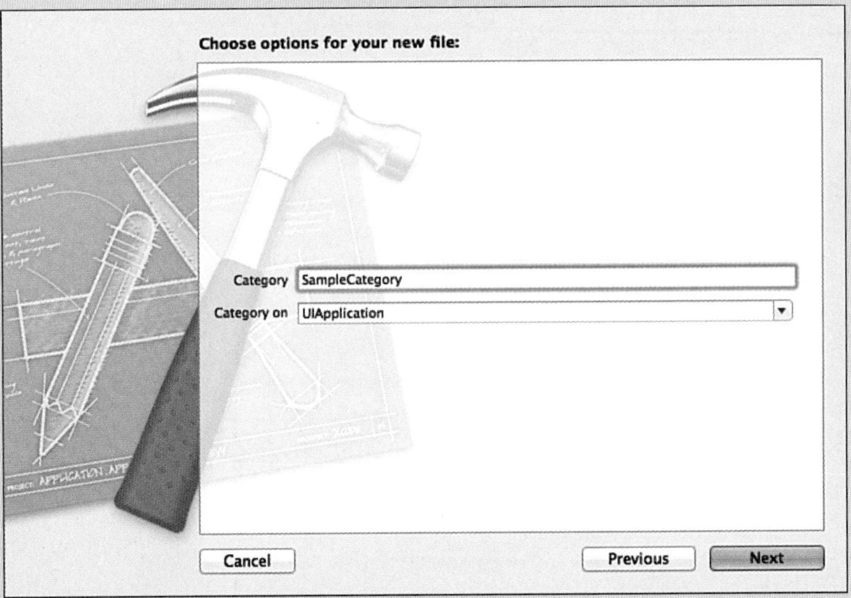

Choose options for your new file:

Category   SampleCategory

Category on   UIApplication

Cancel   Previous   Next

FIGURE 18.2
Name the category and specify its class.

8. In the `.m` file, provide the method definition. You can use an empty method such as the following for now:

```
#import "UIApplication+SampleCategory.h"

@implementation UIApplication (SampleCategory)

- (void) testCategory {


}
@end
```

9. Add a message to the category test method in `application:didFinishLaunching WithOptions:` in AppDelegate.m.

```
- (BOOL)application:(UIApplication *)application didFinishLaunchingWithOptions:(NSDictionary *)launchOptions
{
    [application testCategory];
}
```

10. Make certain you add an `import` for the header file of the category to the top of AppDelegate.m.

```
#import "UIApplication+SampleCategory.h"
```

11. Place a breakpoint at the beginning of the method you built in the category in step 7.

12. Build and run the app. You should see the results shown in Figure 18.3. The app stops at the breakpoint in the category.

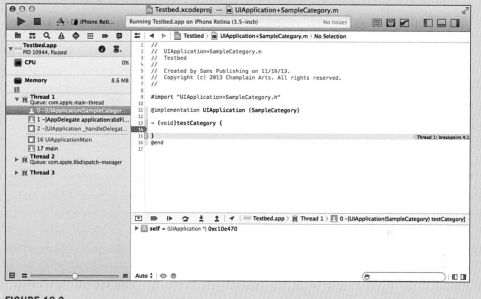

FIGURE 18.3
The method in the category is executed.

Using Class Extensions

Class extensions are also known as anonymous categories. They can be used to redefine properties, variables, and methods that you do not want to expose in the class's interface file. Over the past several years, they have gained in popularity, and they are created by default in many of the Xcode templates. These class extensions are often empty, but they are ready for you to use them to define properties and methods that aren't visible in the public interface.

You can redeclare properties in an anonymous category (changing `readonly` to `readwrite` for example) or declare methods that you want to totally hide from people who have access to the interface file of the class.

Class extensions have the same syntax as named categories, but instead of the name in parentheses, the parentheses are empty, as in this example:

```
@interface MyClass ()
...
@end
```

The methods in an anonymous category must be implemented in the main `@implementation` section for the class rather than in a separate category `.m` file. If they are not implemented there, the compiler warns you.

Named categories are implemented in their own `.m` files. If a method implementation is missing, you are not warned.

Working with Informal Protocols

The category structure was used in the past to create informal protocols in which some methods are optional. (This legacy code still exists.) As noted in the previous section, methods declared in a named category do not trigger compiler warnings if they have no definition in a `.m` file. As a result, you can consider the methods optional. Until the ability to specify `@optional` in a protocol (in Objective-C 2.0), this was the only way to implement that functionality: a named category with some missing definitions. Now that `@optional` is available for protocol methods, there is little need for informal protocols implemented as named categories.

Summary

This hour has shown you how to add or replace methods in a class with methods in a category that is attached to the class. You can use a category to correct a bug in an existing class without recompiling the entire class; you can also use a category to add specific functionality to framework classes.

Categories are also used to organize large projects. (The Cocoa frameworks themselves use categories extensively.)

Q&A

Q. What is the significance of an anonymous class?

A. You must have the source code for the base class.

Q. Why are protocols and categories often discussed together?

A. Both let you add specified methods to a class (categories) or several classes (protocols).

Workshop

Quiz

1. What is the convention for naming files for categories?

2. Are there limits on the number of categories you can create for a class?

Quiz Answers

1. The convention for naming files for categories is ClassName+CategoryName.

2. No, except that each category name (including a blank anonymous name) must be unique.

Activities

Two sample code projects use categories for AppleScript in a progressive way. Check out `SimpleScripting` and then `SimpleScriptingVerbs` from the sample code on developer. apple.com. Particularly if you have used AppleScript, you will find the possibility shown in those examples to be useful for future projects.

Using Associative References and Fast Enumeration

What You'll Learn in This Hour

▶ Simulating adding variables to classes

▶ Using fast enumeration

▶ Using `NSEnumerator` instances with fast enumeration

Catching Up on Objective-C 2.0 Time-Saving Features

Objective-C has been around since the early 1980s (that was the time when most modern object-oriented programming languages or their direct ancestors were developed). It is set apart from many of the other languages by its goal, which was to build on C with the smallest amount of additional code. In part because of this design goal, major changes to the language have been relatively few when compared with some other languages.

NOTE

Comparing C++ and Objective-C Development Strategies

At an Apple Worldwide Developers Conference in the late 1990s, one of the engineers working on Objective-C compared it with C++ by recounting the story of a conference at which a number of new features were proposed for C++. A number of the new features were somewhat similar to one another, but, he said, every single one was added to the language. Coming from the Objective-C world, he considered that the wrong decision.

Objective-C 2.0 was released in 2007 along with OS X 10.5 (Leopard). The release included a new compiler and performance improvements to the runtime. Features such as declared properties, garbage collection, and others appeared for the first time in this release. By comparison, subsequent changes, such as Automatic Reference Counting, have not bumped Objective-C up to a new version number.

Among the Objective-C 2.0 features were the tools that are the topic of this hour: associative references and fast enumeration. Associative references fill a previously unmet need for extending classes, whereas fast enumeration makes programming faster and safer.

Extending Classes by Adding Instance Variables (Sort of)

In Hour 17, "Extending a Class with Protocols and Delegates," and Hour 18, "Extending a Class with Categories and Extensions," you saw how to add methods to classes. In the case of all of those tools, you can only add methods; there is no mechanism for adding instance variables. There are reasons why that feature is not implemented: Two of the most commonly cited are the fact that it is difficult to implement and the notion that being able to add instance variables to classes would lead to sloppy code. Regardless of where you stand on these issues, you cannot add instance variables to classes with any technique other than subclassing and adding the new instance variables to the subclass. See "Getting and Setting an Associative Reference" later in this chapter for another way of addressing this issue.

Associative references (introduced in Objective-C 2.0) simulate the process of adding new instance variables to objects. The process relies on key-value coding (KVC). The terminology is based on KVC: You create a reference from an object to a value where the value is half of the KVC structure.

GO TO ▶ "Getting Familiar with Property Lists" in Hour 15, "Organizing Data with Collections," p. 207, to review key-value coding (KVC).

Adding what appear to be new instance variables is accomplished with a change to NSObject. Each NSObject instance has a set of references to associated objects. These references rely on KVC for their organization.

This implementation enables you to have any number of associated references for an NSObject instance. It also adds very little, if any, overhead because most NSObject instances have no references at all: The feature comes into play only for those objects that do have references.

Associative references let you add a pointer to any object—it need not be a class, but because it frequently is a class, the associative reference has the appearance of an added instance variable on the class. There are three functions that you use with associative references. You write the code, but the action happens at runtime and not during compile or build time.

The three functions are the following:

▶ `objc_setAssociatedObject`—This function sets up the KVC between the object and the value to which it refers. The converse of this function is to call it again with the same object and a value of `nil` so that the previous reference is gone.

- ▶ `objc_getAssociatedObject`—This function uses the key to retrieve the value you set up in `objc_setAssociatedObject`.

- ▶ `objc_removeAssociatedObjects`—This function removes all of the values from the object.

You can hide the first two function calls in the custom setters of a declared property so that it truly appears that you are dealing with added instance variables. However, if you do so, add a comment so that it is clear to others (and yourself!) what is going on behind the scenes.

Adding an Associative Reference

Here is the function to call to add an associative reference:

```
void objc_setAssociatedObject(id object, void *key, id value,
  objc_AssociationPolicy policy)
```

`object` is the object to which you want to add the reference. If `object` happens to be a class, this is parallel to adding a new instance variable to the class. However, remember that this can be any `NSObject` instance.

`key` is the key. It is a unique string that is usually declared with code such as the following:

```
static char myKey;
```

`value` is a pointer to the associated reference object.

Finally, `objc_AssociationPolicy` policy uses pre-ARC terminology to define the choices you have for this argument:

```
OBJC_ASSOCIATION_ASSIGN
OBJC_ASSOCIATION_RETAIN_NONATOMIC
OBJC_ASSOCIATION_COPY_NONATOMIC
OBJC_ASSOCIATION_RETAIN
OBJC_ASSOCIATION_COPY
```

As with the options for declared properties, all setting actions are atomic unless otherwise specified. Also, remember that `ASSIGN` specifies a weak link, whereas `RETAIN` specifies a strong one. At the moment, there are no strong/weak values for these constants.

GO TO ▶ "Managing Reference Counts with Arc" in Hour 16, "Managing Memory and Runtime Objects," p. 225, to review the settings for `objc_AssociationPolicy`.

With a strong link (retain), the associative reference remains valid even if the value for the associated reference is released. This is because the `OBJC_ASSOCIATION_RETAIN` retains (increments the reference count) the value object when the association is created.

Getting and Setting an Associative Reference

After you have an associative reference set up, retrieve it using this function:

```
id objc_getAssociatedObject(id object, void *key)
```

▼ TRY IT YOURSELF

Hide the Associated Reference in a Declared Property

You can hide this code in an accessor for a declared property, as shown in the following steps. The result is that for all intents and purposes you have added an instance variable to the class, although it is implemented with an associative reference at runtime. You can create a new test-bed project based on any project for iOS or OS X.

1. Declare a property in an interface. This should be the interface of the class to which you want to add the associative reference. `AppDelegate` is a good choice.

TIP

Note that not all templates provide an app delegate instance. You may want to try a couple to find one that has it.

```
@property (nonatomic, retain) id myAssociativeReference;
```

2. In your implementation, make it dynamic rather than synthesizing it:

```
@implementation AppDelegate
@dynamic myAssociativeReference;
```

3. Define a constant for the key. Keys must be unique, so if you use this code as a model, be certain to make each one different. This can go in the implementation file:

```
static const char *myARKey = "AssociativeReferenceKey";
```

4. To call the three functions described at the beginning of this section, import the appropriate header file at the top of your implementation file:

```
#import <objc/runtime.h>
```

5. Write the getter to access the associative reference:

```
- (id)myAssociativeReference {
   return objc_getAssociatedObject(self, myARKey);
}
```

6. Write the setter to access the associative reference:

```
- (void)setMyAssociativeReference:(id)myAssociativeReference {
  objc_setAssociatedObject(self, myARKey, myAssociativeReference,
    OBJC_ASSOCIATION_RETAIN);
}
```

7. In a method that is called at startup, set the property to a value. You can add this code to `application:didFinishLaunchingWithOptions:`.

```
NSString *testString = @"Test";
self.myvAssociativeReference = testString;
```

8. Retrieve the value into another variable:

```
NSString *testString2 = self.myAssociativeReference;
```

9. Set a breakpoint and follow how the property value is set and then retrieved. Your accessors are using the associative reference, but the code looks as if it were referencing a property based on an instance variable. You can see the results in Figure 19.1.

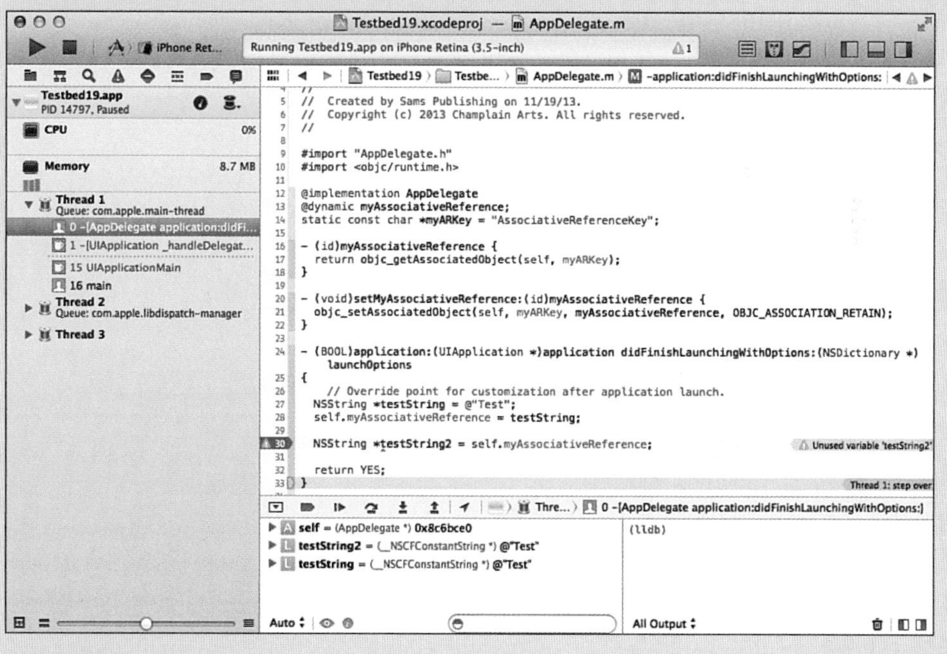

FIGURE 19.1
Test the associative reference.

Removing an Associative Reference for a Key

You remove an associative reference by setting it to `nil` as in the following code:

```
objc_setAssociatedObject(self, myARKey, nil, OBJC_ASSOCIATION_RETAIN);
```

Remember to use the appropriate key. Do not worry about the value of the policy in this case. It has no effect when the value is `nil`.

Removing All Associative References from an Object

It is best to set each associative reference individually, but if you want to remove all of them from an object, you use the following function:

```
void objc_removeAssociatedObjects(id object)
```

Using Fast Enumeration

Whereas associative references provide a feature that did not exist before Objective-C 2.0, fast enumeration makes it much easier to do a very common chore that usually required coding (and recoding) the same control loop. All of the collection objects adopt the `NSFastEnumeration` protocol so you can use it with any of them.

GO TO ▶ Hour 15, "Organizing Data with Collections," p. 205, for more on the collection objects (`NSArray`, `NSSet`, and `NSDictionary`) as well as on `NSEnumerator`.

In a nutshell, fast enumeration gives you an enumerated loop without having to write the control structure. The code is cleaner, and you avoid a potential problem. If you write your own loop, and if the underlying collection is modified while you are looping, you can get into trouble. With fast enumeration, if the underlying collection is modified during the fast enumeration process, an exception is raised so you can handle it.

There are two ways of using fast enumeration: with and without an `NSEnumerator`.

Using Fast Enumeration

This is the simplest way of using fast enumeration.

Use Fast Enumeration Without an `NSEnumerator`

The following steps let you enumerate through any of the collection objects quickly:

1. Start with a collection object that is populated with at least two objects. If you do not have at least two, you cannot tell whether your enumerator is working or not. For the sake of this example, it is assumed that your collection is called `myCollection`. Remember that an `NSArray` contains objects: This array contains two `NSString` objects and one `NSNumber` object.

```
NSArray * myCollection = @[
  @"1", @"2", [NSNumber numberWithInt:3]];
```

2. Create a variable to use in the enumeration. It should be the same type as the objects in the collection. If the objects are of various types, this should be a common superclass—`id` if necessary. This will be set to each object in turn:

```
id myEnumeratedObject;
```

3. Enumerate through the collection and do something with each object:

```
for (myEnumeratedObject in myCollection) {
  // do something with myEnumerationObject
}
```

4. If you need an index, you can create one as you enumerate. This applies only to `NSArray`:

```
NSUInteger counter = 0;
for (myEnumeratedObject in myCollection) {
  // do something with myEnumerationObject
  counter++;
}
```

5. You can combine steps 2 and 3 if you want:

```
for (id myEnumerationObject in myCollection) {
  // do something with myEnumerationObject
}
```

6. You can place any code that you want inside the enumeration block. A common thing to do is to test the enumeration object. As a result of the test, you can use a standard C `break` statement to jump out:

```
if (condition) {
    break;
}
```

Using Fast Enumeration with an `NSEnumerator`

An `NSEnumerator` can let you enumerate an `NSArray` forward or backward. With `NSDictionary` collections, an `NSEnumerator` lets you enumerate over the values or the objects.

`NSEnumerator` instances are created by `NSDictionary` and `NSArray` on demand. For `NSArray`, there are two methods that return `NSEnumerator` objects:

```
- (NSEnumerator *)objectEnumerator
- (NSEnumerator *)reverseObjectEnumerator
```

For `NSDictionary`, two methods return `NSEnumerator` objects that enumerate through the keys and objects, respectively:

```
- (NSEnumerator *)keyEnumerator
- (NSEnumerator *)objectEnumerator
```

You use these methods as in the following code:

```
NSEnumerator *myEnumerator = [myArray reverseObjectEnumerator];
```

No matter which type of `NSEnumerator` you use, the basic process is the same. After you have your collection, create the `NSEnumerator` you want to use. The syntax in steps 3 and 5 changes to use the `NSEnumerator` instead of the collection:

```
for (id myEnumerationObject in myEnumerator) {
}
```

Summary

In this hour, you saw how to use associative references to simulate adding instance variables to classes and fast enumeration to make your collection loops safer and easier to read. Both features were added to Objective-C 2.0. This means that if you are maintaining old Objective-C code, you might be able to simplify it and sometimes speed it up by using these features. However, because this is happening at runtime, remember to ensure that your keys are unique so that there is no confusion about what is being added to the class.

Q&A

Q. What is the variable in the fast enumeration loop for?

A. It contains each enumerated object.

Q. What is the performance penalty for using fast enumeration?

A. None. It is faster than other techniques.

Workshop

Quiz

1. How can you use associative references as if they were properties?

2. In what way can fast enumeration make your code safer to run?

Quiz Answers

1. Declare a property and make it dynamic in your implementation file. Build your own getter and setter that use the associative reference functions behind the scenes.

2. Fast enumeration can raise an exception if the underlying collection changes as you are enumerating across it.

Activities

Take some existing code that uses traditional loops and convert it to fast enumeration. Look for the gnarliest and ugliest looping code so that you can see what the conversion to fast enumeration can give you. If you are new to a project, ask people who have worked on it for a while to show you the nightmare looping code. They'll probably know just where to look.

HOUR 20
Working with Blocks

What You'll Learn in This Hour

- ▶ Comparing blocks to callbacks
- ▶ Using `typedef` and function pointers
- ▶ Declaring blocks
- ▶ Using blocks

Revisiting Blocks

Blocks are not new; they were a part of Smalltalk and other languages 30 or more years ago. (In some cases, they were referred to as closures for reasons that you see in this section.) They show up in Ruby, Python, and Lisp as well. For a variety of reasons, they were not implemented on OS X until Snow Leopard (10.6); they have been in iOS since version 4. Because of their long history, for many people using blocks on OS X or iOS, it is a matter of revisiting concepts they might know from other languages or even from long-ago basic programming courses.

Blocks take advantage of one of the most basic principles of computers in the twentieth century; computers store and manipulate digital data. And here is the critical principle: Digital data can represent data in the sense of numbers or text just as easily as it can represent computer instructions. It is all digital, and it is all managed in basically the same way.

GO TO ▶ Hour 22, "Grand Central Dispatch: Using Queues and Threading," p. 283, for additional information on blocks.

A *block* is a chunk of code that can be assigned to a variable or property similarly to the way in which you would assign an `int` or a `struct` or an object to a variable or property. You need not assign the chunk of code to a variable or property; you can also reference it in an expression.

Whether assigned to a variable or property or used in an expression, a block can access variables that are defined at the time it is assigned or used. The closure terminology refers to the fact that the block closes around the values of variables at the time it is defined. In this way, those variables differ from arguments that could be passed into a function.

Blocks are frequently used in loops. They are also frequently used in framework methods in much the same way as callback functions have been used in C and its derivative languages. Methods such as `enumerateObjectsUsingBlock:` in `NSArray` let you pass in a block as an argument to be used in the enumeration. A similar method in `NSSet` is used in the same way, whereas in `NSDictionary`, `enumerateKeysAndObjectsUsingBlock:` is available. Not to be outdone, `NSString` has `enumerateLinesUsingBlock:`.

NOTE

Finding More on Enumerate Methods Using Blocks

These classes and methods are described more fully later in this hour.

Looking at Callbacks

Blocks are similar in some ways to callback functions, which have long been used in C and Objective-C as well as other programming languages. Callbacks are often used in real-time processing, so you find them in Core Audio and similar frameworks of Cocoa. A callback is typically passed in as a parameter in some code that manages an event that might occur (and recur) over time.

At some point (the end of a movie clip, for example), the process is over, and certain completion code needs to be called. This is a common example of a callback. You pass in a pointer to the completion routine, and it is called at the appropriate moment. Callbacks used in this way are often a more elegant and efficient way than polling the ongoing event to see if it is finished and then performing the completion routine.

GO TO ▶ Hour 17, "Extending a Class with Protocols and Delegates," p. 231, for information on delegates, which in some cases can provide similar functionality to blocks.

One way of looking at callback functions is that in some ways they are like supercharged functions. A function can take any number of arguments that you pass in when you call it (as long as they are defined). This goes to the heart of what a function is—code that can function on data that is passed into it at runtime.

Callback functions are functions that can be passed in at runtime, just as is the case with data (again, as long as the definition allows them). Being able to change not only the data on which a function acts, but also the functions that it may call in the course of its processing allows for a great deal of flexibility.

The only tricky part of callback programming is that you need to somehow package a C function in a format that can be passed in as a parameter to the function or method that is going to call it. You do that by passing it in as a function pointer. There are two versions of function pointers:

▶ Function pointers using `typedef`

▶ Inline function pointers

The two styles are shown in the following sections.

TRY IT YOURSELF ▼

Use a `typedef` Function Pointer

Using a `typedef` function pointer can make your code more readable (not everyone agrees with this, however), and the following steps make the process fairly explicit. Inline function pointers (described in the next section) may be more compact.

1. Create a new testbed project, as shown in Figure 20.1. The example shown here uses the iOS Single View Application template.

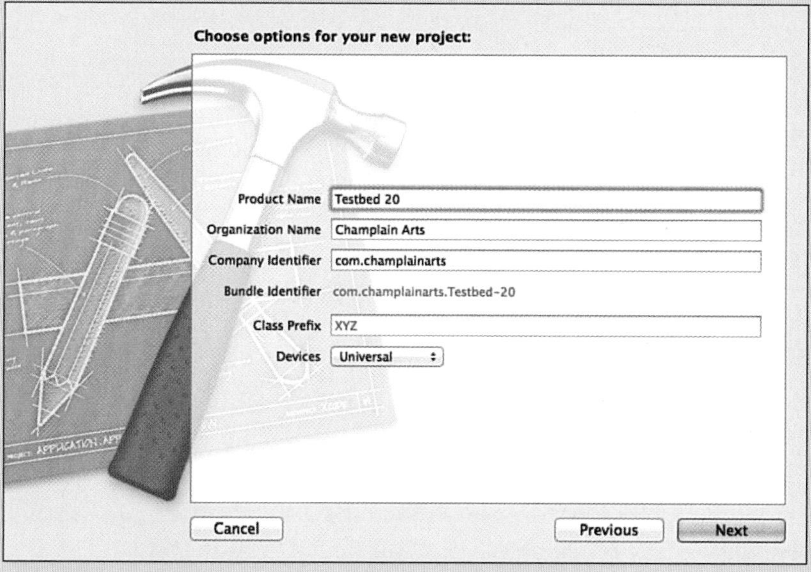

FIGURE 20.1
Create a new project.

2. In AppDelegate.m, create a `typedef` for a pointer to a function that will be used as a callback routine. The function pointer's name is enclosed in parentheses with the asterisk. If you place the asterisk outside the parentheses, it means that the function is returning a pointer. Instead of that, you want a pointer to the function itself.

```
typedef float(*TypeDefFunction)(int myInt);
```

3. Declare a method that will use the `typedef` that you declared in step 2. In this example, the method will pass in a pointer as defined in step 2 as well as a `float` value. For demonstration purposes, that float value will be passed into the function pointer as you will see in step 5).

```
float useTypeDefFunctionPointer (TypeDefFunction myTypeDefFunction, int
inputInt);
```

4. Declare a callback function that will be passed into `useTypeDefFunctionPointer`:

```
float myCallBack (int anInt);
```

5. Define the method that will use the `typedef` you created in step 3. The critical line is the first one after the comment: There the function that is passed in (`myTypeDefFunction`) is called and the argument that is passed in (`inputFloat`) is passed into that function:

```
float useTypeDefFunctionPointer (TypeDefFunction myTypeDefFunction, int
inputInt) {
    // do something with the function pointer and argument
    float myFloat = myTypeDefFunction (inputInt);
    return myFloat;
}
```

6. Define the callback function. As you can see, it is a simple function that takes a single argument, divides it by 2, and returns it. The function and the argument to be passed in are the two arguments declared in step 2:

```
float myCallBack (int anInt) {
    // do something with the argument
    return anInt / 2.0;
}
```

7. Call the function declared in step 3 and defined in step 6. You can place it in `application:didFinishLaunchingWithOptions:` to make sure it is called:

```
float myReturnedFloat = useTypeDefFunctionPointer (myCallBack, 17);
```

8. Place breakpoints in the code, as shown in Figure 20.2. You can trace the sequence of execution as the line of code in `application:didFinishLaunchingWithOptions:` dynamically calls the callback function at runtime with a value that is also set as a parameter at runtime.

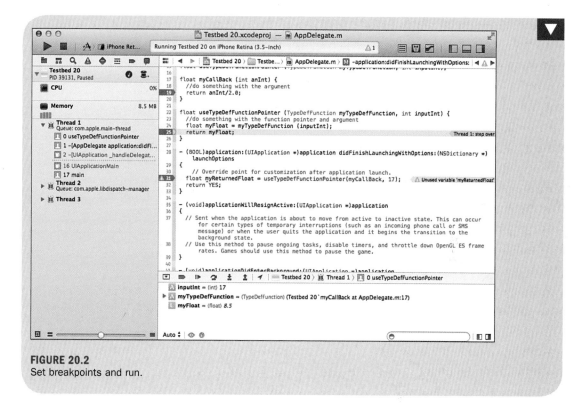

FIGURE 20.2
Set breakpoints and run.

Instead of using a `typedef`, you can use an inline function pointer to achieve the same result. This means a bit less typing (some people would say it is less clear for that reason).

Considering Callback Routines

Callback routines are part of C and many other languages. In C, they are implemented with basic constructs of the language that may be put together in a way that people are unfamiliar with, but there really is nothing new there.

The most important point to remember is that with both the inline function pointer and the `typedef` declaration, the name of the function is a dummy. You replace it in your use with a function that you declare.

Introducing Blocks

Blocks in Objective-C are implemented differently from callback functions in three important ways:

▶ Objective-C blocks are objects at runtime.

▶ Blocks can access data from the scope in which they are defined. This means that when a block is called, it has access to the data available where it was defined even if that data is no longer available. The access to this data is read-only.

▶ The syntax of a block declaration uses a special character (^), and for many people this makes the block syntax more readable.

NOTE

Callbacks, Delegates, and Blocks

Blocks have similarities to callback functions. Also, as noted previously in Objective-C, the functionality of callback functions is often implemented using delegates. Bear in mind that these three concepts are related, but they are certainly not identical. In this section, you will see the basics of how to work with blocks. The main example is roughly comparable to the example shown for callbacks, but it is not identical.

Just as with callback functions, you can create a block as a variable or as a `typedef`; you can also create a block inline. Although it is slightly more verbose, declaring a block as a variable or using a `typedef` is somewhat clearer, and as you will see, in some cases, it is preferred.

As noted previously, this section is generally similar to the preceding function pointer section.

Creating a Block as a Block Variable

You can declare a block as a variable. The main difference in the syntax is that block declarations use a carat (^) rather than an asterisk, as is the case with pointers. You can declare a block using syntax such as this:

```
float(^myBlock)(int, float);
```

This represents a block named `myBlock` that will take two arguments, an `int` and a `float`. It will return a `float`.

The `typedef` method shown for function pointers is preferred if you are going to be using this pattern several times. It can put your block declarations together in one place, and the same definition can be used for several blocks. The previous declaration can become a `typedef` as follows:

```
typedef float(^MyBlockType)(int, float);
```

To create a variable, use the `typedef` just as you ordinarily would, and provide the code for the block:

```
MyBlockType myBlock = ^(int myInt, float myDivisor) {
  return myInt / myDivisor;
};
```

Using a Block Variable

Use a block variable just as you would a function:

```
float myFloat = myBlock (17, 2.0);
```

Make a Block from a Callback Function

Using the callback function example from the previous section, you can convert it into block syntax using the following steps:

1. Create a `typedef` for the block. This is similar to the `typedef` for a function pointer, but it is introduced by a ^.

   ```
   typedef float(^TypeDefBlock)(int, float);
   ```

TIP

Note that this code is simplified for the sake of example. Following the name of the block, the pair of parentheses can contain a list of arguments to the block that you can fill in when you use the block. If there are no arguments, use `void`.

2. Create a function that uses that `typedef` to declare a block for a function that can be passed in at runtime:

   ```
   TypeDefBlock myBlock = ^(int myInt, float myDivisor) {
     return myInt / myDivisor;
   };
   ```

   This definition of the block can reference variables in scope at the time the block is created with this code. They are evaluated and placed into the block as read-only values, but they are available to you as the block executes.

3. Call the function you declared in step 1 with the replacement function you declared in step 2:

```
float myFloat = myBlock (17, 2.0);
```

4. Set a breakpoint on the line you entered in step 3 and run.

NOTE

Finding Out More About Blocks and Block Syntax

The code in the previous steps is deliberately basic and bare bones. Continue to the next section, "Exploring Blocks in Cocoa," to see real-life examples of blocks and how they can be used. You also see how to use a block variable as a function argument in Cocoa methods.

Exploring Blocks in Cocoa

Some of the major enumeration methods are described in this section, but you should be aware that they are far from the only enumeration methods in Cocoa that use blocks. Also, these are just the highlights of the methods for some of the classes that implement block-based enumeration. Check the class reference for the classes you are interested in to find more enumeration methods.

All of these methods use the same basic structure: They enumerate over an object that may be a collection object or an object that otherwise consists of discrete entities such as lines in a string. They specify the format of the block that you pass in (that is, its signature). One of the arguments in the block is typically a `BOOL` named stop. You set this to `YES` to stop the enumeration at that point.

Here is an overview of the major block enumeration methods in Cocoa. Each has a companion method that includes an `options` argument. Thus, `NSArray` has `enumerateObjectsUsing-Block:` as well as `enumerateObjectsWithOptions:usingBlock:`.

The options are as follows:

▶ `NSEnumerationConcurrent`—This is taken as a hint but might improve the speed on multicore devices. Your block's code must be safe against concurrent invocation (that is, it must be able to be performed on two cores at the same time without each copy interfering with the other).

▶ **NSEnumerationReverse**—This is undefined for NSDictionary and NSSet objects because they are unordered. When selected together with NSEnumerationConcurrent, it is also undefined. It is a good idea to stay away from undefined operations. They are not errors, but their behavior is indeterminate.

TIP

You Can Enumerate Small Objects

When you think about enumerating over items, it is reasonable to think about the computer whirring away through collections with hundreds or even thousands of objects in them. That is a reasonable thought, and, particularly with today's multicore computers running Cocoa-based apps, the speed is impressive.

However, small-scale enumerations are just as valuable, and an argument can be made in favor of using block enumerations over only a single object to be enumerated. The rationale for using small-scale enumerations is that the blocks structure your code and focus your attention very well. Among other things, this means that if at some time in the future you need to do the same thing to 1,000 objects that you do to a single object in a special-case part of your app, the conversion to a block-based enumeration is simple.

NSString enumerateLinesUsingBlock:

This is a frequently used method that enumerates each line in a string and applies a block to it. Note that in this and other interfaces, the actual block code is shown as {...}. Here is the interface:

```
- (void)enumerateLinesUsingBlock:(void (^)(NSString *line, BOOL *stop)){...}
```

To help you construct this and the following method calls, here is a typical basic implementation. You can use a block that you have declared as described in the previous section, "Using a Block Variable." However, just as with function pointers, sometimes an inline declaration instead of a variable is easier and faster to write. It may be less clear to future code maintainers, and if you are using it in several places, the block declaration is preferable.

```
[myString enumerateLinesUsingBlock: ^(NSString *line, BOOL *stop) {
  // extract value from line using something like
  // if value is END...
  *stop = YES; }
];
```

As each line is enumerated, your block is called with that line stripped of its terminators so that you can quickly deal with it. The two typical things that you might want to do are the following:

▶ Evaluate the line and possibly store its data in an object or other location.

TIP

If you convert each line to an object, chances are you will be storing them in a collection.

▶ Based on your evaluation, you may stop the enumeration.

NSArray `enumerateObjectsUsingBlock:`

This method starts from the beginning of the array and continues with each item until it reaches the end or until you set the block variable `stop` to `YES`.

Note that you get each object in turn back in `obj`; you also get its index in `idx`. Based on either value (or something else entirely), you can stop the enumeration.

```
-    (void)enumerateObjectsUsingBlock:(void (^)(id obj, NSUInteger idx, BOOL
*stop)){...}
```

Listing 20.1 shows an example of how you would use that method on an array called `myArray`:

LISTING 20.1   Using `enumterateObjectsUsingBlock:`

```
[myArray enumerateObjectsUsingBlock:^(id obj, NSUInteger idx, BOOL *stop) {
  do something with obj and/or idx
  if (someTest)
    {stop = YES};
}];
```

NSSet `enumerateObjectsUsingBlock:`

Sets are not ordered, so if you compare the `NSSet` method with the `NSArray` method, you will see that the index is not returned or set:

```
- (void)enumerateObjectsUsingBlock:(void (^)(id obj, BOOL *stop)) {...}
```

NSDictionary `enumerateKeysAndObjectsUsingBlock:`

Dictionaries are not ordered, but for each value there is a key. Thus, the basic enumeration method for `NSDictionary` looks a bit like the method for `NSArray`, returning a value and a key for `NSDictionary` compared with a value and an index for `NSArray`:

```
- (void)enumerateKeysAndObjectsUsingBlock:(void (^)(id key, id obj, BOOL *stop))
{...}
```

Looking Deeper into Cocoa Blocks and Memory

Blocks are objects that, by default, are allocated on the stack. When execution leaves the scope in which the block is defined, it means they are gone—unless you copy them to the heap.

To copy a block to the heap, declare it as a block variable and then copy with this code:

```
[myBlock copy];
```

There are also C functions: `Block_copy()` and `Block_release()`.

You can use the `__block storage` type modifier for local variables as in this case:

```
__block double myDouble;
```

This places the variable in a storage location that is shared between the normal scope of the variable and all blocks declared or created within that scope. This means that you can import this variable into any of those blocks and modify it if you need to.

Summary

This hour explored blocks and how they are different from C callback functions. You have seen how to create them as the syntax to use them with basic Cocoa objects, such as the enumeration methods for `NSArray`, `NSDictionary`, and `NSet`.

Q&A

Q. What variables can a block reference?

A. A block can reference variables declared as `__block` in the scope in which the block is declared as well as the arguments passed into it.

Q. What is the preferred way to declare a block?

A. Using a `typedef` is the preferred way to declare a block. If you are declaring it inline, that can be more concise.

Workshop

Quiz

1. How long can a block be?

2. If you are using a __block variable in a block, what happens when control exits the scope in which the variable is declared?

Quiz Answers

1. There is no hard-and-fast rule, but most blocks are short and to the point.

2. It is still valid in the block until the block is exited.

Activities

Experiment with the enumeration methods described in this chapter, adding NSLog methods to see what is happening as you enumerate and evaluate items in the collections.

HOUR 21
Handling Exceptions and Errors

What You'll Learn in This Hour

▶ Using exceptions in today's software

▶ Throwing exceptions

▶ Working with the try/catch/finally blocks

▶ Logging incidents

Rethinking Exceptions and Errors

Most programming languages today provide some method for handling exceptions and errors—events that must interrupt the normal flow of processing because that normal flow of processing cannot handle the event that has occurred. Modern exception handling usually provides a structure that lets you react programmatically to the type of error and, if possible, take remedial action.

Compared with software from a decade or longer ago, today's best software is much less verbose. Instead of reporting each problem as it occurs, software increasingly attempts to either prevent problems or to resolve them automatically. Sometimes problem resolution techniques are simple, such as automatically retrying a communication link three times before giving up and reporting a failure instead of reporting the problem on the first try. In cases such as this, you may well want to log the failed attempts even though you do not interrupt the user until you are certain you cannot recover. This makes debugging easier.

As software, operating systems, and hardware have evolved, people are doing more complex tasks with software than they were doing in many cases in the past, and, in many cases, they are doing those tasks with less support from traditional sources. The rise of crowdsourcing problem-solving sites, which was initially opposed by many corporate developers, is now widely accepted—because it often works.

All these changes in the computing environment mean that exception handling is, in many cases, focused on somehow completing either the task the user has asked for or a task that moves the user forward and stops at a point that is knowable and logical for both computer user and whatever support resources are available.

NOTE

Moving to a Logical and Knowable Place

In a large number of cases, when a user and app get into trouble, the issue can only be unraveled with the assistance of people with two separate skills, such as software engineering and domain knowledge. If an exception can be handled by moving to a place where either a software engineer or a domain specialist can resolve it, it can save a great deal of time and expense.

What most users desire is software that continues to behave as they expect it to. They do not want to even know about failures that they cannot resolve themselves or that do not matter. Today's developers try to oblige.

The commonly used distinction between errors and exceptions is that errors can usually be recovered from—perhaps automatically. Exceptions may be fatal. Furthermore, errors often are caused by users, while exceptions are the result+ of action (or inaction) on the part of the developer. (These concepts are rooted in Java.) Apple's Human Interface Guidelines for their various devices (particularly for the iOS devices) have a number of ideas on how to keep apps from visibly failing. *Error Handling Programming Guide* and *Exception Programming Topics* also provide additional information. In addition, searching for NSException and NSError on the developer site will reveal dozens of sample code projects.

Introducing the Exception and Error Classes

Two direct subclasses of NSObject are used in Cocoa and Objective-C to handle unexpected events. They have different structures and different uses. Exceptions and errors are described in the following sections. After that, you look inside the classes that implement them (NSException and NSError).

Although there are distinctions between exceptions and errors, ultimately the decision of which to use is up to you. This has become more important with the advent of 64-bit executables. The reason is that throwing exceptions in 64-bit is much more expensive than it was in 32-bit executables. On the other hand, @try blocks are much more efficient in 64-bit. Apple's advice for 64-bit is that, "you should throw exceptions only when absolutely necessary."

Using Exceptions

Exceptions are typically *thrown* (or *raised*) as the app runs. They include conditions such as attempting to access a nonexistent object or variable whether it is through an invalid array subscript or a dangling pointer. They also can arise from passing invalid arguments into methods.

Be Careful with Dynamism

A great deal of the power of Objective-C comes from its dynamic features. You can use `id` variables that can refer to any object in many cases. This lets you do remarkable things, such as write a method with an argument that you expect at runtime to be either an `NSWindow`, or an `NSView`. (Some object-oriented hierarchies link the two classes.) However, if you do so, the burden is on you and the developers who use your code to check that what actually is in that `id` variable at runtime is not a totally different object, such as an `NSDocument`. Many people believe that using `id` only when static typing is not feasible might be a good way to go—particularly if you are new to Objective-C. When you are comfortable with the dynamic features and the introspection methods such as the `NSObject class` method, you can relax.

You often cannot predict when these conditions will arise, but in many cases you can write brief snippets of code to test if they might arise before you do something (such as reference an object that might be `nil`) and then prevent them from arising. After an exception is raised, the app normally quits soon thereafter. It is common (but not necessary) to subclass `NSException`.

Using Errors

Unlike exceptions, errors are for issues that don't require the app to quit. They have features allowing you to localize an error string so that you can present detailed error information to users. These include conditions such as low (or no) memory, a communication link that does not exist (or that has suddenly disappeared), and the like. Sometimes the app can simply retry the task; other times the user needs to be involved. There are cases where both strategies may be used. For example, in the absence of a communication link, the app may retry to connect three times. If that doesn't work, the user is brought into the picture to try to troubleshoot the connection.

NOTE

"Error 17" is not detailed error information.

In keeping with the trend to not be verbose, the basic error message might not need to explain that three attempts have been made and failed, but that information can be logged so that users can access it if necessary.

Looking Inside NSException

Inside every NSException instance are three properties (one is optional):

▶ **name**—This is an NSString that uniquely identifies the type of exception. (Methods of NSException—such as callStackSymbols—can identify where this particular exception occurred.)

▶ **reason**—This is an NSString that contains a human-readable string explaining the exception. You can pass it along to users or use it as the basis for an NSError.

▶ **userInfo** (optional)—This is an NSDictionary containing key-value pairs with additional information that is primarily for developers to use in choosing what actions to take to ameliorate or bypass the exception. It also can be used to log the problem in the console.

GO TO ▶ "Reading and Writing Dictionaries" in Hour 15, p. 213, for more on dictionaries and how they can be used to pass structured data through as a single object in a method call.

Looking Inside NSError

Three different properties are inside NSError (two are required, and one is optional):

▶ **code**—This is an NSInteger that identifies the error (the values for the Cocoa domain are shown in Table 21.1).

▶ **domain**—This NSString identifies the error's domain (the values are shown in Table 21.2).

▶ **userInfo** (optional)—This is an NSDictionary that may contain key-value pairs further describing the error.

TABLE 21.1 NSError Domain Codes

NSMachErrorDomain
NSPOSIXErrorDomain
NSOSStatusErrorDomain
NSCocoaErrorDomain

TABLE 21.2   NSError **Error Codes in the Cocoa Domain**

NSFileNoSuchFileError

NSFileLockingError

NSFileReadUnknownError

NSFileReadNoPermissionError

NSFileReadInvalidFileNameError

NSFileReadCorruptFileError

NSFileReadNoSuchFileError

NSFileReadInapplicableStringEncodingError

NSFileReadUnsupportedSchemeError

NSFileReadTooLargeError

NSFileReadUnknownStringEncodingError

NSFileWriteUnknownError

NSFileWriteNoPermissionError

NSFileWriteInvalidFileNameError

NSFileWriteFileExistsError

NSFileWriteInapplicableStringEncodingError

NSFileWriteUnsupportedSchemeError

NSFileWriteOutOfSpaceError

NSFileWriteVolumeReadOnlyError

NSKeyValueValidationError

NSFormattingError

NSUserCancelledError

NSFileErrorMinimum

NSFileErrorMaximum

NSValidationErrorMinimum

NSValidationErrorMaximum

NSFormattingErrorMinimum

NSFormattingErrorMaximum

```
NSPropertyListReadCorruptError

NSPropertyListReadUnknownVersionError

NSPropertyListReadStreamError

NSPropertyListWriteStreamError

NSPropertyListErrorMinimum

NSPropertyListErrorMaximum


NSExecutableErrorMinimum

NSExecutableNotLoadableError

NSExecutableArchitectureMismatchError

NSExecutableRuntimeMismatchError

NSExecutableLoadError

NSExecutableLinkError

NSExecutableErrorMaximum
```

In addition, four methods provide localized assistance for users:

- ▶ `localizedDescription` (NSString)

- ▶ `localizedRecoveryOptions` (NSArray)

- ▶ `localizedRecoverySuggestion` (NSString)

- ▶ `localizedFailureReason` (NSString)

(For more information, consult the `NSError` class reference in Xcode or on developer.apple.com.)

These let you localize the description, recovery options (these are presented as button names), as well as a suggestion and reason for the failure.

Using Errors in Cocoa and Cocoa Touch

Although the internal structure of `NSError` is the same on Cocoa and Cocoa Touch, you use it in different ways in part due to the difference in the interfaces. The documentation for each OS on developer.apple.com provides you with details of using `NSError` with sheets and alerts (on OS X) and with pop-overs (on iOS).

With both `NSException` and `NSError`, the structure that you set up for name values (`NSException`) and domain values (`NSError`) is crucial. With the right sets of names and domains, you can use the `userInfo` dictionary to refine the problem that has been encountered.

Many of the domain values for NSError are shown in Table 21.1. The error codes for the Cocoa domain are shown in Table 21.2. As you scan through the error codes, you will see the types of errors that can be caught. (Note that some of them are placeholders for ranges of errors; they are the error codes that contain minimum and maximum to delimit the range.) It's a fact of development life that as more features and frameworks are added to Cocoa and Cocoa Touch, more domain values and error codes are added.

Identifying an Exception

The most common exception pattern in Objective-C (and many other languages) is based on try/catch/finally blocks. The conceptual structure is shown in Listing 21.1.

LISTING 21.1 Objective-C Try/Catch Block

```
@try {
    // code that could fail
}
@catch (NSException *exception) {
    // code to perform if there has been a failure
}
@finally {
    // code that is performed regardless of success/failure
}
@end
```

This is the conceptual structure. There is a code snippet for an Objective-C try/catch/finally block that you can drag from the Code Snippet library into your code, as shown in Figure 21.1.

TIP

Make sure you pick up the Objective-C snippet because there is also a C++ snippet. The snippet contains placeholders that you replace with your own code. As you do that, the errors you see in Figure 21.1 will disappear.

The @try block contains code that might raise or throw an exception. This can happen because you deliberately raise or throw it based on a condition that you have found in your code or the environment, or it can happen because an exception is thrown while control is in that block, but it is thrown by something other than an explicit action in your code. For example, if a line of code in your @try block calls a method that calls another and another, an exception may be thrown several calls away when, perhaps, a dangling pointer is dereferenced. The exception is passed up the exception chain until it finds an @catch block that traps it. All of this is managed for you; all you have to do is declare the @try block along with @catch and @finally.

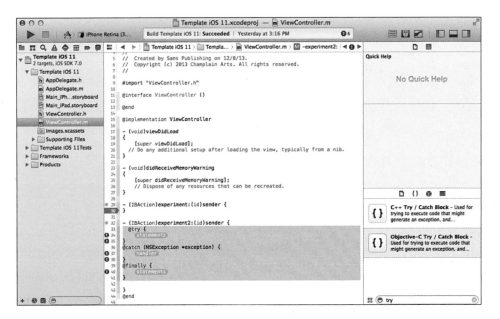

FIGURE 21.1
Drag a try/catch snippet from the library into your code.

@finally is the code that is performed at the end of the block regardless of success or failure. It may set a value—perhaps from temporary values set in @try and @catch.

TIP
Note that @finally can be an empty block.

Throwing an Exception

Throwing (or raising) an exception is a two-step process:

▶ Create an NSException instance (or an instance of a subclass).

▶ Throw (or raise) it.

For many people, the simplest way to create an NSException instance is to use the class factory method:

```
+ (NSException *)exceptionWithName:(NSString *)name
   reason:(NSString *)reason
   userInfo:(NSDictionary *)userInfo
```

There are other techniques described in the NSException class reference on developer.apple.com and in Xcode Help.

Throw an Exception

You may throw or raise an exception yourself. If you do, it will be passed up the exception chain until it hits an @catch block. These steps show you how to throw an exception:

1. If you will be passing in a dictionary, create it and fill the key-value pairs.

TIP

The dictionary keys vary by the specific subclass (if any) of NSException.

GO TO ▶ Hour 15, "Organizing Data with Collections," p. 205, for more information on creating dictionaries.

2. Prepare the name and reason strings. If you have constant strings, this code will do, but it is preferable to declare these strings in defines so that they are all in one place.

```
NSString *myName = @"MyExceptionName";
NSString *myReason = @"MyExceptionReason";
```

3. Create the exception instance with code such as this:

```
NSException *myException = [NSException exceptionWithName: myName
    reason: myReason
    userInfo: myDictionary];
```

TIP

Remember that userInfo is optional: You can pass nil.

4. Throw or raise the exception. Use only one of these lines of code. raise is used only for NSException objects. It is possible, but not particularly common, to throw other types of objects.

```
@throw myException; //use only one of these lines
[myException raise];
```

Catching an Exception

You catch an exception in an `@catch` block, as shown previously in Listing 21.1. You can have several of these blocks with each one catching a separate exception. They are selected at runtime based on the class of the exception. As noted previously, you can subclass `NSException` for different exceptions. Each `@catch` block handles one class or subclass of `NSException`. The last block may handle a totally generic `id` exception. In addition to handling different exceptions in different ways, you can also create a new `NSException` instance and throw it. In that way, you can transform one exception into another.

GO TO ▶ Hour 23, "Working with the Debugger," p. 293, to find out about using the log and `NSConsole`. They are used with errors and exceptions as well as the debugger.

Summary

This hour has shown you the ways to handle exceptions that are typically fatal issues and errors that can often be worked around. As noted, the distinction is conceptual and practical—exceptions are more expensive to use than errors on 64-bit architectures.

Q&A

Q. What changes in error handling have occurred in the last few years?

A. Apps are becoming less verbose as they handle issues on their own without bothering users.

Q. How can you prevent exceptions?

A. Typical methods are to check for dangling or `nil` pointers before dereferencing them and making certain that objects exist. If you are worried about performance, test with and without these small tests. Typically, unless you are in a very tight loop, there is no reason not to make these basic tests.

Workshop

Quiz

1. How do you implement separate `@catch` blocks?
2. Should you quit after posting an error alert to a user?

Quiz Answers

1. Use different subclasses of `NSException` and `NSException` itself and create a catch block for each one.

2. Typically, exceptions are followed up by the app quitting. With errors, the user can often continue.

Activities

Browse discussion boards for apps and review the comments about error handling and what people do not like about it in various apps. This should not be difficult. Error handling is a common complaint, and you should be able to see what really bothers people.

Grand Central Dispatch: Using Queues and Threading

What You'll Learn in This Hour

▶ Exploring the Grand Central Dispatch mechanism with blocks

▶ Using a queue

▶ Using a concurrent queue

Getting Started with Concurrency

Concurrency refers to the ability of a computer to run more than one task at the same time. Because all processor operations are carried out by the computer's processor, the capabilities of the processor come into play with concurrency.

NOTE

Running Multiple Tasks at the Same Time—What It Doesn't Mean

When talking about concurrency, people are referring to processor tasks. A program can send a request to a printer to print a page, and the computer can continue processing other tasks while the printer chugs away. The computer can further send a request to a disk drive to read or write some data, and that operation can proceed without concurrency; printers and disk drives frequently chug away at the same time. The processor is normally only involved with sending an instruction to print or an instruction to read or write. The peripheral devices receive the instruction and then carry on their own processing. Computers actually have a number of separate processors, including processors to control communications. This discussion is in regard to the central processor.

Looking at Processors Inside Computers

Many people refer to the computer and its processor synonymously. One computer has one processor, and that is the end of the story—at least until the advent of multicore chips. Each core on a chip is its own processor, and the chip contains management software that often allows each core to access shared data. (Note that this is a high-level conceptual overview.)

For computers with a single processor (or core), concurrency is pretty much irrelevant. There are many of those devices in use today, but Apple's current lineup of computers is multicore. The first iPad and iPhone models before the 4S were single core, but the newer versions use multicore chips.

As soon as you have multiple cores, the question naturally arises: How do you use the processing power they contain? Going back to the days of mainframe computers, engineers have devised various ways to use the power of multiple processors. Most of these techniques involve rewriting code because code written for a single processor does not naturally or automatically adapt to running on multiple processors.

Using Concurrency Without Rewriting User Apps

Fortunately, rewriting code to take advantage of multiple processors need not pose a significant burden on developers. This is because, on most computers, the biggest single user of the processor is the operating system itself. The high-level programming instructions that developers write are converted during the compile/build process to the actual processor instructions (and there may be several layers of abstraction involved in the process).

As Apple started to explore multicore chips for their hardware, it also started exploring the changes to the operating systems that would enable the OSs to take advantage of the multicore chips. Apple shipped its first multiprocessor computer with the Power Mac Gigabit Ethernet model in the summer of 2000. One of the considerations involved in moving to NeXTSTEP was the hope that it would make the transition to multiprocessing Macs easier and faster than other alternatives.

In addition to starting to implement concurrency in rewrites of the operating system, Apple used Xcode to explore ways in which concurrency could be used to speed up application programs. Over time, the concurrency code in the operating system has become much more sophisticated, and the number of multicore processors has proliferated, as has the number of cores on multiprocessor cores themselves.

Using Threads for Concurrency

Threads are sequences of tasks running inside a single process. In a single-processor environment, one thread can run at a time. However, the operating system can swiftly switch from one thread to another, which can give the impression that multiple threads are running at the same time.

With multicore processors, multiple threads can, indeed, run at the same time. In documentation, you frequently find references to the concept of thread-safe code. Because multiple threads in the same app might be accessing shared memory at the same time, thread-safe code contains safeguards so that two threads do not corrupt the shared store.

Programming with threads can be a bit tricky because it is up to the implementer to manage the threads. Furthermore, in today's world of multicore processors in various configurations, using threads can involve significant amounts of code that are aware of the configuration of cores on which they are running. Thus, threads can be a challenge to implement in general as well as being challenging with regard to the environment in which they are running. In some ways, this aspect of threads is a throwback to the 1940s and 1950s in which, in many cases, programs were written for specific computers. The situation still exists today in some areas of software development.

NOTE

Processors, Chips, Cores, and CPUs

Each of these terms has a different, specific meaning. However, in Apple's diagrams and in this book, CPU, the abbreviation for central processing unit, is used in the context of Grand Central Dispatch (GCD) to describe what is usually a core within a chip. This avoids repeating the fact that what is called a CPU in this context might be a chip or a core within a chip.

Introducing Grand Central Dispatch (GCD)

GCD is the technology that Apple uses to manage concurrency on iOS and OS X. It was introduced with iOS 4 and OS X 10.6 (Snow Leopard) and has continued to evolve.

Looking at the Overall GCD Design

GCD is built on the concept of queues, which is described in the following section. Queues are designed to be easily accessed by developers in an abstract environment. The specific processing that you often have to specify with regard to threads is now implemented deep in the operating system (specifically, in the Darwin kernel).

GCD is what helps make your multicore Mac or iOS device perky. The enormous amount of processing power required to make the user interface responsive at the same time processing power is required to compile and build your latest app can be managed with GCD.

Using GCD

Between the iOS and OS X operating systems and Xcode on OS X, if you are using Apple hardware that is fairly recent, you are using GCD and concurrency (and so, most likely, are your users). GCD is automatic in many cases, but you can also write explicitly to use the features of GCD.

Apps that benefit most from GCD are those that do intensive and often repetitive calculations; computing the square root of a single number might benefit from concurrency in the implementation of the square root function that you and other apps call, but that single process is unlikely to benefit from concurrency.

Calculation-heavy processes that might benefit from concurrency and multicore processors have typically been found in image- and video-processing apps as well as apps for long-term weather and climate forecasts and calculation-intensive apps such as brute-force decryption of data as well as artificial intelligence applications, including language and image recognition. In addition to calculation-intensive apps, real-time apps that must run at a given speed also traditionally have used multiprocessing and concurrency to stay on top of their changing data.

Introducing Queues

Queues are at the heart of GCD and of many other computer structures. A *queue* is a line of objects, whether those objects are people at a bus stop or tasks to be run in a computer. The queues used in GCD are first in, first out (FIFO) just like the queue at a bus stop. If you are the first person in line, you are the first person on the bus.

Just as with the bus queue, there are exceptions to the FIFO rule. Passengers with disabilities may jump the queue at the suggestion of a dispatcher or bus driver. In some societies, passengers may also jump the queue by brute force; others may jump the queue by bribing their way onto the bus ahead of other people.

At this point, the real-life instance of bus queues is left behind with the note that jumping the FIFO queue in GCD is possible at the behest of the developer. The chaos of brute force or bribery have no parallels in GCD.

GCD has several types of queues, which are outlined in this section. In thinking about these types of queues, remember that their characteristics are designed not only to allow developers to use the appropriate features for the concurrent processes, but also to create queues that, by their characteristics, are amenable to being managed by the kernel. You do not worry about scheduling your queues; you just set them up and the operating system does the scheduling.

Here are the types of GCD queues:

▸ **Dispatch queues**—These are based on C, but they can contain Objective-C objects.

▸ **Dispatch sources**—These are for system events that are handled asynchronously. They are also based on C.

▸ **Operation queues**—These use Cocoa for their management. They are the queues you generally focus on in your code.

Dispatch Queues

Dispatch queues are FIFO queues that can contain either function pointers or block objects. The queue objects are generically referred to as tasks.

GO TO ▶ Hour 20, "Working with Blocks," p. 259, for more about blocks and function pointers.

A dispatch queue can be either serial or concurrent. Both types dequeue each task in the queue in turn. Serial queues execute the dequeued task and, when it is complete, execute the next task. Concurrent queues dequeue the tasks in turn, but, instead of waiting for completion, if there is a CPU available, the next task can be dequeued and execution can begin without waiting for the completion of the first one.

TIP
***

Synchronizing Using Locks

In concurrent processing that you have to manage for yourself (such as using threads rather than queues), you can lock resources so that only one thread can access it at a time. With serial queues, you do not have to worry about locking. The nature of the serial queue is that only one of your tasks runs at a time.
***

It is GCD that handles this dequeuing and starting of processes from queues as well as managing the availability of CPU.

Dispatch Sources

Like dispatch queues, *dispatch sources* are C-based; they process system events asynchronously. They handle events such as timers, signal handlers, Mach port events, and custom events. They are beyond the scope of this book.

Operation Queues

These are the queues that you most frequently worry about with GCD. They are manipulated through Cocoa (and Cocoa Touch) using the NSOperationQueue class, and the tasks they contain are instances of NSOperation. You construct your NSOperation instances and enqueue them. Go to the NSOperation class reference in Xcode or on developer.apple.com for more information.

NOTE

True Stories from Developers

The release of Xcode 4 and a new generation of Macs, including the MacBook Pro, provided an interesting example of the power of multicore processors interacting with the tuned operating system and Xcode. More than one developer reported performance improvements that subjectively appeared to be much greater than the revised specs for the new hardware would have suggested. Much of the performance improvement appears to have been the result of better use of concurrency.

Using Dispatch Queues

Dispatch queues are the simplest type of queues you can use to achieve concurrency.

GO TO ▶ Hour 20, "Working with Blocks," p. 259, for the simplest way to work with queues using blocks.

TIP

Using Block Pseudocode

For simplicity, blocks used in the pseudocode in this section are shown as

^ { ... }

Replace the { ... } with your own code.

Using Global Concurrent Dispatch Queues

GCD does its best to use your queues and the tasks within them as efficiently as possible with the available CPUs. As you design your app (and particularly the concurrent sections of it), bear in mind that you can make life easier for GCD and your users by using concurrent rather than serial queues. With serial queues, a task might wait for a previous one to complete, and during that time, a CPU might be idle. For the same basic reason, asynchronous tasks, rather than synchronous tasks, allow GCD to improve performance on multicore processors.

NOTE

Keeping these points in mind is important. You might want to revise the structure of some very computation-intensive sections of your app so that you can take advantage of concurrent and asynchronous processes.

There are three global concurrent dispatch queues for each app. You do not have to create them because they are ready for your use. You access a global concurrent dispatch queue with the following code:

```
dispatch_queue_t myQueue =
  dispatch_get_global_queue (DISPATCH_QUEUE_PRIORITY_DEFAULT, 0);
```

`dispatch_queue_t` is a `typedef` that is declared in the GCD framework code.

The zero as the last argument is a placeholder for future expansion. You can get the other three global dispatch queues using these terms:

```
DISPATCH_QUEUE_PRIORITY_LOW
DISPATCH_QUEUE_PRIORITY_HIGH
DISPATCH_QUEUE_PRIORITY_BACKGROUND
```

These provide lower and higher priorities than the default queue. Using the different queues can improve performance because you can send tasks to one or the other depending on considerations such as the task itself and the data that it is using. Tasks that are going to be updating the user interface usually should run at a higher priority than a task designed to index data that is not currently displayed.

Adding a Task to a Global Concurrent Queue

As noted previously, asynchronous tasks generally provide greater concurrency throughput. You distinguish between synchronous and asynchronous tasks when you add them to a queue. Note that synchronicity is a property of each task and not of the queue as a whole.

TRY IT YOURSELF ▼

Add an Asynchronous Task to a Queue

If you have created a block to encapsulate a task, you can add that block (and, thus, the task) to a queue using the following steps:

1. Get the appropriate queue for your task. Most commonly, it is the default queue:

```
dispatch_queue_t myQueue =
    dispatch_get_global_queue (DISPATCH_QUEUE_PRIORITY_DEFAULT, 0);
```

2. Add the block to the queue:

```
dispatch_async (myQueue, ^{ ... } );
```

This function returns immediately (it is atomic so it completes within one cycle). You can continue and add other tasks to the queue.

TIP

Remember that because this is a concurrent queue, the tasks may execute in an order other than the order in which they are added to the queue.

Designing with Queues

You can create your own queues to manage specific tasks or types of tasks. In general, the smaller and more focused your tasks are, the more they benefit from GCD and queues. The best way to get familiar with queues and GCD is with the sample code on developer.apple.com.

Remember that you can use __block specifiers for variables that you want to access within a block, and that you can have read-only access to variables declared in the scope where your block is defined. Together, these tools let you communicate into and out of blocks in queues.

TIP

More on Grand Central Dispatch

There is a good deal of information available for you on blocks and GCD. Look at the sample code on developer.apple.com, videos from the Worldwide Developers Conference, and discussion lists on developer.apple.com. It can help to appreciate an overview of GCD such as this and then to explore it when you are actually confronted with an issue that lends itself to concurrency. Most people find it much easier to learn about concurrency in the context of a real-life problem they are trying to deal with.

Summary

This hour has provided an introduction to queues and Grand Central Dispatch, the generalized replacement for threading in Cocoa and Cocoa Touch. Because of the complexity of working with threads (not to mention the fact that multicore processors were not widely available), many developers stayed away from all of the issues of concurrency. With Grand Central Dispatch, concurrency and highly efficient (automated) use of multicore processors is readily available.

Q&A

Q. What is the biggest difference between Grand Central Dispatch and thread-based concurrency?

A. With GCD, the actual scheduling of the queue tasks is handled by the Unix level kernel, deep in the operating system. From a developer's point of view, the biggest difference is that Grand Central Dispatch is much easier to use than threads.

Q. Why are asynchronous tasks and concurrent queues particularly advantageous when using GCD?

A. CPUs are not idle while tasks are waiting for completion of another task.

Workshop

Quiz

1. What are the four default global concurrent queues?

2. What is a good replacement for locking when using queues?

Quiz Answers

1. The four default global concurrent queues are default, low, high, and background priority.

2. Use serial queues.

Activities

On developer.apple.com, search for sample code using Grand Central Dispatch (GCD). Also on developer.apple.com, search the WWDC videos for sessions demonstrating GCD. Furthermore, look at Apple Developer Forums for discussions. GCD can be intimidating at first, but as you get into it and communicate with other developers, you will become more comfortable with it.

Because concurrency is important to different types of apps and in different ways, you will probably feel more at home if you look at examples and discussions of concurrency for the type of processing that you are doing (processing images or video, handling real-time data streams, and so forth).

HOUR 23
Working with the Debugger

What You'll Learn in This Hour

▶ Understanding how to communicate with yourself and other developers from an app

▶ Using the log entries for messages

▶ Enhancing breakpoints with actions, conditions, and iteration control

Logging Information

When you want to communicate with your users, you have a wide variety of tools available to you in the Cocoa and Cocoa Touch frameworks. In this book, the emphasis is primarily on the Objective-C language, so the Cocoa frameworks are outside the scope of this book. What this means is that you have to use the communication tools of the language itself and Foundation on both iOS and OS X, which is a good way of summarizing a few of the communication tools you need to communicate with yourself and your co-developers on a project.

Leaving aside the user interface features in Cocoa, there are two primary ways of communicating:

▶ **Console logs**—You can write to the console as you can in most languages.

▶ **Breakpoints**—You can insert breakpoints into your code; when the code stops at a breakpoint, the current variables and their values are displayed.

Using Console Logs

OS X contains an app in the `/Applications/Utilities` folder called Console. It lets you view the various log files on your Mac. Figure 23.1 shows an excerpt from Console.

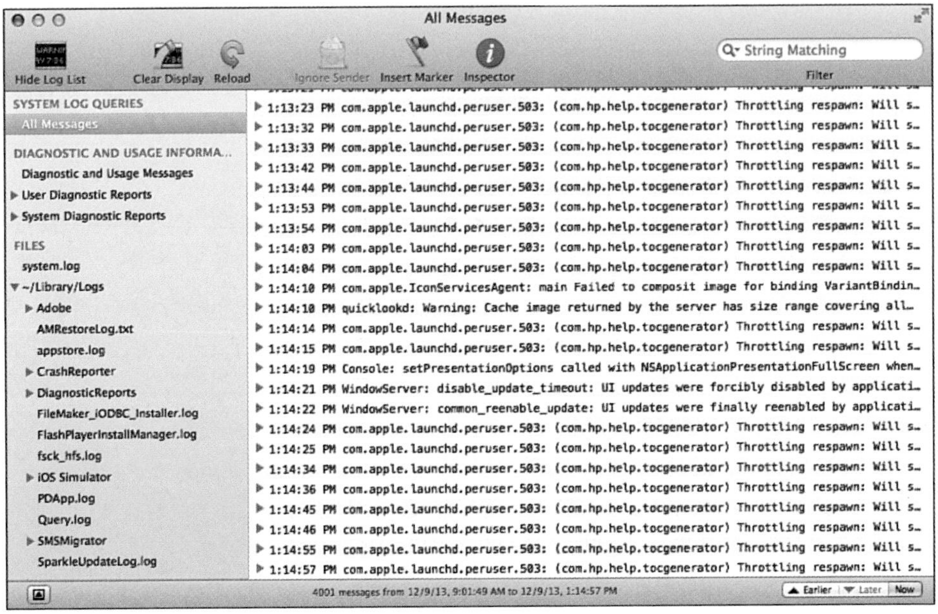

FIGURE 23.1
View logs on OS X with Console.

Well-behaved apps use the system logging facility to generate log entries in the hard disk root at `/Library/Logs/<app name>` or in `<home>/Library/Logs/<app name>` depending on the nature of the log. Console can see all of them. The logs are listed at the left of the window. Each entry is automatically time-stamped. As you can see at the top right of the window, log entries are searchable.

Because your system software is constantly updating various logs, you can launch Console and explore log entries for yourself.

TIP

Using Logs for Troubleshooting

Console is valuable to you for routine troubleshooting. You can track down unusual slowdowns and other strange behaviors with the help of the Console log. Furthermore, note that you can save a log to a file so that you can ship it off to technical support at Apple or elsewhere.

Using NSLog

You use the Foundation function NSLog to generate your log entries. The time stamp and the process ID that you saw at the left of each entry in Figure 23.1 are automatically generated for you by NSLog. Here is the syntax for NSLog:

```
void NSLog (
   NSString *format,
   ...
);
```

Note that NSLog takes a variable list of arguments. In fact, it puts them together and calls NSLogv, which has two arguments—an NSString format argument and a variable argument list (va_list), which contains the elements of the variable argument list. You rarely worry about NSLogv.

It is important to note that the format argument (the NSString) is a standard C format string, although it can be augmented with additional information. For example, here is a typical invocation of NSLog:

```
NSLog (@"Finished conversion routine");
```

This simply writes a time-stamped log entry with the format string, which, in this case, is simply a string.

You can use the format string to format data as in this example:

```
NSLog (@"Finished conversion routine with result %d", myResult);
```

Here, the format string contains an informational string followed by a standard C format string for an integer representation of a decimal number (%d).

TIP

Using the Format String in Log Messages

In the relatively rare case that you are printing out a C string variable, you should format it (probably with %s) in the format string. Otherwise, your string variable will be used as formatting information, which might (but probably won't) be satisfactory. (NSString variables should normally use %@.) Remember that the format string is enclosed in @" and ".

Enhancing NSLog

There are some built-in macros and expressions defined in the C preprocessor that are useful for logging. Table 23.1 shows the macros for the C languages (Objective-C, C, and C++).

Note in this table that the macro names begin and end with two underscore characters.

TABLE 23.1 Logging Macros for the C Languages

Macro	Format	Description
__func__	%s	Function signature
__LINE__	%d	Current source code line number
__FILE__	%s	Current source code file
__PRETTY_FUNCTION__	%s	Similar to __func__ but provides additional information for C++

Table 23.2 shows you the Objective-C expressions.

TABLE 23.2 Logging Expressions for Objective-C

Expression	Format	Description
NSStringFromSelector (_cmd)	%@	Current selector (note that _cmd is a single underscore)
NSStringFromClass([self class])	%@	Current object's class
[[NSString stringWithUTF8String:	%@	Source code filename __FILE__] lastPathComponent]
[NSThread callStackSymbols]	%@	NSArray of current stack trace

This enables you to create defines such as the following SLOG define, which is based on the Simple Scripting example on developer.apple.com. The define wraps a call to NSLog that uses some of the macros shown in Table 23.1. The only tricky point is that the format string from the invocation of the SLOG define is passed through, and the variables in the define for the filename, line number, and function are also automatically added to the log entry. The ##__VA_ARGS__ is the define for the variable arguments. A define such as this can appear in a precompiled header if you use it throughout your project, but it can also appear in a shared interface file or even an implementation file.

```
#define SLOG(format,...) NSLog( @"SLOG: File=%s line=%d proc=%s "
  format, strrchr("/" __FILE__,'/')+1, __LINE__, __PRETTY_FUNCTION__,
  ##__VA_ARGS__ )
```

Here is what a typical invocation of that define looks like:

```
SLOG (@" returning application's ready property");
```

And here is the corresponding output:

```
2014-01-17 09:15:14.608 Test[1159:70b] SLOG: File=AppDelegate.m line=23
  proc=-[AppDelegate application:didFinishLaunching]
  returning application's ready property
```

TIP

Logging

One guideline to which many developers subscribe is that you shouldn't waste a log message. By that, they mean that if you go to the trouble of creating a log message, don't throw it away. It only takes a few moments to bracket a log message in compiler directives so that you can choose to compile verbose log messages or not based on a single compiler option that you create. Just about as much effort can be expended so that a runtime variable can be turned on and off by users and testers. Not even compiling the log messages obviously improves runtime performance.

Using Smart Breakpoints

Several times in this book you have seen how to set breakpoints: You click in the gutter of the Xcode editor next to the line on which you want to break. As shown in Figure 23.2, just before that line is executed, the debugger appears and shows you the current values of variables.

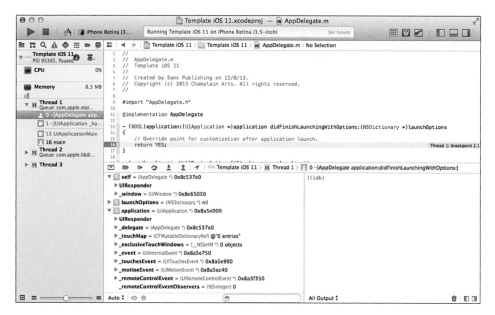

FIGURE 23.2
Use a breakpoint.

Enhancing Breakpoints with Messages

You can edit a breakpoint to provide more information and to control how it behaves.

▼ TRY IT YOURSELF

Edit a Breakpoint

Here are the basic steps to use to edit a breakpoint:

1. Set a breakpoint. In this case, set it on the last executable line of the method shown in Figure 23.2 (that is, set it on RETURN YES).

2. Control-click on the breakpoint to open the menu shown in Figure 23.3.

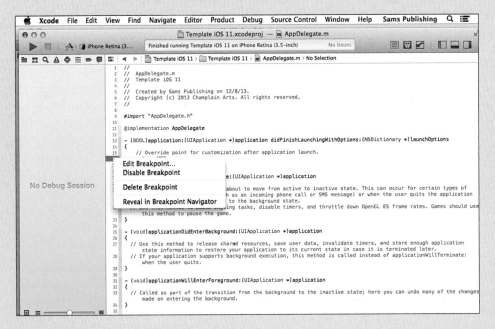

FIGURE 23.3
Start to edit a breakpoint.

3. Select Edit Breakpoint to see the window shown in Figure 23.4.

   You can set a condition on which to break; if you are inside a loop, you can set a number of iterations to ignore before breaking. You can also check the value of one or more variables and only break if those values are or are not in certain ranges. Basically, if you can express the condition in terms of variables to which you have access at that point in the code, you can use the condition for a breakpoint.

Remember that this expression is evaluated at runtime, however, so make certain you have done any necessary casts for it to function properly.

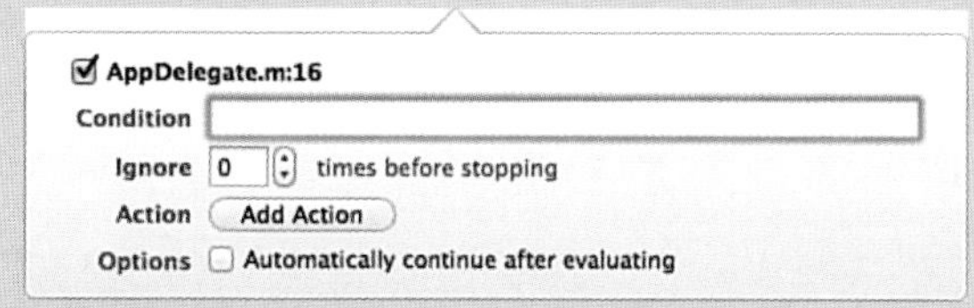

FIGURE 23.4
Review the editing options.

The actions are a set of types of actions that can be performed automatically when the breakpoint is hit:

- ▶ AppleScript

- ▶ Capture OpenGL ES Frame

- ▶ Debugger Command

- ▶ Log Message

- ▶ Shell Command

- ▶ Sound

You can choose which of these you want to have happen at the breakpoint. Notice the + and – at the top right of the Actions section in Figure 23.5. You can have multiple actions on a single breakpoint.

Finally, you can choose whether or not to automatically continue after the actions are evaluated. If you do not automatically continue, you can use the debugger window to inspect variables. However, you might want to just run one or more actions and review the output at a later time.

4. If you choose Log Message, you can specify the message to log, as shown in Figure 23.5.

5. Click Done.

6. Click Run at the top left of the toolbar (or choose Product, Run or ⌘+R).

7. You should see the message, as shown in Figure 23.6. (The message is shown in the console at the right of the debugger area.)

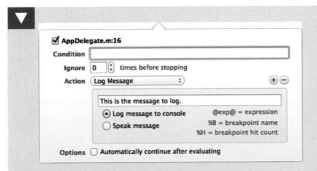

FIGURE 23.5
Specify a log message.

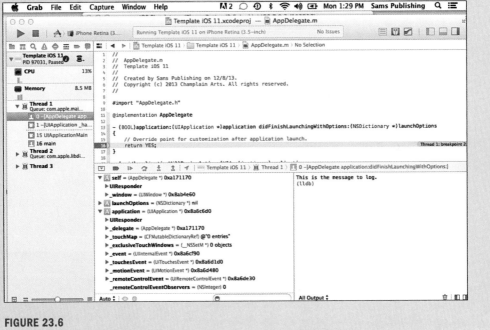

FIGURE 23.6
View the breakpoint message.

Breaking on a Condition

Customizing the breakpoint message is very useful, but there is much more that you can do. The easiest way to demonstrate this is to modify the code so that it is inside a loop that repeats several times. The simplest way to do this is to use the Code Snippet library: Drag the For statement into your code, as shown in Figure 23.7.

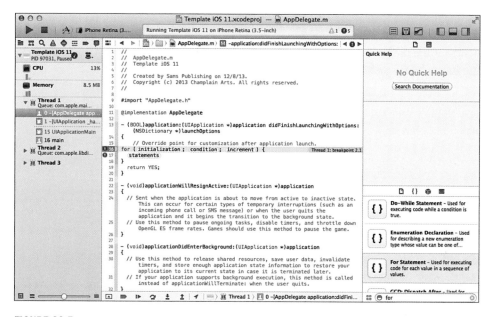

FIGURE 23.7
Add a for loop to the code.

Do a bit of rearranging to put the existing code inside the loop and to add a counter variable, as shown in Listing 23.1.

LISTING 23.1   Implementing a For Loop for the Code

```
- (BOOL)application: (UIApplication *)
  applicationDidFinishLaunchingWithOptions:(NSDictionary *)launchOptions
{
  // Override point for customization after application launch

  for (int counter = 1; counter < 10; counter++) {
    NSNumber * myFactor = [NSNumber numberWithFloat:8];

    NSNumber * myUnits = [NSNumber numberWithFloat:5];

    self.converter = [[Converter alloc] initWithFactor:myFactor];
    NSNumber *result = [self.converter units: myUnits];
  }
}
```

Move the breakpoint into the loop (it does not matter where). Make certain that it logs a message as before, but now use the Options check box to have it automatically continue. Make certain to click Done when you are finished.

Run the app again from Xcode, and view the results. Because the app is continuing after the action, the debugger is not shown as messages are written to the console. However, if you show the debugger (or use the Console app in the Utilities folder) later on in the project (just set a breakpoint anywhere), you see all of the action messages.

Change the breakpoint so that the action fires for the condition counter > 5 and run it again. Continue with the various options (and add more with the + and –) to see how you can control the breakpoint's behavior.

TIP

OS X Debugging Magic

Don't let the title of Tech Note 2124 mislead you: These are tips for both OS X and iOS debugging commands and options. You can find it at https://developer.apple.com/library/mac/technotes/ tn2124/_index.html.

This tech note, as well as the Xcode debugger documentation, show you how to inspect and change variable values while the app is paused in the debugger as well as other very useful techniques.

Summary

In this hour, you have explored some of the debugging tools available in Xcode and Objective-C. You have seen how to use NSLog as well as how to enhance it with defines that provide additional debugging information. You have also seen how to enhance breakpoints so that they perform actions based on conditions as well as on iterations through a loop.

Q&A

Q. **What is the purpose of continuing with execution after a breakpoint fires?**

A. If the breakpoint contains an action such as a log message or an AppleScript script, it continues running and generates output for you to review later. You do not have to sit there and click your way through each iteration of a debugged loop.

Q. **How is a breakpoint condition useful?**

A. For pesky bugs that only seem to happen sometimes, you can set a breakpoint on a value so that you find out exactly when that value is set to a peculiar number (such as zero, causing a divide by zero). You do not have to watch to find out when this happens; the breakpoint does the watching for you.

Workshop

Quiz

1. How do you choose what action to use for a breakpoint?

2. How do you specify values to be logged at a breakpoint?

Quiz Answers

1. You do not need to choose because you can use + and – at the top right of the breakpoint-editing window to add as many actions as you want.

2. To explore values at a breakpoint, do not use the check box to continue execution at the breakpoint. You drop into the debugger and can explore on your own.

Activities

Use one of the more complex examples on developer.com or in an Xcode template to explore breakpoints. A good test case is the Master-Detail Application in Xcode templates for iOS. Set a breakpoint at the end of `insertNewObject`: in MasterViewController.m and explore what happens each time you add another object with the + in the master view controller.

HOUR 24
Using Xcode Debug Gauges for Analysis

Putting Debug Gauges in Perspective

Broadly speaking, there are four steps to developing and implementing an app whether it is for an iOS device, a Mac, or any other computer, including a Windows computer, an old-fashioned mainframe, or even more obscure devices:

▶ **Define and design**—Decide what your app is supposed to do.

▶ **Compile**—If you cannot pass this hurdle, no one can run your app.

▶ **Work as expected**—This means that calculations are correct and that the app delivers on the design promise.

▶ **Work properly in the computing environment**—This section explores this point.

In any development process, some people stop after any of these steps. Being unable to agree on the definition and design of a project is common, and, in many ways, it is positive. It is much less expensive to cancel a project if you decide at the start that it will not work than it is to cancel the project after it has flopped.

Some developers think their work is done when they get a clean compile and build, but most know that the app still needs extensive testing to make certain that it works as expected. Many think that is the end of the road.

The last step—working properly in the computing environment—is critical. Almost every app today runs in a shared environment, and it has to work well with the other components in that environment. Perhaps nowhere is this so critical as when your app runs in a shared environment that includes telephony and battery power.

In fact, except for some very specialized apps that work in single-purpose environments (guiding a spacecraft far from earth or managing a complex industrial machine, for example), almost every app today runs with at least one other app—the operating system. In modern computing environments such as iOS or OS X, it is easy to have more than a hundred separate processes running simultaneously. The operating system itself might account for many of these, while end-user apps such as Numbers, Xcode, or Safari can account for others.

When an app runs in a shared environment like this, its behavior has to mesh with the behavior of the other processes. That means releasing exclusive holds or locks on resources such as memory quickly as well as allowing the operating system's management tools to function efficiently by not hogging the processor(s) in ways that prevent them from being shared from time to time.

When an app fails at the third level (working as expected), you might be lucky to discover that a specific user action (choosing a menu command, for example) causes it to crash. You might not like this, but it is a deterministic problem that can eventually be tracked down and corrected.

If an app does not work properly in the shared computing environment, the problem is often hard to track down because if it does cause a crash (and, from a debugging point of view, that is a great help), that crash might come almost randomly at some point depending on what is happening elsewhere on the computer at that time.

A good example of this is memory leaks. In pre-Automatic Reference Counting (ARC) days, forgetting to call `release` or `dealloc` allowed you to litter the heap with now-unused and even unusable objects. Gradually, the amount of free memory dwindled. Modern operating systems do not function properly under extremely limited memory or disk conditions. Some users of modern Macs believe that having less than 1GB of free space on their startup disks renders the system practically unusable. Others peg that number at 10GB. Regardless of the number, if the free space on disk is too small, a ripple of bad consequences starts to play out.

As discussed in Hour 23, "Working with the Debugger," you have tools available to let you inspect what is happening at critical points in the app. Although that helps you make certain that the app is functioning correctly, the debugger is of limited help in helping you monitor how it is behaving in its computing environment.

This is where debug gauges come in.

Monitoring CPU Utilization

Xcode now presents graphic gauges that monitor resources as your app runs. They are located in the Xcode debug navigator, as shown in Figure 24.1. Gauges show resource utilizations, while at the lower section of the window a timeline moves along showing the trends. In some gauges such as iCloud, more specialized information such as iCloud interactions is shown.

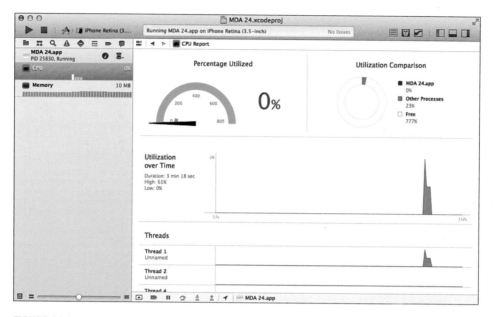

FIGURE 24.1
Use debug gauges for CPU utilization.

In Figure 24.1, you see the CPU gauge. In general, what you're looking for here are the values shown in the utilization graphics at the top of the screen, but you're also looking at how those values change over time on the running timeline.

As you run your app (either in the simulator or on your Mac or device), you should see utilization spike when you perform some action, such as open a new document or select a new item in a Master-Detail Application app. You're watching to see that the spike comes down when the operation is finished. Remember that you're looking only at your app, so it's not unreasonable to expect its usage to come down to 0% even if you're running plenty of other apps on your device.

Monitoring Memory Utilization

Compare the spikes in Figure 24.1 to the graphic in Figure 24.2 that shows memory utilization. Note at the beginning of the timeline (all the way at the left) that the memory usage jumps up quickly. It remains at a high level in Figure 24.2.

Thus, you expect a spike in CPU utilization when you open or close a document with a quick up-and-down motion. When it comes to memory, you expect a longer-term increase because while the document is open, the memory remains in use.

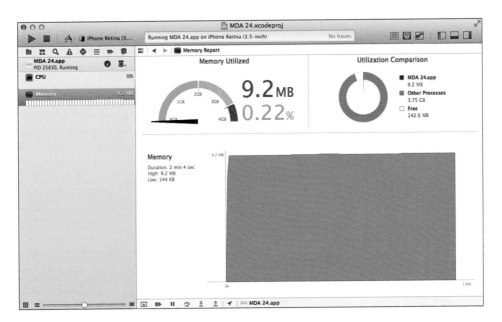

FIGURE 24.2
Use debug gauges for memory utilization.

On top of this, if you close a document, you expect a CPU spike for the close operation and a fairly rapid drop in memory use as the document objects are released. Every app is different, but in general as you close or dismiss items, you should see a decrease in memory.

NOTE

This is not an absolute rule because sometimes you deliberately leave objects around so that they can be brought back onscreen quickly. To properly debug your app, you have to understand what it does so that you have a good feeling for when memory and CPU usage should go up, stay up, and go down.

Monitoring Energy

On a Mac, you see the Energy Impact gauge, as shown in parts (a) and (b) of Figure 24.3.

The Energy Impact timeline is particularly useful because it not only shows you the Utilization, Napping, and CPU Wake Overhead, but it also indicates periods when energy is impacted by App Nap Prevention, Idle Wake Prevention, and other events (those are the Xs below the time-line). The Energy Impact timeline is useful if you are exercising your app and noticing how it behaves in response to your actions. It's also useful when you think nothing is happening and notice that you're running down the battery (timers are often a culprit here). Unlike CPU and memory where you should have a basic idea of what will go up and down, it's these occasional incidents where utilization and overhead occur that can impact your app's energy use.

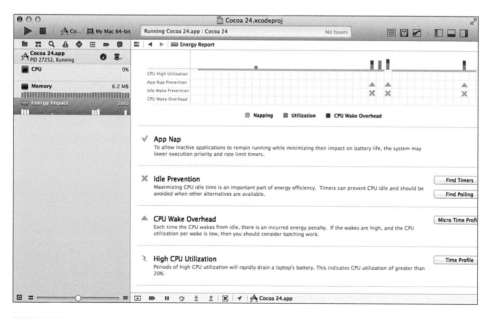

FIGURE 24.3
Use debug gauges for energy impact.

Using Instruments

Instruments is an app that runs alongside everything else on your computer. It is a collection of tools in which each monitors a particular type of activity, from memory leaks to network access and garbage collection. Instruments feeds the debug gauges, so if you want to drill down deeper, you can switch to Instruments for more information. (You can also write your own instruments.)

With Instruments, you can observe what is happening inside your app in graphical and numerical displays. By looking for aberrations, you can start to track down these problems that can cause your app not to work well in the shared computing environment. What you are looking for varies from app to app. For example, there might be no concern with network access in a computation-intensive app that works solely from user-entered data.

This hour gives you an overview of the basic Instruments functionality. The *Instruments User Guide*, downloadable from developer.apple.com, provides more than a hundred pages of details.

There are certainly some apps where you need to use all of the Instruments capabilities, but fortunately, for many apps, you can focus your attention on specific areas that you know in advance are likely to be troublesome. These include specific areas that are relevant to your app's processing as well as some general concerns (such as memory leaks) that apply to most apps.

NOTE

Memory Leaks and Battery Usage

Some people believe that memory leaks and battery usage concerns are specific to iOS devices, and that they do not apply to plugged-in computers sitting on a desktop. Others (including the author) think that this assumption is wrong. They matter everywhere. The fact that they are often hidden by plugged-in power sources and vast amounts of built-in memory is, in the long term, generally misleading. At some point, they will matter.

Instruments is shown in Figure 24.4. You can switch to Instruments using the button at the top right of debug gauge displays. Instruments provides you with a great deal of data, but for many people, debug gauges provide a solid and easy-to-understand picture of your app.

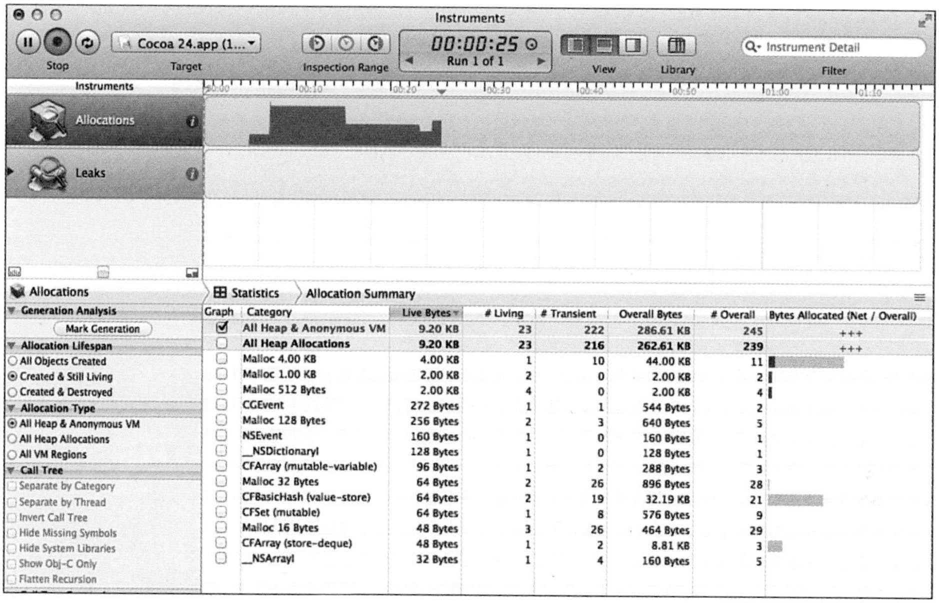

FIGURE 24.4
Use Instruments.

Summary

This hour showed you an overview of how to work with debug gauges and Instruments to monitor your app's performance in the computer environment as it runs. This type of analysis is typically done after you have designed, compiled, and tested your app. However, there are cases early in the development process where you might hit a bump in the road and use Instruments to try to track down what is happening. Most of the time, though, in the development process you rely on the debugger; Instruments and debug gauges come into play later on.

Q&A

Q. Why should you always assume your app is running in a shared environment?

A. With very few exceptions, it is. It must coexist (appropriately) with the operating system and other apps.

Q. What apps can you connect to with Instruments?

A. You can target any apps running on your Mac, on the iOS simulator on your Mac, or on an iOS device set up in Xcode. You can watch the behavior of complex apps such as Xcode and Safari to begin to understand the data that Instruments presents to you.

Workshop

Quiz

1. Do you have to worry about memory leaks if you use ARC?

2. What is the best set of instruments to use when you start using the Instruments app?

Quiz Answers

1. Although it is much more difficult than in the past, you can still create memory leaks if you use ARC.

2. When you are starting out, you might like Activity Monitor template but you should also focus on particular areas of concern to your app.

Activities

Go back to the code that you have written in the earlier hours of this book and explore it with Instruments. Do you find memory leaks or other problems? Cleaning up your practice code can get you positioned well for moving on to more complex projects. (It also can help you form good habits for writing new code.)

APPENDIX A
C Syntax Summary

Objective-C is a thin layer built on top of C, but you do not need to be a C expert in order to use it. In fact, only a relatively small subset of C is used for most Objective-C projects. The reason is that the classes in the Cocoa frameworks implement many of the functions that you might otherwise work with in C. For example, with a few exceptions, handling of strings and numbers in Cocoa is done in the Cocoa classes and not in raw C. This appendix lists some of the key syntax elements that you use with Objective-C.

You can find tutorials about C on the Web and in books such as *Sams Teach Yourself C in 21 Days* by Bradley L. Jones and Peter Aitkin. The classic reference is *The C Programming Language* (2nd Edition) by Brian W. Kernighan and Dennis M. Ritchie.

Data Types

C supports the same basic types as most programming languages today: signed and unsigned `char`, `short`, `bool`, `int`, and `long` as well as `float` and `double`. Most of the time, you either use Cocoa classes or Core Foundation references to these types such as `NSString` (a class) or `CFString` (a reference).

Enumerated Type

Instead of defining types by characteristics such as integer, you can define a type by its values. They are implicitly numbered from zero, but you can also add specific numbers.

```
enum days {
  monday,
  tuesday,
  wednesday,
  thursday,
  friday,
  saturday = 101,
  sunday = 102
};
```

Struct Type

These are based on structured records. You can combine primitive types into a single structure that can be manipulated. structs are used in various places in Core Foundation, but if you have a background in C and are used to using structs, ask yourself if you are actually better off creating a class with instance variables or declared properties.

```
struct bankAccount {
  float balance;
  float creditLimit;
};
```

Declare a variable of the struct type:

```
struct bankAccount myAccount;
```

Access an internal struct element:

```
myAccount.balance = 0;
```

Pointers

Pointers are used constantly throughout Objective-C. They point to primitive types or to structures (such as objects) as in this line of code:

```
NSError *error = nil;
```

Pointers can be dereferenced with & so as to get to the underlying data. This is commonly used with NSError. Some methods use double indirection in their declaration as shown here for outError:

```
- (BOOL)readFromURL:(NSURL *)url error:(NSError **)outError
```

You can invoke it with code such as

```
myResult = [myDocument readFromURL:myURL error: &error];
```

The argument url is a pointer to the NSURL class. outError is a pointer to a pointer to the NSError class (this is called double indirection). If the method makes a change to URL, it affects the object passed in via the argument. With the double indirection of outError, the method can change the pointer so that it points to another object. Typically, it is used to change it from its initial value (nil) to another instance of NSError. In this way, a method can return a new value not only as its result (BOOL in this case) but also through a doubly indirected argument.

Arrays

In Objective-C, arrays are frequently declared with the Core Foundation opaque CFArray reference. More often, arrays are used as one of the collection objects (NSArray, NSSet, and NSDictionary).

Control Structures

As in most other programming languages, control passes from one statement to the next one. Functions or methods can be called; they might return a value that is used in a subsequent statement. In common with other object-oriented languages, long sequences of step-by-step code ("spaghetti code") are frowned on. Anything that organizes the control structure makes the code more maintainable. Three basic control structures (other than function and method calling) are used extensively.

if Statements

Here is a typical use of an if statement.

```
if (someConditionIsTrue ) {
    return (YES);
} else {
    return (NO);
}
```

switch Statements

For many people, omitting the break at the end of each case is a very common error.

```
switch(type) {
  case oneCase:
    doSomething ();
    break;

  case anotherCase:
    doSomethingElse ();
    break;
  }
```

Repeat Statements

Look at the fast enumeration and the NSEnumerator class in Cocoa when you are tempted to use a repeat statement. If you do want to use a C repeat structure, here are the three basic forms:

```
do
<code>
while ( <condition> ) ;

while ( <condition> )
<code>

for ( <condition> ; <condition> ; <condition> )
<code>
```

APPENDIX B
Apps, Packages, and Bundles

Apps, packages, and bundles are interrelated terms that describe the way in which apps and other software products are distributed. *Bundles* provide a convenient and structured way to keep together the various files that make up a project. These files can include the code itself, resources such as images and sound, localizable strings, icons, and various other files. Some file types, such as resource files, are standard (txt, rtf, mov, and the like), whereas others, such as property lists (plist files), are specific to the Apple frameworks and operating system.

Bundles are used to assemble files for apps, frameworks, plug-ins, and Dashboard widgets. Each type of bundle has its own structure. This means that, given a bundle, the operating system can determine its type and, therefore, what should happen if the user tries to do something with the bundle.

NOTE

The most common thing that a user does with a bundle is to try to launch it if it is an app.

The bundle structure is the same on both OS X and iOS, although there are differences in the presentation of the bundle to users. On OS X, bundles are presented in the Finder as packages. A *package* is a directory of files that is displayed on the desktop and in Finder windows as a single file.

If you Command-click on a package, you bring up a shortcut menu containing the commands that are relevant for that object. In the case of a package, the first command is Show Package Contents, which opens a new Finder window focused on the top level of the bundle. With that window, you can navigate through the package directory and open other files.

Looking Inside a Project Bundle

Most of the time, people do not open a bundle's package. If you are a developer, you use Xcode, and it opens the files for the project; you can view them in the project navigator. When you build a project, Xcode creates a bundle that assembles the various files into a bundle.

The files in a bundle are visible in Xcode, and you normally use it to modify them. There are occasions when you need to know exactly where the files are and what their names are. For those occasions, you need to know the bundle's layout.

Perhaps the most common reasons for writing code to locate files in your app's bundle is when you want to distribute the app with extra features. For example, it is common to include an SQLite database for Core Data as part of an app's bundle. The app can then check to see if a database exists in a known place on the user's computer (such as in a Documents folder or some other appropriate location). If no database is found in the known location, the database from the app's bundle is copied there, and the app is ready to run.

This method of distribution relies on the database or other user files being in a known location, and that is happening more and more with iOS and OS X sandboxing. It also relies on the app being able to locate the database or whatever file is in question within its own bundle so that it can copy it.

There are some special folders within a project folder on disk. The folders and files show up in the project navigator in Xcode in various ways. These are the special folders.

`lproj` **Files**

`lproj` files are used for localization. These files are placed in folders such as `en.lproj` (which contains English localized strings), `fr.lproj` (for French), and so forth. Recently, there has been a new "language" for `lproj` folders—Base. This folder typically contains the storyboards for an iOS project.

Storyboards may contain text for button titles and the like. The files in `Base.lproj` are used by default when the app runs, unless localized files are provided and they match a user's localization choice. This structure means that `Base.lproj` can be any language at all, and English may be just another localization of the base files (which might be Portuguese, for example).

Strings are placed in the appropriate language `lproj` folder in files that end with the extension `.strings`. Inside the project navigator, they typically appear in a Supporting Files group.

Asset Catalogs

Starting in Xcode 5, *asset catalogs* let you organize resources, including launch images and icons. These appear on disk in folders such as `Images.xcassets` in your project. Within such a folder, you typically have an `AppIcon.appiconset` and a `LaunchImage.launchimage` folder. You can create additional imageset folders for your app's resources.

`plist` **Files**

Property list files (with the extension `.plist`) contain your app's basic settings. They also show up in the Info project tab. Most people manage them through Xcode, but you can edit the files directly if you want. There can be several `plist` files in your project, but the basic one is typically named `MyApp-Info.plist`. You can use a file with another name if you want. Specify your app's `plist` file in the Build Settings tab of the project in the Packaging section.

Precompiled Header Files (.`pch`)

Precompiled header files provide compiler information; they are not localized. Precompiled header files can use the version macros, as well as any other information you choose to place there.

Precompiled header files can use version macros that are part of the frameworks. Here is a precompiled header file for an iOS template in Xcode. Note that it checks for availability of features (in the Availability.h file).

```
//
// Prefix header for all source files of the 'Testbed iOS 11' target in the
// 'Testbed iOS 11' project
//

#import <Availability.h>

#ifndef __IPHONE_5_0
#warning "This project uses features only available in iOS SDK 5.0 and later."
#endif

#ifdef __OBJC__
  #import <UIKit/UIKit.h>
  #import <Foundation/Foundation.h>
#endif
```

These are examples of precompiled header files that you will find in your Xcode templates as well as in downloaded sample code. Many people customize their precompiled header files with their own custom defines and the like. Precompiled header files typically appear in the Supporting Files group in the project navigator.

APPENDIX C

Archiving and Packaging Apps for Development and Testing

Although this book focuses on Objective-C itself, there is no point learning Objective-C if you do not use it at least to build some test code. A key part of development is packaging and distributing the code so that you can run it on various devices and share it with other people.

Archiving

Xcode has an archiving feature that you use to package your code. You get to it from Product, Archive in Xcode.

NOTE

If you are building an iOS app, you must make certain that your Scheme setting is for an iOS device and not for a simulator. If you are building for a simulator, the Archive command is not available. In order to build for an iOS device, you must be a registered Apple developer and you must have configured your developer account for the device you want to use.

TRY IT YOURSELF ▼

Create a Mac Archive

After you have a project in Xcode, you can create an archive for the App Store (either one of them) or to distribute. The process is slightly different for Mac and iOS apps. This is the Mac process:

1. Build and test your app.

2. When you are satisfied, choose Product, Archive to build the archive. If you have syntax or build errors, you are not able to proceed.

3. When the archive has been created, the window shown in Figure C.1 opens to show you the new archive and any previous ones.

4. Select the archive you want to work with.

5. Click Distribute to build a sharable copy.

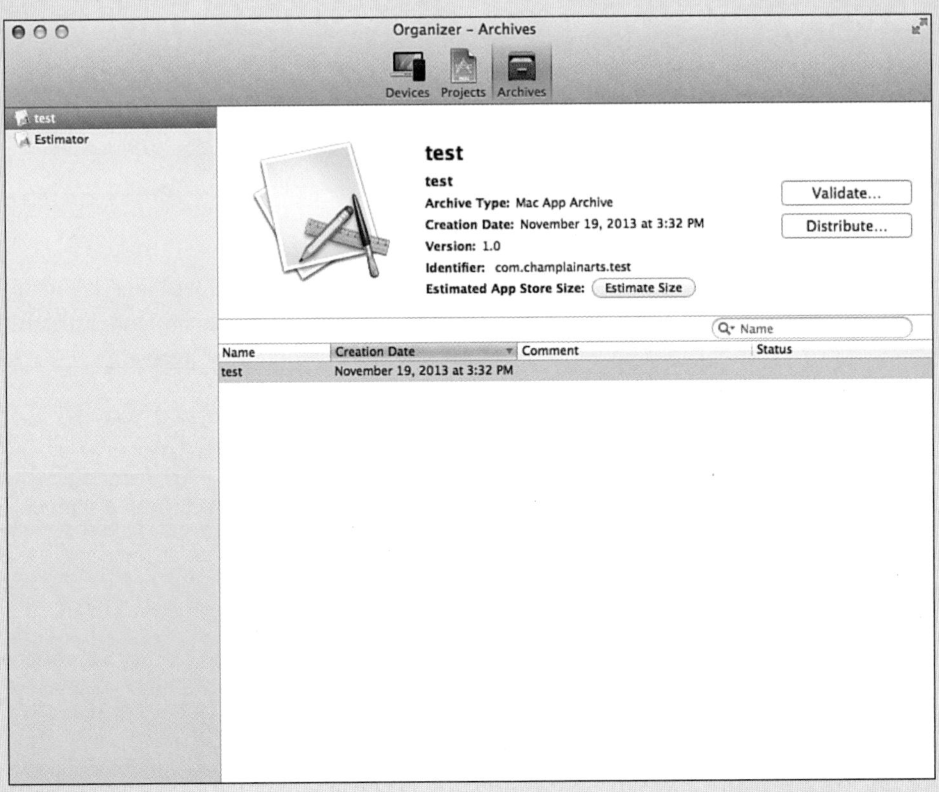

FIGURE C.1
Open the project archive window.

6. For sharing with friends and colleagues, choose Application from the sheet shown in Figure C.2.

   If you have a paid Mac developer account, choose Export Developer ID-signed Application. Otherwise, the app can be run only by a user with Anywhere chosen in the download preferences of the General tab in Security & Privacy in System Preferences.

7. Name the application and select the place you want it to be stored. You now have an application that you can share with friends and colleagues.

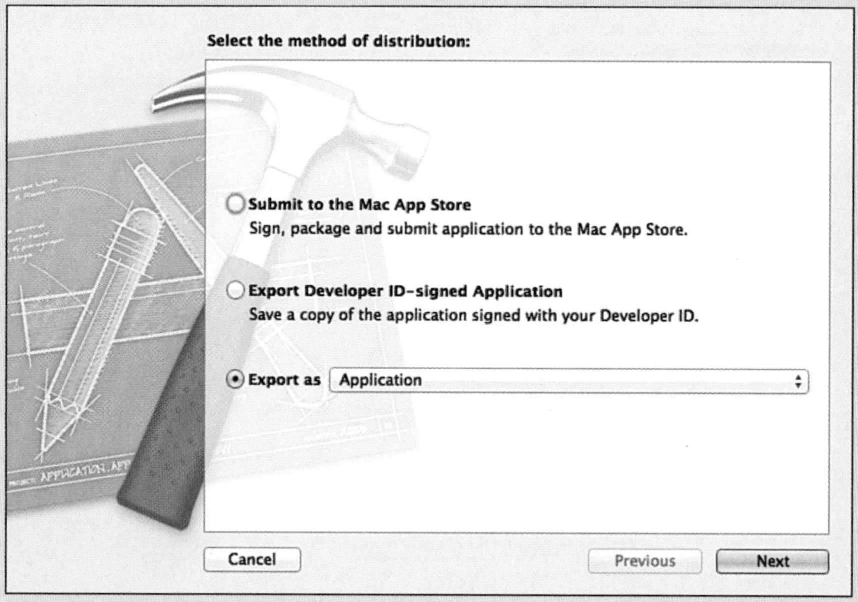

FIGURE C.2
Create the application.

TRY IT YOURSELF ▼

Create an iOS Archive

The process is basically the same as for a Mac app, but you must have registered your iOS device and perhaps the devices of friends to whom you want to send the app. Follow these steps:

1. Build and test your app.
2. Make sure you are building for an iOS device and not for a simulator, as shown in Figure C.3.

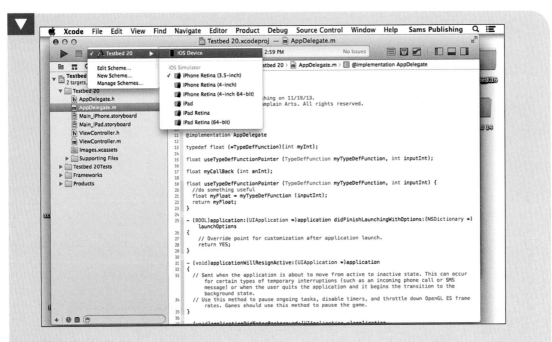

FIGURE C.3
Make sure you are building for an iOS device.

3. You can validate the archive or submit it to the App Store. You need to provide your iTunes Connect credentials.

   If you are a registered developer, you can distribute your apps to up to 100 users for testing. You need to have their device ids so that you can attach them to the profile for the app in Xcode. (See developer.apple.com for more information about working with an iOS device.)

Index

G

H

I

with Interface Builder, 171

overview, 166

performSelector, 169-171

SEL data type, 168-169

setting, 174

testing whether instance can respond to selector, 175-176

sending messages to text fields, 92-94

setArgument method, 174

setByAddingObject method, 214

setByAddingObjectsFromArray method, 214

setByAddingObjectsFromSet method, 214

sets

Git, 50-56

discarding changes, 56

history of, 48

tracking changes, 52-55

overview, 42-47

remote repositories, 58-60

repository tips, 48-49

Subversion, 58

square brackets ([]), **94**

statements

if, 315

repeat, 316

switch, 315

static typing, **117-122**

step-by-step conversion routine, building, 194-200

at symbol (@), **74**

synchronizing with locks, **287**

@synthesize directive, **130-132, 138**

T

targets

overview, 12

setting, 173

tasks, adding to queues, **289**

testbed apps

building on iOS, 78

building on OS X, 79

creating, 193-196

message syntax, 94-95

overview, 77-78

text fields, 81

adding in iOS, 82-84

adding in OS X, 85-87

connecting to code in iOS, 89-91

connecting to code in OS X, 91

sending messages to, 92-94

testing

membership in collections, 217

whether instance can respond to selector, 175-176

text fields, 78

adding in iOS, 82-84

adding in OS X, 85-87

Sams **Teach Yourself**

When you only have time
for the answers™

Whatever your need and whatever your time frame, there's a Sams **Teach Yourself** book for you. With a Sams **Teach Yourself** book as your guide, you can quickly get up to speed on just about any new product or technology—in the absolute shortest period of time possible. Guaranteed.

Learning how to do new things with your computer shouldn't be tedious or time-consuming. Sams **Teach Yourself** makes learning anything quick, easy, and even a little bit fun.

Sams Teach Yourself Android Game Programming in 24 Hours

Jonathan S. Harbour
ISBN-13: 9780672336041

HTML, CSS and JavaScript All in One
Julie C. Meloni
ISBN-13: 9780672333323

Sams Teach Yourself JavaScript in 24 Hours
Phil Ballard/Michael Moncur
ISBN-13: 9780672336089

Sams Teach Yourself Node.js in 24 Hours
George Ornbo
ISBN-13: 9780672335952

Sams Teach Yourself jQuery Mobile in 24 Hours
Phillip Dutson
ISBN-13: 9780672335945

Sams Teach Yourself Objective-C in 24 Hours, Second Edition

In Full Color

SECOND EDITION

Figures and code appear as they do in Xcode

Jesse Feiler

FREE Online Edition

Safari Books Online

Your purchase of *Sams Teach Yourself Objective-C in 24 Hours, Second Edition,* includes access to a free online edition for 45 days through the **Safari Books Online** subscription service. Nearly every Sams book is available online through **Safari Books Online**, along with thousands of books and videos from publishers such as Addison-Wesley Professional, Cisco Press, Exam Cram, IBM Press, O'Reilly Media, Prentice Hall, Que, and VMware Press.

Safari Books Online is a digital library providing searchable, on-demand access to thousands of technology, digital media, and professional development books and videos from leading publishers. With one monthly or yearly subscription price, you get unlimited access to learning tools and information on topics including mobile app and software development, tips and tricks on using your favorite gadgets, networking, project management, graphic design, and much more.

Activate your FREE Online Edition at informit.com/safarifree

STEP 1: Enter the coupon code: YIVNJFH.

STEP 2: New Safari users, complete the brief registration form. Safari subscribers, just log in.

If you have difficulty registering on Safari or accessing the online edition, please e-mail customer-service@safaribooksonline.com